The United Na
and Civil Socie

About UNRISD

UNRISD, the United Nations Research Institute for Social Development, is an autonomous agency engaging in multidisciplinary research on the social dimensions of contemporary problems affecting development. Its work is guided by the conviction that, for effective development policies to be formulated, an understanding of the social and political context is crucial. The Institute attempts to provide governments, development agencies, grassroots organizations and scholars with a better understanding of how development policies and processes of economic, social and environmental change affect different social groups. Working through an extensive network of national research centres, UNRISD aims to promote original research and strengthen research capacity in developing countries.

UNRISD's current research programmes include: Civil Society and Social Movements; Democracy, Governance and Well-Being; Gender and Development; Identities, Conflict and Cohesion; Markets, Business and Regulation; and Social Policy and Development. For further information on UNRISD work, visit www.unrisd.org.

About the author

Nora McKeon studied history at Harvard University and Political Science at the Sorbonne, before joining the Food and Agriculture Organization (FAO) of the United Nations. She held positions of increasing responsibility there, culminating in overall direction of the FAO's relations with civil society. She now divides her time between writing and lecturing on development discourse, peasant farmer movements and UN–civil society relations; and coordinating an exchange programme for African and European farmers on agriculture and trade policy issues. She recently published (with Michael Watts and Wendy Wolford) *Peasant Organizations in Theory and Practice*.

The United Nations and Civil Society

Legitimating Global Governance – Whose Voice?

Nora McKeon

Zed Books

LONDON & NEW YORK

The United Nations and Civil Society: Legitimating Global Governance – Whose Voice? was first published in 2009 by Zed Books Ltd, 7 Cynthia Street, London N1 9JF, UK and Room 400, 175 Fifth Avenue, New York, NY 10010, USA

www.zedbooks.co.uk

Distributed and typeset in the UK
by Long House Publishing Services
Cover designed by Rogue Four Design
Printed and bound in Great Britain by CPI Antony Rowe, Chippenham and Eastbourne

Distributed in the USA exclusively by Palgrave Macmillan, a division of St Martin's Press, LLC, 175 Fifth Avenue, New York, NY 10010, USA

A catalogue record for this book is available from the British Library.
Library of Congress Cataloging in Publication Data are available.
/ 0 0 6 / 6 3 / 5 7
ISBN 978 1 84813 274 0 hb
ISBN 978 1 84813 275 7 pb
ISBN 978 1 84813 276 4 eb

Contents

Tables and Boxes

Tables

Boxes

Abbreviations

ACP	Africa Caribbean Pacific
ADB	Asian Development Bank
AIDS	acquired immune deficiency syndrome
ANEC	Asociación Nacional de Empresas Comercializadoras de Productores del Campo (National Association of Rural Producers, Mexico)
ANGOC	Asian NGO Coalition
ARPA	Agricultural Rehabilitation Programme for Africa
AS-PTA	Assessoria e Serviços a Projetos em Agricultura Alternativa (Advisory Services for Alternative Agricultural Projects, Brazil)
CBOs	community-based organizations
CCA	Common Country Assessments
CEB	Chief Executive Board
CFA	Comprehensive Framework for Action
CFS	Committee on World Food Security
CLONG	Comité de Liaison des ONG (Liaison Committee of Development NGOs to the European Union)
COAG	Committee on Agriculture
COASAD	Coalition des Organisations Africaines pour la Sécurité Alimentaire et le Développement Durable (Coalition of African Organizations for Food Security and Sustainable Development)
CSA	Collectif Stratégies Alimentaires
CSD	Commission on Sustainable Development
CSO	civil society organization
DAW	Division for the Advancement of Women
DPI	Department of Public Information
EC	European Commission
ECOSOC	United Nations Economic and Social Council
ECOWAS	Economic Community of West African States
ENDA	Environmental Development Action
EPAs	Economic Partnership Agreements
ETC Group	Action Group on Erosion, Technology and Concentration

EU	European Union
FAO	Food and Agriculture Organization of the United Nations
FFA	Food for All Campaign
FFD	Financing for Development
FFHC/AD	Freedom from Hunger Campaign/Action for Development
FIAN	Foodfirst Information and Action Network
FONGS	Fédération des ONG du Sénégal (Federation of Senegalese NGOs)
FTAA	Free Trade Area of the Americas
G-8	Group of 8
G-77	UN Group of 77
GATT	General Agreement on Tariffs and Trade
GMOs	genetically modified organisms
HIV	human immunodeficiency virus
HLTF	High Level Task Force
IAAH	International Alliance against Hunger
IATP	Institute for Agriculture and Trade Policy (US)
ICARRD	International Conference on Agrarian Reform and Rural Development
ICDA	International Coalition for Development Action
ICFTU	International Confederation of Free Trade Unions
ICN	International Conference on Nutrition
ICT	information and communication technology
IEE	Independent External Evaluation
IFAD	International Fund for Agricultural Development
IFAP	International Federation of Agricultural Producers
IFI	international financial institution
IFOAM	International Federation of Organic Agriculture Movements
IGWG	Intergovernmental Working Group
ILO	International Labour Organization
IMF	International Monetary Fund
INGO	international non-governmental organization
IPC	International CSO Planning Committee for Food Sovereignty
IPM	Integrated Pest Management
IRED	Innovations et Réseaux pour le Développement (Development Innovations and Networks)
ISC	International Support Committee
ISWG	Intersessional Working Group
ITDG	Intermediate Technology Development Group (now Practical Action)
IUF	International Union of Food, Agricultural, Hotel, Restaurant, Catering, Tobacco and Allied Workers' Associations
MAI	Multilateral Agreement on Investment
MDGs	Millennium Development Goals
Mercosur	Common Market of the South
MG	Major Group

MIF	Montreal International Forum
MNC	multinational corporation
NEPAD	New Partnership for Africa's Development
NGO	non-governmental organization
OECD	Organisation for Economic Co-operation and Development
PAIA	Priority Area for Interdisciplinary Action
PrepCom	Preparatory Committee
PRSPs	Poverty Reduction Strategy Papers
RAFI	Rural Advancement Foundation International
ROPPA	Réseau des Organisations Paysannes et des Producteurs Agricoles de l'Afrique de l'Ouest (Network of Farmers' and Agricultural Producers' Organizations of West Africa)
SARD	Sustainable Agriculture and Rural Development
SOFA	State of Food and Agriculture
SPFS	Special Programme for Food Security
TCD	Technical Cooperation Department
UN	United Nations
UNAIDS	Joint United Nations Programme on HIV/AIDS
UNCCD	United Nations Convention to Combat Desertification
UNCED	United Nations Conference on Environment and Development
UNCTAD	United Nations Conference on Trade and Development
UNDAF	United Nations Development Assistance Frameworks
UNDESA	United Nations Department of Economic and Social Affairs
UNDP	United Nations Development Programme
UNEP	United Nations Environment Programme
UNESCO	United Nations Educational, Scientific and Cultural Organization
UNICEF	United Nations Children's Fund
UNIFEM	United Nations Development Fund for Women
UN-NGLS	United Nations Non-Governmental Liaison Service
UNRISD	United Nations Research Institute for Social Development
WABA	World Alliance for Breastfeeding Action
WFC	World Food Conference
WFP	World Food Programme
WFS	World Food Summit
WFS:fyl	World Food Summit:five years later
WHO	World Health Organization
WRI	World Resources Institute
WSAA	World Sustainable Agriculture Association
WSSD	World Summit on Sustainable Development
WTO	World Trade Organization

Foreword

This volume has emerged from a research project of the United Nations Research Institute for Social Development (UNRISD), *UN World Summits and Civil Society Engagement* (2003–2005), which looked at the way and extent to which different civil society actors have used the opportunities created by United Nations summits and related processes to advance their networking activities and advocacy impacts. Originally commissioned as a thematic paper (*Building Links between Global and Local in the UN System: The Civil Society Dimension*), Nora McKeon's inquiry grew into the present book in which she traces the relationship between the UN system and civil society, from the early days to the present.

Intergovernmental processes within the United Nations have opened up to civil society voices over the past two decades, notably in the context of the UN global summits of the 1990s. The book examines the dynamics of change that the global summits have helped to set in motion. According to McKeon, the UN system has not yet moved beyond episodic participation toward meaningful, durable incorporation of non-state actors into global political processes.

McKeon uses the World Food Summit and its follow-up (1996, 2002 and 2006) to ground her analysis in this volume. It is a timely and persuasive case for several reasons. Food is a basic human need, and agriculture provides a livelihood for the majority of the world's population. Enormous geopolitical and corporate interests revolve around food and agriculture. The food crisis that hit the headlines in 2008 has dramatically brought home the dangers of food dependency faced by many of the poorest developing countries. It has demonstrated the fallacy of treating food as any other commodity, and has placed reform of global governance of food and agriculture high on the world's agenda. It is not surprising that the World Food Summit and its follow-

up attracted considerable attention from a sector of civil society –
organizations representing small-scale producers in the South – underrepresented in most other summit processes. Furthermore, the UN
Food and Agriculture Organization has been the site of innovative
experimentation in relations with civil society.

McKeon sets the FAO case study into a broader context by reviewing
the results and implications of steps taken by the UN over the past
decade to reform the rules and procedures of its engagement with civil
society organizations, based on a survey of civil society offices
throughout the UN system. In doing so, she identifies important
principles to be respected in UN–civil society interaction, promising
tendencies and practices to be pursued, and many remaining challenges.

The research project was funded by the Ford Foundation. And, as
with all UNRISD projects, the work would not have been possible
without core funding provided, during the years the research was
carried out, by the governments of Denmark, Finland, Mexico, the
Netherlands, Norway, Sweden, Switzerland and the United Kingdom.

Thandika Mkandawire
Director, UNRISD

The levels of decision-making seem to be jumping around like frogs. From the national scene, where our farmers' platform is well in place now, to the UEMOA [Union Economique et Monétaire Ouest Africaine/West African Economic and Monetary Union], where we are managing to make our voice heard. But tomorrow it will be the ECOWAS [Economic Community of West African States] with the challenge of relating to a mammoth like Nigeria, and the day after NEPAD [New Partnership for Africa's Development], the European Union, the WTO [World Trade Organization] … How to decide which end of the stick to grab in order to make progress quickly? The temptation of just huckling down to work in one's own field is strong. But it is no longer an option.

(West African farmers' leader, interviewed in Thiès, Senegal, January 2002)

A clear paradox is emerging: while the substance of politics is fast globalizing (in the areas of trade, economics, environment, pandemics, terrorism, etc.) the process of politics is not; its principal institutions (elections, political parties and parliaments) remain firmly rooted at the national or local level. The weak influence of traditional democracy in matters of global governance is one reason why citizens in much of the world are urging greater democratic accountability of international organizations.

(United Nations 2004a:8)

1
Setting the Stage

The past two decades have seen so rapid an evolution in the space and pace of world affairs that it is difficult to discuss them in a straightforward fashion. A whole industry of disposable terminology has cropped up, with 'globalization' heading the catalogue, whose products seem shopworn and outmoded before they reach home. New, border-crossing problems such as pandemics twine incestuously with old ones like poverty. Individuals and communities are called upon to process vastly expanded ranges of information and experience, most often without the tools they need to exercise discernment but draw the line at judgmental discrimination. Political ideologies of different kinds have loosened their grasp on people's interpretations of reality. Problems may be understood to be complex, responsibilities diffuse, solutions all but self-evident. But fundamentalist sectarianisms, self-protective individualisms, pseudo-hedonisms move in to fill the ideological gap. Basic shared values and consensus on a concept of common goods have never seemed more needed, more elusive, more difficult to enforce. Multilateralism is besieged by public and private unilateralisms, like a lovable but ineffectual beast bumbling along the path to extinction.

By design or by default, the United Nations (UN) system finds itself invested with the thankless responsibility for refereeing this global match. The gap is noteworthy between what is needed in the way of worldwide clout and the UN's capabilities, given its design, authority and resources. A memorable documentary some years back panned from compelling shots of human suffering in a war-torn country somewhere in the southern hemisphere to suited and tied diplomats in a soft-lit, plush-carpeted meeting room negotiating the placing of a comma. It was an unfair image, given the range of efforts and people that the UN deploys between the two extremes and on the front line of misery itself, but an effective illustration of the disproportion between ends and means.

1

These discrepancies, between ends and means, between people's expectations and the UN's capabilities, between a rapidly changing world and institutions set in their ways, are a source of the dialectic that has fuelled the interaction between the UN system and civil society over the past 15 years. This study will seek to tell a piece of the story and to say something about how it is impacting on the UN. To what degree and in what ways is the UN adapting to accommodate a range of actors who can help to strengthen its focus on the values on which it was founded and to defend them in a complex and evolving global context?

The thesis defended here is that the UN system has indeed opened up to civil society voices since the early 1990s, most significantly in the exceptional setting of the global summits, but that it has failed thus far to move from generic and often episodic participation to meaningful incorporation of these actors into global political process. The bases for such incorporation are far more solid than they were a decade and a half ago, particularly in terms of the structures and capacities of civil society organizations (CSOs) and the thickness and quality of their networking. At the same time, however, the geopolitical and economic powers that have underwritten the neoliberal agenda that these civil society actors contest are more determined than ever to defend their interests. The challenge before the UN is to provide a terrain – or rather a series of intercommunicating terrains – on which meaningful confrontation and negotiation can take place, as it did 60 years ago when the Universal Declaration of Human Rights was crafted around a table fractured by the cold war. The political context and the cast of actors have changed, but the significance of this role and the urgency of assuming it masterfully and authoritatively are unaltered.

Scope and Methodology

This study attempts to assess the longer-term dynamics of change that the global summits, as strong mobilizing moments in a broader process of interaction between the UN and civil society, have helped to set in motion.[1] We trace the ground that has been covered since the early 1990s and identify the present challenges faced by both the UN and its civil society interlocutors, exploring the following parameters in particular:

• What impact has interaction between civil society and the UN system had in terms of changing *development discourse* within the UN system?

How has it influenced the issues that find their way onto the global agenda, the way in which they are framed and – more profoundly – the paradigms on which agenda setting is based?

- To what degree has this interaction contributed to *institutional change* within the UN – both formal and informal – to accommodate civil society input into global policy debate and normative work? What new political spaces have opened up, and for what kinds of CSOs?
- How is the UN system performing in terms of building two-way *links between global policy dialogue and action at country level* to implement summit outcomes, and how is civil society being involved in this vital task?

We address these questions in three steps. First, in Chapter 2, we take an in-depth look at a specific terrain of UN–civil society interaction, that of the Food and Agriculture Organization of the United Nations (FAO) and global governance of food and agriculture issues. This focus is motivated by several considerations. The World Food Summit process of 1996 and 2002 is the least documented among the UN international conferences of the 1990s so far as the involvement of civil society is concerned.[2] And yet the food and agriculture nexus of issues plays an exceedingly important role in the world policy arena. Food is perhaps the most basic human need. Agriculture provides a livelihood for most of the world's population and the majority of the poor who have been the object of so much summit attention. The geopolitical and corporate interests that revolve around these issues are enormous, as demonstrated by the difficulties encountered during the World Trade Organization (WTO) Doha Round negotiations and by the food crisis that erupted on the global scene in 2008. For these reasons, the World Food Summit and its follow-up have attracted considerable attention on the part of organizations representing social movements of the South, a highly significant category of civil society that has been underrepresented in most other summit processes. Finally, the FAO has been the locus since the mid-1990s of an innovative experiment in UN–civil society relations, one that figures forward some of the principles and practices on which more effective UN outreach to civil society could be based.

Chapter 3 sets the FAO case study into a broader context. It reviews how the practices and procedures of the UN system as a whole are evolving as a result of interaction with civil society in a changing political context in which the summit processes constitute valuable observation posts. This review is based on several sources of information, underwritten by many years of personal experience, observation and analysis. It draws on the views of UN system practitioners themselves through an inquiry which asked them to discuss how their organizations are handling civil society involvement in global policy dialogue and in country-level action, and what links exist between the two levels. This inquiry is supplemented by the insights emerging from a series of interagency exchanges organized by the United Nations Non-Governmental Liaison Service (UN-NGLS) over the past few years, of which the most valuable for the purposes of this study are the informal 'off-the-record' networking meetings which enable participants to speak freely, without concern for institutional face-saving. Chapter 3 also draws on the growing body of literature which the summits have spawned outside of the UN itself.

The chapter takes a look at system-wide efforts to ensure integrated implementation of summit outcomes through the Millennium Development Goals (MDGs), and approaches being adopted to involve civil society in these efforts through the Millennium Campaign. Finally, it reviews the implications of steps taken by the UN since the mid-1990s to reform rules, procedures and practices governing relations with civil society, culminating with the report of the Panel of Eminent Persons on United Nations–Civil Society Relations appointed by Kofi Annan (United Nations 2004a) and its follow-up under the reign of a new UN Secretary-General.

Finally, in Chapter 4 we draw out conclusions regarding the state of play in the democratization of global governance. We identify important principles to be respected in UN–civil society interaction, promising tendencies and practices to be pursued, challenges for the future and areas meriting further research. Our consideration of these issues is enriched by the body of analytical work that has been built up over recent years by students both of social movements and of international relations,[3] work to which we refer throughout this study. The literature to date has focused above all on the more exciting of the two members of the couple we are examining, civil society. It has a lot to say about the phenomenon of transnational civil society networks, how they are organized, the dynamics of their relations to national protest movements, the conditions under which they are most likely to emerge and to be effective, the repertoire of frames and actions on which they draw, their strategies and targets.[4] Our study corroborates many existing hypotheses. It also, however, adds some new dimensions, stemming in particular from the fact that the civil society network at which we take an in-depth look in the FAO chapter is one of the rare instances in which it is people's organizations and social movements in the South that call the shots.

At the same time, we take a closer look at the less researched 'poor sister' in the interaction, the UN system.[5] Observers sympathetic to the aims of civil society advocacy assess the political opportunities the UN affords in terms that cover a range of options. 'Why bother?' is the verdict of some (see Bullard 2005). Others have taken a selective approach by identifying certain frames, such as human rights, and certain activities, such as international norm setting, as congenial both to global civil society objectives and to what has been called a 'boomerang' effect on national situations (see, for example, Keck and Sikkink 1998 and Smith 2008). Still others hold out for wholesale 'democratization' of UN governance through the institution of a world parliament (as in Falk 2005). The FAO case study and the cross-system review, both strongly grounded in a perspective internal to the institutions, contribute a more nuanced understanding of hindrances to, and opportunities for, change in the UN system than is current in the literature. It is important to match up this area of understanding with the relatively thorough exploration of transnational civil society networking that is already available if we want to capture the full richness of the potential dynamics of interaction between the two spheres.

A World Context in Flux: Re-examining Global Governance

When 50 nations gathered in San Francisco in 1945 to witness the birth of the United Nations, the most compelling motivation for embarking on a new experiment in world governance following the failure of the League of Nations was 'to save succeeding generations from the scourge of war'.[6] The 'We the Peoples of the United Nations' posited at the opening of the UN Charter as the authors and the actors of this intention were assumed to exercise their agency through the sovereign states that represented them or, in the case of the millions of people whose countries had not yet reached independence, through the colonial powers who ruled over them.[7] One major transformation of the world political scene since that founding moment was the decolonization of the vast majority of these countries by the mid-1960s, an evolution which multiplied and diversified the membership of the UN and shifted problems of development and North–South inequalities from the dockets of individual metropolitan powers to the heart of the world agenda. Another, some 25 years later, was the end of the cold war and the profound recasting of the dynamics that had governed international politics for decades.

Awareness of the need to re-examine the architecture of world governance mounted rapidly during the early 1990s. Among the most comprehensive proposals were those that emerged from the Commission on Global Governance, an independent group of 28 eminent individuals that started its work in 1992 with the endorsement of UN Secretary-General Boutros-Ghali.[8] In its report (Commission on Global Governance 1995:26–7),[9] the commission predicated its advocacy of global governance on the belief that the world was ready to accept 'a global civic ethic' based on 'a set of core values that can unite people of all cultural, political, religious, or philosophical backgrounds' (Commission on Global Governance 1995:26–7). Painting the backdrop for its recommendations, the report recalled that

> When the United Nations system was created, nation-states, some of them imperial powers, were dominant ... Thus the establishment of a set of international, intergovernmental institutions to ensure peace and prosperity was a logical, welcome development.
>
> Moreover, the state had few rivals. The world economy was not as closely integrated as it is today. The vast array of global firms and corporate alliances that has emerged was just beginning to develop. The huge global capital market, which today dwarfs even the largest national capital markets, was not foreseen. The enormous growth in people's concern for human rights, equity, democracy, meeting basic material needs, environmental protection, and demilitarization has today produced a multitude of new actors who can contribute to governance (Commission on Global Governance 1995:26–7).[10]

What was – and is – at stake is a major recasting of the world governance system. An authoritative United Nations University study (Rittberger 2001) suggests that core governance goals in the present world context can be considered to include ensuring people's security, livelihoods, and legal certainty, defending the natural environment, promoting channels of participation that facilitate the development of a sense of collective civil society, and correcting inequalities resulting from markets. *International* governance, essentially intergovernmental,[11] finds it increasingly difficult to attain these goals, prompting a transition to *global* governance 'characterized by the decreased salience of states and the increased involvement of non-state actors in norm- and rule-setting processes and compliance monitoring' (Rittberger 2001:2).[12] Three factors are frequently cited as key contributors to the crisis of international governance. The technological revolution, particularly in information and communications, enables citizens and CSOs to enter the stage of world politics directly, as in the case of the 'anti-MAI campaign'.[13] Globalization has widened the gap between rich and poor and altered the relationships among states, market forces and civil society actors, necessitating corrective action to ensure balanced and equitable participation in governance processes. Finally, the end of the cold war has enlarged the scope of action of all three actors and potentially enhanced the autonomy of the UN itself as a fashioner of world polity no longer subservient to a paralysing polarized conflict between a few powerful members (Rittberger 2001:23).

Yet fulfilling this potential has not been an easy or automatic process. In the field of peace and security, multilateralism is threatened by the unilateralism of the world's superpower and its closest allies. The economic and social objectives of the UN mobilize only tepid levels of political interest as compared with the financial and trade agendas. The UN system in the strict sense is felt by many to be increasingly sidelined by the international financial and trade institutions governed by a neoliberal policy consensus and limited, weighted-vote forms of multi-lateralism.

The crisis of governance also affects the level of national governments, the building block of UN legitimacy. What has been termed a 'democracy deficit' (see United Nations 2004a:24) is not limited to Southern countries whose political systems may be weak or authoritarian, corrupt, insufficiently accountable. In Northern democracies as well there is a significant gap between the formal political sphere of party politics and parliaments and the real world of societies and citizens. National governments are losing their monopoly of representing their societies on the international scene as influential new actors emerge, often contesting the legitimacy of official positions. At the same time, national governments' policy-making autonomy is eroded by the advancing encroachment of international norm setting and conditionalities, particularly through structural adjustment regimes and the WTO regulations. Regional entities are playing an increasing role in determining and enforcing the rules of the game. Yet the institutional existence of such entities most often does not coincide with a deep sense of common political identity, as the fate of the draft EU Constitution demonstrates. In short, throughout the world citizens feel alienated by their minimal influence over global decision making on problems that formerly were treated closer to home.[14]

Global Actors in Evolution: From International NGOs to Transnational Social Movements

Changes in the world political scene since the early 1990s have thus opened the door to more significant involvement of non-state actors in UN affairs. But these relatively recent developments are not the beginning of the story.[15] The Charter of the United Nations, unlike that of the League of Nations fashioned just a few decades earlier, already specifically provided that 'the Economic and Social Council [ECO-SOC] may make suitable arrangements for consultation with non-governmental organizations [NGOs] which are concerned with matters within its competence'.[16] This rather indeterminate article was refined in practice when the UN set up shop. Clearer limits of NGO involvement were delineated, excluding them from the General Assembly, denying them voting rights and equal status with governments, and dividing them into three categories with differentiated privileges. Although the UN Charter foresaw that consultative arrangements might be extended to national NGOs with the agreement of the concerned members of the UN, in fact formal status was confined to international NGOs (INGOs) for the first 50 years of the UN's life. The organizations on which consultative status was conferred in this first phase of relations were valued as interlocutors because of their high international standing and the moral and intellectual input they could bring to UN deliberations. They included bodies such as the international trade unions, faith-based organizations, international councils of women and of youth, and a range of professional and business associations. Like their status, their interaction with the UN was formal.

But it is misleading to limit a view of early interaction between the UN and civil society to what transpired in the UN meeting rooms in New York and Geneva. The United Nations Associations of the first generation, grouped globally into a dynamic world federation, were active in their promotion of public information and reflection on the issues on the table of the UN, as were the national chapters of many of the INGOs in formal status. And some of the UN system programmes and specialized agencies were ahead of the UN secretariat itself in the civil society game. The International Labour Organization (ILO) is a special case, founded in 1919 with a tripartite statute involving employers' and workers' organizations as well as governments. The United Nations Children's Fund (UNICEF) set stock by its public outreach from the outset and invested time and resources in the effort. But FAO's Freedom from Hunger Campaign, with its national committees, and the United Nations Educational, Scientific and Cultural Organization (UNESCO), with its national commissions and international scientific councils, also reached deeply into civil society and brought its concerns to bear on the governing bodies of the two agencies, separate from those of the UN secretariat itself.

A new chapter in UN–civil society relations opened up in the early 1960s with decolonization and the introduction into the UN scene of North–South dynamics and development agendas that were conditioned by cold war logic but were not subservient to it. The Non-Aligned Movement, inaugurated in 1961, was the basis for the formation of the UN Group of 77 (G-77) in 1968. At its instigation, the United Nations Conference on Trade and Development (UNCTAD) was established in 1964 as a permanent organ of the General Assembly. The Declaration on the Establishment of a New International Economic Order saw the light in 1974 and the Declaration on the Right to Development was adopted by the General Assembly in 1986. NGO leaders, many of them children of the social movements of the 1960s and 1970s, followed these evolutions with passion, giving birth to new, less formally and rigidly constituted non-governmental institutional mechanisms such as the International Coalition for Development Action (ICDA).

Networking across national borders in the southern hemisphere was also an evolution of the 1970s and 1980s, of necessity discreet and informal in regions like Latin America and parts of Asia where NGOs constituted a fragile bulwark against the oppression of military dictatorships. It is important to recall the dialectical relation that existed between the practice and the reflection of these organizations.[17] Issues, concepts and approaches which this area of the non-governmental world brought to the UN were not moral or intellectual abstractions but the fruit of active engagement in often difficult socioeconomic and political struggles. The dialectic of reflection and local action has subsequently been perturbed to some degree by the gigantism and the globalization of the UN forums of the 1990s, contributing to a widely lamented delink between proclamation and practice. It continues, however, to operate in the world of social movements and the NGOs that work closely with them, and constitutes a solid potential basis for the task of building bridges between global commitments and national action in the post-summit era, which we will discuss in Chapter 4.

It is also important to remember that world summits were not an invention of the 1990s. Over 150 global conferences took place under UN auspices from 1961 through the mid-1980s (see Foster and Anand 1999:77–9). Some of these were direct forerunners of the 1990s summits, for instance the 1972 UN Conference on the Human Environment, the 1974 World Food Conference, and the women's conferences of 1975, 1980 and 1985. The conferences of the 1990s cannot be understood without appreciating what they built upon, both within the UN and in the world of civil society.

This said, there was something new at work in the 1990s. The changing political context did undoubtedly help to open up the space of international deliberations and offer CSOs a more visible and effective role. The contribution of non-state actors to the solving of world problems was increasingly recognized in a paradigm of structural adjustment and redefinition of public/private spheres and responsibilities. As a study of NGOs, the UN and global governance conducted in the mid-1990s put it, 'NGOs are emerging as a special set of organisations that are private in their form but public in their purpose', particularly relevant to the 'low politics' issues that were rising on the international agenda (Weiss and Gordenker 1996:364). The summits revisited the themes, the cast of characters, the settings, the language and the rhetorical devices of international affairs. The scenario shifted dramatically, moving from diplomats confronting each other behind closed doors in cold war conflict mode to indigenous peoples offering governmental delegates an occasion to commune with nature in the UN atrium, or women giving public testimony to the domestic violence to which they are subjected. The summits were experienced as agenda setters, dealing with the desperately unfinished business of the twentieth century and ringing up the curtain on the twenty-first. The world community looked to them as occasions to frame emerging global issues and mobilize political will to deal with them. They were expected to establish international standards and commitments which would guide national policy, and to set in place monitoring mechanisms enforcing accountability. They represented an effort to sidestep the stifling institutional setting of UN deliberations and experiment with more effective approaches to global governance. A civil society presence was essential for all of this to happen.

On their side, CSOs were attracted to the summits by the spaces they opened up and the opportunities they offered both to influence the substance of the discussions and the decision-making processes themselves and to build their own networks and alliances. They achieved the first objective to varying degrees in different venues, and the second beyond expectations.[18] The conference fatigue many of them developed during the course of the decade stemmed in good part from the gap between commitments and action. The principles and values that had been reaffirmed by the UN summits, it became increasingly evident, were simply no match for the neoliberal agenda promoted by the international financial institutions (IFIs), global economic actors and some powerful governments. Frustration at the continued impermeability to civil society participation of the UN as a global governance system was another contributing cause. As the decade advanced, civil society actors felt increasingly that they were in serious and growing danger of being co-opted to serve watered-down intergovernmental agendas rather than advancing their own visions and objectives.[19]

Getting the Terms Straight

Before moving on to the main body of the study we need to devote a moment of attention to clarifying the terms of the interaction we will be discussing: both the vague and fluctuating category of civil society and the more circumscribed but not univocal world of the UN. We will not be concerned with achieving a definitive and objective definition of reality. Rather, we will try to get a better grasp of how each of the two parties tends to view the other, since these perceptions themselves have a dynamic effect on how they interact.

How, then, has the UN's perception of the world of non-state actors evolved over the past years? What concepts and categories has the UN adopted to get a handle on this universe, which was originally situated discreetly on the periphery of its space but has increasingly demanded a protagonist's role? As we have seen, the Charter of the United Nations defines these actors, by opposition to the governments who are its members and masters, as *non*-governmental. The original physiognomy of NGOs was that of well-established non-profit, apolitical international councils grouping people or associations that felt themselves to be families on the grounds of their professions, their academic fields, their beliefs, their ages, their status, their activities, their experiences. This perception of structured civil society was a Western one, and the first generation of INGOs that interfaced with the UN were almost exclusively headquartered in Europe and North America, with some 'mirror' organizations in the East, particularly where trade unions were concerned. Although many had branches in the developing world, the way these organizations conducted their business and presented themselves to the world followed a Western pattern, with interesting instances of synchronism.[20] Questions of representation were not major issues, except in the case of the ILO, with its governance structure involving trade unions and employers' associations. INGOs were expected to represent their own members but not society as a whole, which was the purview of the member states. Issues that arose in the ECOSOC NGO committee responsible for granting INGOs formal status with the UN were more likely to have to do with real or suspected cold war affiliations than with who was claiming to speak for whom.

The term 'NGO' remained dominant for four decades. It stretched uncomfortably over the years to cover new generations of national development, advocacy and solidarity NGOs in both the North and the South, and local people's associations in those countries that have been the object of successive development decades. One reason for the persistence of this terminology was undoubtedly institutional consecration. 'NGO' figured in the constitutions of both the UN and the specialized agencies, and procedures were in place for recognizing and dealing with such organizations. The term also tended to increase the comfort level of UN officials by delineating a parallel universe that was defined by reference to the world of governments, one with which they themselves could communicate directly through their own professional or religious affiliations. The bottom-line, day-to-day perception of most UN staff was that NGOs were the 'do-gooders' or the 'good conscience' of the UN, calling it back – sometimes a bit sanctimoniously – to the basic values on which it was founded.

Increasingly, however, the category was contested by pieces of the universe it was expected to describe. Tensions developed between Northern and Southern NGOs as the latter sought to gain greater autonomy. People's organizations, established by and accountable to specific constituencies – like peasant farmers, rural women, artisanal fisherfolk – became impatient with the habit of NGOs speaking (and fundraising) on their behalf. Contrasts grew between the INGOs, to whom access to the UN had been reserved through the mechanism of consultative status, and the broader range of actors who now began to show interest in the international arena. At the same time, within the UN the term 'NGO' was increasingly felt to be inadequate to compre-hend the kinds of more complex roles and relations that were emerging.

The concept that began to come into use to replace it was 'civil society' and 'civil society organizations', of which NGOs were assumed to be one important variety. Agenda 21, the action plan adopted by the United Nations Conference on Environment and Development (UNCED) in 1992, rather adventuristically divided this space into nine 'major groups' ranging from women to business and industry.[21] In the report of a stocktaking exercise on 'The United Nations, NGOs and Global Governance: Challenges for the 21st Century', organized by UN-NGLS in 1995 (UN-NGLS 1996), the dominant term throughout was 'NGO', although several speakers referred vaguely to civil society as the universe for which NGOs were somehow speaking. By 1997 the two terms were coupled in a fashion that clearly spoke of transition. And by 2000 'civil society' and 'civil society organizations' were winging it alone in many documents.

The concept of civil society, of course, was not a new one. It had come into vogue in the West in the early modern period to describe the space that opened up between the household, government and the marketplace once all-invasive monarchies began to wane, in which people began to organize to pursue their interests and values. There was a neat correspondence in the fact that the concept of 'civil society' was being elevated into global usage in the late twentieth century in a moment in which the state's role and its relation to the two other actors were once again undergoing redefinition. The end of the cold war was very much a part of the story, as regimes which had occupied all of the space up to the threshold of the home collapsed and Western powers and foundations rushed into Eastern Europe with recipes and resources to promote the growth of civil society. But so was structural adjustment in the developing world, with its effect on the state's sphere of action, as well as the subsequent discovery on the part of the underwriters of the Washington consensus that markets cannot function in a social and governance vacuum.[22]

There was – and is – a considerable amount of confusion within UN circles as to just what is in and what is out of the civil society basket. The World Bank defines it as 'the wide array of non-governmental and not-for-profit organizations that have a presence in public life, expressing the interests and values of their members or others, based on ethical, cultural, scientific, religious or philanthropic considerations' (World Bank 2008). An FAO policy paper on cooperation with NGOs and other CSOs published in 1999 expressed the distinctions in these terms:

The expansion and diversification of the non-governmental sector and of its relations with the UN is being accompanied by an evolution in terminology. 'NGO' now tends to be reserved for formally constituted organizations which often do not represent sectors of the population but provide services and/or mobilize public opinion in areas of relevance to the UN system. The term 'civil society' refers to the sphere in which citizens and social movements organize themselves around objectives, constituencies and thematic interests. 'Civil society organizations' include both NGOs and popular organizations – formal and informal ... The term 'non-state actors' is even more comprehensive, also including for-profit businesses (FAO 1999a:3–4).

But as late as 2003 the document establishing a UN Secretary-General's Panel of Eminent Persons to examine UN–civil society relations included the private sector in its terms of reference as falling within the category of civil society (United Nations 2004a:74). However clearly the frontier may be drawn, there are ample areas of overlapping between civil society and the private sector. Small farmers' organizations pursue the economic interests of their members but, at the same time, promote social values and visions that go far beyond the profit motive. To compound confusion, institutional procedures have not kept pace with the changing terminology. Accreditation and formal relations continue to be accorded to 'NGOs' rather than CSOs. Private sector interests normally reach UN meeting rooms via business associations, which are formally non-profit NGOs, or through the delegations of member governments, which may include for-profit enterprises.

While the UN was still trying to digest the new terminology of civil society, the crowds hit the streets in Seattle in 1999 and the world discovered a global form of the kind of social movements that had rocked the USA in the era of civil rights and anti-Vietnam war protest. The UN's relationship with this social phenomenon is ambivalent in the extreme. On the one hand, social movements are feared because they threaten established bases and forms of international interaction. On the other, they are courted since the values they defend, the energy they mobilize, and their capacity to attract young people seem to hold a key to the relegitimization of the UN. Just what is meant by the term within the UN is far from clear. At times a superficial shorthand operates, and social movements are equated with noisy and sometimes violent anti-globalization advocates. At times the term 'social movement' is used as a synonym for people's organizations – organizations of peasants, fisherfolk, workers and others – as contrasted with NGOs. Or, again, it is understood to refer to phenomena of social change that include structured organizations but go beyond them, such as the student and women's movements of the 1960s or, today, the conglomeration of various kinds of organizations and groups that populate Social Forums. In this latter sense social movements are equated with what a growing literature terms 'global civil society'[23] or 'transnational advocacy networks' (Keck and Sikkink 1998; Marchetti and Pianta 2007). But most UN staff are unfamiliar with the literature and encounter the phenomenon in the course of their work with the same cognitive preparation as the average citizen.

On the other side of the field, even civil society actors that have had long frequentations of the UN tend to view it, erroneously, as a single monolithic entity. This is a serious misapprehension.[24] A fundamental distinction has to be drawn between the governing bodies of the UN system, where the real political decision making takes place, and the secretariats, which set the scene for decision making through the information and analysis they provide and the way in which they orchestrate the deliberative process. Even the category of 'member governments', however, is not univocal: different ministries relate to different UN forums and do not necessarily take the same positions on the same issues. A multi-level perspective is also necessary. Government spokespersons are often more malleable and subject to peer pressure regarding dialogue with civil society at global level than when the interaction shifts to the national scene.

Within the UN system itself, it is necessary to differentiate between offices, programmes and funds that fall under the direct authority of the Secretary-General and the General Assembly, such as the United Nations Department of Economic and Social Affairs (UNDESA), the United Nations Development Programme (UNDP), UNICEF and the United Nations Development Fund for Women (UNIFEM), and the specialized agencies which have separate and autonomous governing bodies, such as the FAO, UNESCO, the World Health Organization (WHO) and the ILO. The former type of entity most often exercises either policy forum or operational functions but not both, while the latter combines the two.[25] Small, new, focused agencies such as the Joint United Nations Programme on HIV/AIDS (UNAIDS) find it easier to innovate in the involvement of CSOs in governance than older, larger, more institutionalized structures. The IFIs have distinct mandates and governance mechanisms, not based on the 'one country one vote' UN rule but weighted according to levels of contributions. The WTO, outside the UN family, is yet another case. Within the secretariat of each organization, top management is likely to have one view of civil society relations, the unit responsible for managing them another, and the rest of the staff a range of perceptions depending on the nature of their work and their own individual experience and convictions. Innovation in civil society relations can operate at different rhythms in headquarters and in field offices.

Both terms of the civil society–UN equation, then, harbour a range of realities. We will see how these variables come to play in practice as we turn now to take a closer look at specific interaction processes. It is important to guard against notional shorthand that disguises these complex dynamics, since they are the most promising terrain for change in UN–civil society relations.

2
The FAO, Civil Society and the Global Governance of Food and Agriculture

Background

Throughout the history of humanity, procuring sufficient food to keep oneself and one's family alive has headed the list of what it was once fashionable to call 'basic needs'. Doing a better job of it was the most compelling enticement for families to gather together into communities and start building societies. That this number one basic need was not always being met for all people has thrust its way into the consciousness of governors and governed periodically over the past centuries. Interpretations of why this was so and of how to address the problem have varied considerably, of course, and continue to do so today as different actors barter their views of what to do about the global food crisis that hit the media in early 2008.

Within the United Nations (UN) system, this controversial issue has been most strongly associated with the Food and Agriculture Organization of the United Nations (FAO). Already between the two world wars the League of Nations had witnessed a split between the theses of the 'economic Malthusians' (Cépède 1984) who blamed the agricultural overproduction of 1929 for the ensuing economic crisis and prescribed reduction of production as a cure, and the work of a group of nutritionists – backed by trade unions and farmers' organizations – who were uncovering the scandal of widespread malnutrition[1] despite the global overavailability of food. A 'marriage between health and agriculture'[2] was in the brokering, and civil society was involved from the outset. It was consummated when the FAO was established in 1945 as a specialized technical agency of the UN, with the strong backing of the US President Franklin D. Roosevelt.

Not surprisingly, the new institution was fashioned to fit the perceived policy interests of the rich surplus-producer states.[3] The FAO's functions, as defined by its founding members, gave it little effective power to deal with fundamental problems such as that of international management of agricultural markets.[4] Its first director-general, Lord Boyd Orr of the UK, has recalled that he accepted the post reluctantly because he believed that the major powers would seek to limit the FAO's purview to that of 'collecting statistics, engaging in research and holding conferences' (FAO 1970:11). He resigned when it became clear that his forecast was proving correct. The occasion was the failure of his proposal to establish a World Food Board designed to reorganize international agricultural trade on a non-free-market basis in order to address the problem of world hunger and malnutrition.[5] A more modest project, for the creation of an International Commodities Clearing House, put forward in 1950 by his successor, N.E. Dodd, was also rejected. From the outset, the gap between the dimensions of the problem of world hunger and the lack of political will to solve it has been evident, leading many sensitive actors to view an appeal to the pressure of public opinion as the only way forward.[6]

This was certainly clear to Dr B.R. Sen of India, who took over the direction of the FAO in 1956. Sen brought with him the sense of urgency he had developed in his position as food commissioner in India during the Second World War, as he witnessed mass deaths from starvation yet was powerless to access food supplies from abroad (see Weitz 1999:73–90). As he worked to restructure and refocus the FAO, he became increasingly convinced that he had to reach beyond governments and the bureaucrats of the secretariat to deal with 'the old enemies of mankind: hunger, poverty, injustice and the denial of human rights and human dignity' (FAO 1970:13). In his strategy, the convening of a World Food Congress went hand in hand with an innovative appeal to civil society through the launching of a Freedom from Hunger Campaign (FFHC) to focus public attention on the problem of hunger and to mobilize national and international effort toward its solution. The idea was endorsed by the United Nations Economic and Social Council (ECOSOC) and adopted by the FAO Conference in 1959. The FFHC was launched on 1 July 1960, making the FAO one of the first UN agencies to establish a structured programme for cooperation with the non-governmental sector.

The first 15 years of the FFHC were marked by three international meetings focused on food and hunger. The First and the Second World Food Congresses, held respectively in Washington, DC, in 1963 and in

The Hague in 1970, were called at the initiative of the FAO. They were people's gatherings, not intergovernmental conferences. Nominations were solicited from governments, non-governmental organizations (NGOs), scientific societies, church organizations and other bodies, but participants were invited in their personal capacity.[7] The Congresses' results, hence, were not binding on member states, but their moral weight was not inconsiderable, given the level of the participants.[8]

The 1974 World Food Conference (WFC), in contrast, was an intergovernmental meeting called by the UN in response to the serious food shortage of 1972–73 which, many felt, could not be addressed solely through the kind of agriculture-oriented technical measures associated with the FAO. There is some irony in the fact that the FAO was being criticized for lack of political authority by the same powers that had ensured it remained toothless during its first years of life and who, in the view of knowledgeable observers, profited from the 1974 conference by operating a further dismantlement of global food and agriculture governance (see ETC Group 2008). The WFC introduced into the halls of the FAO the flavour of the North–South ideological debate that characterized the discussion on the New International Economic Order taking place at that time in the UN General Assembly[9] and triggered off the expression of divergent views on the merits of isolating technical and scientific endeavour from political considerations.[10] Observer status was granted to 161 international NGOs, but an attempt was made to limit their access to the plenary sessions by parking them in a parallel and separate NGO forum with little opportunity to engage with government delegates.[11] The NGO platform diagnosed the causes of the food crisis as predominantly political and structural. It highlighted the need for regulation of international markets in accordance with the needs of vulnerable and disadvantaged populations. It condemned the use of food aid as a political weapon and called for defence of rural producers' access to resources and capacity for food production. Although the official Universal Declaration on the Eradication of Hunger and Malnutrition that the conference adopted did not take these concerns on board, it did reaffirm the 'inalienable right to be free from hunger and malnutrition' and the primary responsibility of governments to ensure it. On balance, the 1974 WFC was judged by the NGOs themselves to have been an important catalyst for NGO advocacy work. 'Rome drew the attention of a whole new set of NGO actors and propelled them onto the international stage' (Van Rooy 1997:98).[12]

Punctuated by these international gatherings, the FFHC developed an innovative approach to networking, dialogue and action with civil society organizations (CSOs) over the three decades of its existence. In many ways it anticipated the UN system-wide evolutions of the 1990s.[13] During the 1960s, enjoying the full personal support of the FAO's Director-General, 'freedom from hunger' became the central theme of the organization's activities, a 'rededication to the objectives of the Charter' (Sen 1982:274). National FFHC committees were established in some 100 countries in all regions of the world as forums bringing together civil society and government to reflect and act to alleviate hunger and malnutrition. Regional and international FFHC conferences met just prior to the FAO regional and global conferences and fed NGO concerns and recommendations directly into the discussions of the FAO's governing bodies. 'People-to-people' FFHC projects combined civil society solidarity with FAO technical support. A 'Young World Appeal' mobilized the energy and idealism of young people concerned with world hunger. Regional FFHC liaison officers appointed in the field moved the focus from the global stage to the national. The campaign's bulletin, *Ideas and Action*, developed into a widely known and appreciated instrument for exchange of views and experience among national and local civil society groups in all regions.

During the decade of the 1970s, the FFHC and its partners moved to situate problems of hunger within a broader development context. Considerable attention was devoted to contacting the rapidly growing NGO world in the South and developing close relations with it, and to facilitating networking among groups in political situations in which cross-border contacts were difficult.[14] FFHC partners subjected the traditional development tool, the 'project', to critical scrutiny and reconceived it as a time-bound instrument of local development processes which had to be mastered by the people directly concerned, a concept later termed 'empowerment'. This led them to evolve participatory approaches to project formulation and to identify the kinds of 'non-project' support that NGOs needed to be effective 'empowerers',[15] two decades before 'capacity building' became a mainstream concern. The FFHC backed Northern NGO partners in their efforts to build up an informed, committed body of public opinion on issues related to food and development.[16] NGO advocacy networks were facilitated to participate in intergovernmental processes being negotiated in the FAO in such areas as biodiversity and fisheries resources. Throughout the 1980s, the FFHC increasingly provided a forum for intense dialogue between Northern and Southern NGOs,[17] while its projects constituted a laboratory for testing NGO alternative proposals.[18] The fact that the FFHC could count on liaison officers in the field and a modest but strategically significant budget of seed money programmed in consultation with civil society partners made it a focus for emerging regional and thematic civil society networks concerned with development issues.

The 1980s, however, also witnessed the progressive demise of the FFHC programme. In part this was due to the personality and priorities of the man who acted as the FAO's Director-General from 1975 to 1993. Eduoard Saouma was not a great lover of civil society, particularly when it voiced criticism of his policies; nor was he a particularly adept practitioner of partnerships in general. He kept NGOs at arm's length from the early days of his leadership, even when he organized initiatives of which they were backers, such as the World Conference on Agrarian Reform and Rural Development of 1979.[19] He exploded at them in anger when they attacked the FAO toward the end of his tenure in a special issue of the *Ecologist* published in 1991.[20] Leaving the personality of this particular leader aside, it is a fact of institutional life that top management are more committed to initiatives linked to their own administration than to those of their predecessors.[21] When the FAO encountered financial difficulties during the 1980s, the FFHC was a preferred target for cuts. The international and regional NGO consultations were discontinued. The regional liaison posts were eliminated and *Ideas and Action* was abolished despite a formidable campaign to keep it alive. The headquarters staff was reduced. In 1990 it was moved to an external relations office ill-suited to pursuit of the programme's reflection-and-action agenda, whose director glacially rejected the very idea of a budget jointly programmed with civil society partners.

But Saouma's distaste for civil society does not suffice to explain the death of the FFHC.[22] The first coordinator of the FFHC has suggested that the campaign's early promoters erred in failing to use the period of maximum dynamism and support of the FFHC to push for institutional changes in procedures for civil society participation in the governance of the FAO (Weitz 1999:90). Whether such changes would have got through at the time is a moot question. What is certain is that the fate of the FFHC in the 1970s and 1980s was bound up with broader issues of development paradigms and divergent views of institutional mandates and responsibilities. Already in the 1970s the FAO had been the theatre of the first staff strike in the UN system. This strike was sparked not only by demands regarding conditions of work but also by the convictions of an ample and articulate network of staff members who felt that it was illusory for the FAO to masquerade as a neutral technical forum and that the Green Revolution technology the organization was promoting was, in fact, politically and economically loaded. This was a radical internal statement of two related problems that have haunted the FAO from the outset: the gap between what is technically possible and the political will necessary to attain it, on the one hand, and the difficulties of conjugating technical and political dimensions of food and agricultural issues in a meaningful and transparent way, on the other.

The staff protest was quashed in the end and FAO's technical assistance programme settled back into the standard technology- and capital-driven sectoral programmes that characterized the period, hardly amenable to the empowerment approach that the FFHC and its partners were developing. A good illustration of this gap was the Agricultural Rehabilitation Programme for Africa (ARPA) – formulated by the FAO in response to the drought in Ethiopia, the Sahel and parts of Southern Africa in the mid-1980s – which consisted of country portfolios of separate sectoral proposals for crops, livestock, fertilizers and other components. When the FFHC office came forward with a participatory programme designed to help drought-affected communities in Ethiopia formulate and implement their own integrated rehabilitation proposals, the reaction of the FAO's management was to throw it out since it did not fit into the schema of the ARPA.[23] As the anthropologist Mary Douglas has put it, 'Institutions systematically direct memory and channel perceptions into forms compatible with the relations they authorize … The solutions they proffer only come from the limited range of their experience' (Douglas 1986:92). The FFHC was far distant from mainstream paradigms and practice and proved unable to have a significant impact on them.

A final important factor contributing to the fate of the FFHC was the relative weakness of civil society advocacy on food and agricultural issues at the time. Technically competent advocacy groups on issues like plant genetic resources or artisanal fisheries tended to work each in its own corner without making connections among themselves and developing overall visions and strategies. Non-state actor influence on the important evolutions taking place in the process of globalization of agricultural trade policy was largely limited to the agricultural economics epistemic community.[24] NGOs in the North and in the South were confronting each other on difficult issues of decision-making power and management of financial resources. And the NGO world in general had not yet woken up to the necessity of building links with people's organizations directly representing the populations on behalf of whom they advocated and acted. Since food and agricultural issues are vital to the livelihoods of the mainly rural poor and directly relevant to the objectives of their organizations – more so than the agendas of some of the other summits of the 1990s – the World Food Summit was destined to become a particularly significant theatre for the emergence on the global scene of these key civil society actors.

The FAO's governing bodies never took an explicit decision to end the FFHC, but under the management of the external relations office it was allowed to drop into oblivion – so much so that the team of consultants hired by Saouma's successor, Jacques Diouf, in 1994 to help him formulate plans for the restructuring of the FAO did not take this experience into account, despite the fact that building cooperation with civil society was a declared interest of the newly elected Director-General. But the knowledge, relations and trust that had been built up between this FAO programme and civil society communities concerned with food and agriculture issues throughout the world were still there. They served as a basis on which to build a renewed relationship when changes in the global context and in FAO's management combined with the proposal to hold a world food summit to create a favourable environment.

Civil Society and the World Food Summit

The 'why' and the 'what' of the summit

The proposal to organize a high-level summit on food issues was a central piece in Diouf's strategy to reinstate agriculture on the world's agenda and the FAO on the map of global institutions. The programme of UN summits which was to mark the decade of the 1990s was in the shaping, and the problem of hunger was up for grabs.[25]

Reanimating an organization that had been ruled by a single person for 18 years required the efforts of a determined and focused manager, and Diouf was one. The first months of his administration were devoted to a thorough review of the FAO conducted by a hand-picked team of outsiders to ensure that reform was not mired down in institutional immobility. His proposals were presented at a ministerial meeting on World Food Security held in Quebec on 16 October 1995 to celebrate the FAO's fiftieth anniversary, and at the 28th Session of the FAO Conference shortly thereafter. In a world context in which Diouf read 'a resurgence of isolationism and the propensity to crawl back into one's shell, with exacerbated criticism of UN and Bretton Woods institutions, a throwing into question of the principle of universality, and a weakened commitment for aid to development', a return to the social and moral values that underlay the FAO appeared essential to him (FAO 1995a). In his address to the Quebec fiftieth anniversary ceremony, Diouf stated that 'it is unacceptable, indeed impossible, to go on living in a world which has 800 million undernourished people' and suggested that 'the crux of the problem is therefore to devise ways to boost food production in Third World countries fast, substantially and sustainably'. Acknowledging that the problem had technical, financial and policy dimensions, Diouf proposed to work on the technical issues through a 'new Green Revolution' designed in such a way as to avoid the adverse environmental and socioeconomic effects of the first edition. Special programmes aimed at having a swift impact on food production in low-income, food-deficit countries would be the operational vehicle for this technical transformation.

The World Food Summit (WFS), in its turn, was intended to address the other two dimensions of the food crisis. As phrased in resolution 2/95 adopted unanimously by the FAO Conference on 31 October 1995, the WFS was expected to 'serve as a forum at the highest political level to marshal the global consensus and commitment needed to redress a most basic problem of humankind – food insecurity' and 'establish a policy framework and adopt a Plan of Action for implementation by governments, international institutions and all sectors of civil society' (FAO 1995b). Issues of trade, investment and environment were high on the policy agenda of the summit, with different segments of the FAO membership taking very different positions. Even obtaining the agreement of the most powerful member governments to the convening of the WFS required substantial efforts of diplomacy and persuasion on the part of the Director-General.

The proposal to hold the summit was subsequently endorsed by the UN General Assembly in December 1995. It thus entered the arena of the UN system of international conferences of the 1990s, although it remained somewhat on the margins of the process compared with the summits organized by offices and programmes directly responsible to the UN Secretary-General and accountable to ECOSOC and the General Assembly.

The FAO's script for civil society involvement

The FAO Conference resolution of October 1995 'stressed the importance of ensuring a process which involved all stakeholders', recalled the contribution that these actors had made to preceding world conferences, and authorized the Director-General to invite to the summit and to preparatory meetings 'observers from relevant non-governmental organizations and private-sector associations'. This text constituted the FAO secretariat's basic mandate to work with civil society in the WFS process.

The organizational machinery for the summit ground into operation while an extensive restructuring of the FAO was under way and staff were still trying to fathom the policies and strategies of their new director. A unit for cooperation with NGOs and the private sector had been created and the staff remaining from the by now defunct FFHC had moved there from the Office for External Affairs. Although the FAO Director-General repeatedly stressed the importance he attached to building partnerships in general, and civil society participation in the WFS in particular, he did not provide any particular policy guidance on how to go about it. The WFS Secretary-General opted to keep responsibility for civil society outreach within the summit secretariat rather than farming this task out to the NGO cooperation unit staff, known for their 'NGO style' of operations. The dialectic internal to the secretariat between an outreach approach firmly sited within the institutional logic and objectives of the intergovernmental organization and an approach that tended to go out on a limb to straddle the two worlds operated throughout the WFS process. The dominant objective of the former approach was to ensure NGO involvement toward attainment of summit objectives while avoiding disruption of the intergovernmental process. The primary aim of the latter approach was to take advantage of the WFS to move in the direction of opening up the organization to more meaningful participation by civil society actors, a process that would inevitably involve revisiting existing intergovernmental procedures.

During the summer of 1995, the WFS secretariat and the NGO cooperation unit worked together to design a strategy framework for NGO involvement in the WFS.[26] Chief among the challenges to be addressed was the need to convince NGOs that the summit would make a difference and that there would be real opportunities for them to influence its outcome. The short build-up time available was identified as a constraint. So was the fact that the FAO had opted to avoid a special preparatory process, using instead the normal sessions of existing bodies. As part of the FAO's governance system, the two major bodies concerned – the global Committee on World Food Security (CFS) and the FAO Regional Conferences – were likely to be more impermeable to NGO intrusion than the ad hoc preparatory committees adopted by other UN summits (UN-NGLS 1995; FAO 1995c).[27] Guidelines for participation of NGOs in the summit were officially communicated to the outside world in an NGO Information Note in early 1996. This envisaged participation at various levels. Within countries, NGOs were invited to contact the national secretariats or committees and become involved in the preparation of national position papers. Instructions to the FAO's Country Representatives encouraged them to facilitate such inclusion. At regional level, subject to availability of extrabudgetary resources, a two-day NGO meeting was planned prior to each Regional Conference. Globally, all interested NGOs were invited to provide written comments on the technical papers prepared for the summit and on the draft declaration and plan of action. Accredited organizations would be invited to attend the sessions of the CFS in which these documents would be discussed. A two-day NGO meeting was scheduled, also subject to availability of resources, just before the final CFS session in September 1996 at which it was expected that the summit documents would be finalized. The NGO Information Note indicated that an NGO forum might be organized in parallel to the summit and made it clear that this was a separate event for which the FAO was not responsible.

Criteria for accreditation of NGOs to attend the summit as observers referred to the open-ended terminology of 'relevant and competent' which had been coined for the United Nations Conference on Environment and Development (UNCED) and adopted by subsequent summits. In the context of the WFS, this was interpreted to mean that NGO observers should have one or more of the following: knowledge of, and experience in, areas related to food security; experience in policy advocacy and public information related to food and agricultural development issues; knowledge of, and experience in, working with food producers and consumers; normative and/or operational cooperation with the FAO in areas of work related to food security. Applying NGOs had to fill in a questionnaire patterned on the UNCED precedent, and to submit what was becoming the standard set of documentation.[28] Priority would be given to organizations that had participated in the preparatory process. National NGOs were invited to seek inclusion in their government's delegation or in that of an invited international non-governmental organization (INGO). In the end some national NGOs were invited to attend the summit, following the UNCED precedent and its procedure of giving the government concerned an opportunity to object. Accreditation to the summit was completely separate from that for the NGO Forum.

One important proposal put forward by the NGO cooperation unit, seconded by the UN Non-Governmental Liaison Service (UN-NGLS) and approved by the WFS Steering Committee that had been set up within the FAO, was, however, not implemented by the WFS secretariat. This was the suggestion that the FAO should encourage the NGO community to establish an interface mechanism with which the secretariat could work in order to involve NGOs not only in the preparations for the summit but in its follow-up as well. This proposal was key to the strategy of the NGO cooperation unit, since it would have moved the FAO toward an interactive stance of dialoguing with the NGO world and increased the negotiating power of the latter. The WFS secretariat, however, preferred to limit interaction with the autonomous civil society mechanism which did emerge to matters concerning the separate NGO Forum, without extending the formal consultative process to participation in the official summit.

Civil society gets itself organized

Like other summits, the WFS constituted an important occasion for various sectors of civil society – coming at the issues under examination from different angles – to build a practice of networking and joint planning. The process was not easy or automatic. Early in 1995, the Italian development NGO federations began consultations regarding the organization of an NGO Forum in parallel to the WFS.[29] On 10 October 1995, they joined with the Liaison Committee of Development NGOs to the European Union (CLONG/Comité de Liaison des ONG)[30] to state formally their willingness to act as hosts to the NGOs coming to Rome for the summit. This commitment was reiterated on 21 October 1995 to a meeting of international NGOs attending the 28th session of the FAO Conference, a group that felt a certain proprietary interest in WFS preparations because of the formal status with the FAO that most of them enjoyed. At about the same time, the CSOs attending the FAO 50th anniversary celebrations in Quebec on 16 October gave birth to a Global Network on Food Security, it too looking toward the summit.

By the end of the year, NGO leaders had diplomatically drawn these networks together into an International Support Committee (ISC) in order to avoid paralysing and self-damaging conflict within the civil society community.[31] The existence of this mechanism was formalized on the occasion of the 21st session of the Committee on World Food Security from 29 January to 2 February 1996. The five original members of the ISC, representing international networks, were all from Europe and North America.[32] Shortly thereafter the committee was broadened to include seven representatives from Southern CSOs – with emphasis on peasants, fisherfolk and indigenous peoples – and one from Eastern Europe.[33] A five-member steering committee supervised forum preparations and acted as a kind of 'political body' during the preparatory process and the forum itself.[34]

The WFS–NGO Forum process got under way just two years after the Rio conference. UNCED had had an enormous impact in terms of bringing new civil society actors into contact with the UN. It had also stimulated communication among sectors of civil society that had previously ignored each other's existence or doubted each other's relevance: development and environment NGOs to cite the most obvious examples. Within this context of great flux, certain dynamics emerged with particular force in the WFS–NGO Forum arena in addition to the well-documented confrontation between Northern and Southern organizations. One of these was the tension between INGOs, which had enjoyed special prerogatives up until then and aspired to represent the civil society of the world at international forums, and the variegated new universe of local and national groups and regional and global networks representing constituencies and modes of organization that bore little relation to those of the traditional INGOs.[35] Although two of the global networks participating in the ISC were composed of INGOs of the traditional type, neither were members of the steering committee and the most powerful voices in planning and running the forum were undoubtedly those of the emerging new civil society world.

A second area of conflict was that between the non-profits and the private sector business associations, which are technically classified as non-profit NGOs within the UN system but in fact most often represent the for-profit interests of their members. This kind of tension was particularly strong in the WFS–NGO Forum process because of the power of multinationals in the agri-food chain and the impact they have on small producers, and on consumers and the environment. The substantive conflict had been exacerbated during the International

Conference on Nutrition (ICN) hosted by the FAO in 1992, by a problem of process. Backed by a number of formal-status INGOs concerned to defend the prerogatives of their private sector INGO associates, the secretariat of the ICN had tried to oblige the NGO observers to let private sector associations participate in their caucusing meetings. In 1996, on the contrary, private sector associations were not admitted to the NGO Forum on Food Security sessions in which civil society positions and statements were formulated.[36]

A third important civil society dynamic that began to take shape during the forum process was that between NGOs, which had heretofore tended to position themselves as spokespersons for the rural poor and the marginalized of this world, and the people's organizations that were emerging in a context of globalization and liberalization and questioned the right of others to speak on their behalf. Ironically, the fact that this dynamic was so evident in the context of the forum was due to the very particular efforts the organizers made to ensure that people's organizations played a protagonist role. Although Via Campesina, the global peasant network born just three years earlier, refrained from underwriting the final declaration of the forum,[37] their contestation was less important than the fact that they considered themselves to be a part of the process. This was the beginning of a relationship that was destined to develop significantly in the period following the summit. Organizations representing other social sectors – pastoralists, fisherfolk, indigenous peoples – were less present at the forum, a reflection above all of their weaker level of structuring. But here too the efforts that had been made to involve them would bear fruit in the future.[38]

To what degree were the CSOs interacting with governments in the run-up to the summit? The line-up of governments on issues of NGO participation in the FAO's policy forums during the first half of the 1990s tended to follow a North–South split, although the motivations of different groups of reluctant Southern countries varied somewhat. Malaysia and other tropical timber producers had been stung by the criticism to which NGOs had subjected them during the negotiations of the Tropical Forestry Action Plan,[39] and they accused Northern environmental NGOs of calling the tune to the detriment of developing-country interests. In Asian countries such as Indonesia and the Philippines, the confrontation between governments and radical popular movements was internal and highly political, to the point of armed conflict. The Latin American group of governments tended to perpetuate the very deep suspicion of the world of civil society that had reigned on the continent during the long period of authoritarian regimes. African governments looked on Northern NGOs as competitors for development assistance and on African CSOs as potential destabilizers of government rule. Europe and North America, on the contrary, were the sources of the positive language about stakeholder participation that figured in the conference resolution.

A few NGO groups were already operating within the FAO policy arena and had developed strong practices of lobbying governments, both at the global level and at home.[40] These networks also tended to be well linked into related processes stemming from other global conferences, Rio in particular. But generally speaking, NGO presence in the technical committees and commissions reporting to the FAO Council and Conference,[41] in which the bulk of intergovernmental decision making under FAO auspices takes place, was scanty and discontinuous in the early 1990s. NGO interaction with the FAO Regional Conferences had been cut back practically to zero with the discontinuation of the FFHC consultations. National-level civil society lobbying on food and agriculture policy was just barely beginning to get under way in many countries of the South, under the pressure of structural adjustment.[42] With the exception of North American and European NGOs, CSOs were not structured and prepared to interact with the regional intergovernmental blocs within which consensus positions were hammered out before the global negotiations ever reached the plenary rooms. Hence, on the rare occasions when civil society spokespersons did make it to global policy forums they arrived too late. The field of interaction between civil society and government on the issues that would be coming up before the WFS was wide open for development.

The official summit and the NGO Forum

As in the case of all UN summits, the resource issue was an important one. How were funds to be mobilized to support civil society participation and who should manage them? The major funder of the 1996 NGO Forum was the Italian government.[43] Negotiations with the government were conducted by the Italian NGO community with the support of the FAO. The funds, deposited with the FAO, were transferred to the Italian Committee for the NGO Forum under the terms of a contract negotiated with the FAO and signed in June 1996.[44] The selection of developing-country participants to receive travel support was made by the ISC steering committee. NGO participation in the official summit process was funded through extrabudgetary contributions to an FAO trust fund set up for this purpose.[45] The WFS secretariat managed these funds and made the final decision on who would receive support.[46]

The preparatory process for the official summit was compressed and intense. In April 1995 the 20th Session of the Committee on World Food Security looked at a draft outline of 'elements for possible inclusion in a draft declaration and plan of action on universal food security' (FAO 1995d). The January 1996 session of the CFS, which had been designated in the meantime by the FAO Conference as the locus for summit preparations, discussed an initial draft of the proposed WFS documents. It established an Intersessional Working Group (ISWG) which held three meetings to negotiate the texts.[47] A steadily growing number of NGOs were accredited to attend the sessions and were permitted to intervene relatively freely in the discussions. The WFS secretariat made a serious effort to facilitate transmission of written NGO comments to government delegations. Comments prepared by individual NGOs were duplicated and distributed, in the original language, as ISWG information documents. A secretariat document presented to the first ISWG meeting synthesized comments that had been received from 14 organizations. NGOs were also encouraged to submit comments on the drafts of 14 technical papers that the FAO secretariat prepared as background for the summit.[48]

At the same time, the planned series of five regional NGO consultations was taking place, from the Near East in late March to Latin America and the Caribbean in early July. The preparation of these meetings had been another area of disagreement internal to the FAO secretariat. The NGO consultation unit proposed that one or more regional NGO networks should be invited to co-organize each consultation and to draft and circulate a discussion paper ahead of time in order to facilitate broader participation and a more coherent and carefully thought-out result. The WFS secretariat preferred to keep organizational responsibility in the FAO's hands. National or regional NGOs were to be involved in the logistics and the last phases of the planning, but preparatory civil society networking and caucusing were not envisaged.

Although the NGO Forum International Support Committee as such was not consulted or involved in the regional meetings, in most cases regional components of the ISC were, if only at the last moment.[49] Lack of careful preparation affected the quality of the discussions. As a European member of the ISC put it:

No preparatory work had been done on the NGO declaration prior to the [European] consultation. As a result it was improvised overnight. The absence of any structure – such as a consultative NGO assembly – gave this consultation an ephemeral and 'light' character. And yet a real and deep work of reflection on the draft WFS declaration and plan of action was being carried out by NGOs outside of the consultation (*Les Brèves du CSA*, August–September 1996:7).

The results of the NGO consultations were reported to the FAO Regional Conferences. The WFS secretariat's NGO Information Note No. 3 circulated summaries of the conclusions of all six meetings. Whatever the shortcomings of the consultations and their concrete outputs, the progression from national to regional to global levels was an effective approach whose results were capitalized upon by the NGO Forum organizers in elaborating their own position and building their networking.

The final act of the officially sponsored preparatory process for civil society was an international FAO/NGO Consultation on the World Food Summit held at FAO headquarters on 19–21 September 1996, immediately before the final negotiating phase for the Rome Declaration and Plan of Action in the CFS. It was attended by more than 400 representatives of some 240 national and international NGOs.[50] The purpose of the consultation, as formulated by the secretariat, was 'to enable participants to discuss the draft Rome Declaration and the Plan of Action in order to produce concrete proposals to be presented to the Committee on World Food Security'. The consultation was also invited to 'propose modalities of civil society contribution to the follow-up to the Summit, including the Food for All Campaign' proposed in the draft Plan of Action. Finally, the ISC would be invited to provide information about plans for the NGO Forum.

In the end, the participants decided not to limit themselves to commenting on the draft official texts but instead to produce an alternative statement of their own. This step was motivated by a recognition that the deep cleavage between the opposing development paradigms to which they and the governments referred could not be bridged by suggesting amendments to the documents under negotiation, amendments that were not likely to be accepted in any event. This was particularly so regarding key issues such as liberalization of international trade, the functions of agriculture, control of multinational corporations (MNCs), and the role of rural people's organizations. A civil society document entitled 'Key Points of the Consultation' was adopted by a very large majority of the participants and presented to the CFS as an information document.[51] This was a turning point in the process, the moment in which the civil society actors took full possession of their preparations for the World Food Summit, deviating from the route that the WFS secretariat had traced. The official and the autonomous NGO preparations were merged, although divergences within the civil society universe continued, of course, to exist. The brief report prepared by the WFS secretariat of the consultation toned down the civil society critique considerably. It constituted an interesting study in the domestication of civil society language and provoked irritated reactions on the part of some NGOs. 'The official synthesis ... illustrates the rupture of perspectives between the NGOs and the FAO. The NGOs are not satisfied with proposing technical measures which can act as safety nets but aspire to change the present model of development' (*Les Brèves du CSA*, October 1996:1).

Participation of NGO observers in the actual CFS discussions was restricted as the negotiations homed in on the most controversial portions of the texts, those concerning sustainable agriculture and international trade above all. The method of negotiation privileged consensus within regional and supra-regional blocks – North America, the European Union and the Group of 77 (G-77). This marginalized isolated countries such as Switzerland and Norway which often took positions more in line with those of civil society. In the end the CFS session was not able to dissolve all of the brackets, and an additional session was required at the end of October in order to get the text into final shape for the gathering of heads of state and government. NGOs were not enthused by the results.

> Late last night, the Green Room produced the single note-worthy 'product' so far surviving the drafting process. If it remains, Summit leaders will pledge themselves to try to cut the number of malnourished people by half over the next 19 years. Staked up against the ringing rhetoric of past food conferences, this is pretty humble stuff (*The [Bread] Bracket* 1996:1).[52]

Outside the official preparatory process, a series of autonomous civil society initiatives produced declarations and position papers that targeted the WFS.[53] A new development was the mobilization of peasant and small farmer organizations, independently of NGOs and of the International Federation of Agricultural Producers – dominantly composed of larger, market-oriented farmers at that time – which had previously constituted the only farmers' voice on the international scene. The second conference of Via Campesina, held in April 1996,

formally decided that the movement should be represented at the WFS
since no solution to the problems of food security could be found
without the active participation of those who produce food. The
constitutive assembly of the Platform of Peasant Organizations of the
Sahel (April 1996) adopted a Memorandum for the World Food
Summit. These autonomous initiatives, networked by the ISC, inter-
sected with the official process at the regional and global NGO consultations organized by the FAO.

The World Food Summit and the NGO Forum for Food Security
were completely separate events although they took place at the same
time and in the same city, just one metro stop away from each other.
The WFS was a very formal affair. The negotiations on the
documents to be adopted had been concluded beforehand and the
programme was essentially composed of a succession of statements by
the heads of delegations of the 186 countries present, 112 at the level
of heads of state or government. Some 800 NGO observers attended,
from about 400 organizations, in addition to some 100 NGO
members of government delegations. A complicated and restrictive
system of passes made it difficult for NGOs to reach the plenary area
and make contact with government delegations. The area assigned to
NGOs was out of the way and practically always empty. The only
provision for NGO observers to speak were 12 four-minute statements allocated to 'constituencies' which were defined and announced
by the secretariat once the summit had already begun, making it very
difficult for them to caucus.[54] The interventions took place late at
night, at the end of the government delegation declarations, before an
empty plenary hall.

Five events were scheduled in parallel to the summit and their
conclusions were reported to the plenary. Of these, the NGO Forum
was by far the biggest and the most significant. The others were a Private
Sector Seminar on food safety and processing, a Parliamentarians'
Meeting convened by the Italian Parliament with the assistance of the
FAO and the Inter-Parliamentarian Union, a Family Farmers' Summit
hosted by the Japanese cooperatives' organization Ja-Zenchu, and an
International Youth Forum organized by the FAO with support from
the International Fund for Agricultural Development (IFAD), the
Belgian government and private firms. This latter meeting, whose
participants were the winners of a worldwide essay contest rather than
self-selected representatives of youth organizations, was criticized by
many of the youth organizations and NGO networks.

The result of this process entirely controlled by FAO and some states was subsequently reported to the WFS in the form of a totally aseptic 'official youth declaration', which sounded more like the discourse of a technocrat than of an international organization of young people *(Les Brèves du CSA,* December 1996:5).

Undaunted, an autonomous alternative youth forum, the Hunger Gathering, staged what was without doubt one of the most effective NGO interventions during the summit, when three young women stripped during the press conference of the US Secretary of Agriculture, unveiling body paint slogans such as 'free trade = hunger', while their companions launched fistfuls of organic soya on the astonished public.

The NGO Forum was housed in a cavernous building intended to serve as a terminal for the airport train and built to hold not more than 1,300 people. The programme was divided into two phases. The first, from 11 to 13 November, was limited to 600 delegates with voting rights, 50 per cent of whom represented local or national organizations of peasants, women and indigenous peoples from the South.[55] This was the only one of the NGO forums held in parallel to the summits of the 1990s that adopted specific procedures of this kind to ensure balanced civil society participation.[56] It was their prerogative to debate and finalize the forum's statement starting off from a text prepared by a regionally balanced seven-person drafting committee.[57] The draft statement was debated in plenary, revised in regional working groups, and again discussed, amended and adopted by the plenary. Via Campesina dissented in the end on the grounds that the text failed 'to express a clear position in favour of oppressed groups and peoples of today's global agricultural systems'. They did, however, state their appreciation that the peasant and farmer organizations they represented had been 'fully accepted and involved throughout the work of the NGO Forum' and their agreement with many of the points contained in the declaration (Italian Committee for the NGO Forum on Food Security 1997:58).[58] The statement was originally scheduled to be communicated to the WFS plenary at 21:00 on 13 November but the NGOs refused to accept such a marginal time slot. In the end they negotiated the right to deliver it to a full hall at noon on 17 November, in the closing plenary session of the summit. The statement was presented by an African NGO representative, while a Via Campesina representative from Latin America was selected by the forum participants to present the declaration of the NGO consultation that had taken place in September.[59]

The second part of the NGO Forum, from 14 to 16 November, was open to all interested organizations subject to a light registration process that served essentially to keep track of who was in the building. Over 800 organizations from 80 countries participated, with an average daily attendance of 1,000 people. Some 300 journalists followed the forum events, which were well reported in the internal WFS journals.[60] The programme included some 30 workshops organized into three blocks: 'Una tierra para vivir' (access to land, biodiversity, sustainable food production), 'Women's Day' (with a workshop on 'Impact of market liberalization on strategies for food security' running in parallel), and 'A Contract of Societies for Global Food Security' (Code of Conduct on the Right to Food and Global Convention). In addition, there was the usual mushrooming of events organized spontaneously by participants as the forum progressed. The closing session on 16 November was intended to identify the next steps for NGO work. The programme included special initiatives, of which the most colourful were a torchlight procession to the Coliseum in collaboration with the City of Rome and a symbolic event in which members of Via Campesina scattered soil and seeds from around the world to create a garden on the unpromising terrain in front of the air terminal.

Not many official summit delegates made the journey to the NGO Forum.[61] Its events were not highly publicized at FAO headquarters and, as we have seen, it was not easy for the civil society organizations themselves to gain direct access to WFS delegates. Participation by the FAO secretariat was also relatively light. The Director-General of the FAO spoke at the opening ceremony on 11 November, the WFS Secretary-General addressed the closing session, and there were three major moments of planned interaction in between.[62] Staff of the two units most concerned with civil society relations[63] were in attendance throughout the forum and some officers from other parts of the organization attended specific events at their own individual initiative. This situation of relative lack of interaction was a product in good part of the 'not too close for comfort' approach to civil society espoused by the WFS secretariat. It would, as we will see, be significantly transformed in the course of the +5 process.

Civil society issues and framing

Turning from process to the content of the NGO Forum, what were the main issues that emerged from the extensive civil society reflection and debate? The final statement, entitled *Profit for Few or Food for All?* (UN-

NGLS 1997), built its case 'first and foremost' on 'the basic human Right to Food', an important affirmation in a period in which a rights-based approach was beginning to move on from the political field to tackle the less charted domain of economic and social rights. The second principle on which the statement rested was the insistence that 'governments have the primary and ultimate responsibility to ensure national and global food security'. Civil society's analysis of the causes of hunger highlighted globalization of the world economy and lack of accountability of multinational corporations leading to unemployment and destruction of rural economies. Industrialized agriculture supported by subsidies and generating dumping practices was seen to be 'destroying traditional farming, poisoning the planet ... and making people dependent on food they are unable to produce'. Structural adjustment and debt repayment imposed by the international community reinforced the tendency of national governments to fashion policies that neglected family farmers and vulnerable people. War, civil conflict and environmental degradation were important accompanying factors. As one NGO bulletin put it:

> The Forum declaration clearly identifies as causes of food insecurity those tendencies which the official declaration presents as solutions: liberalisation of agricultural trade, concentration of farms and capitalistic intensification of production, strengthened role of transnational corporations in the food chain (*Les Brèves du CSA*, December 1996:1).

The NGOs proposed an alternative model based on decentralization, rather than concentration, of wealth and power. They outlined six priority actions to be taken:

1 The capacity of family farmers, including indigenous peoples, women and youth, along with local and regional food systems, must be strengthened.
2 The concentration of wealth and power must be reversed and action taken to prevent further concentration, in particular through agrarian reform and protection of farmers' rights to genetic resources.
3 Agriculture and food production systems that rely on non-renewable resources which negatively affect the environment must be changed toward a model based on agro-ecological principles.
4 National and local governments and states have the prime responsibility to ensure food security. Their capacity to fulfil this role must be strengthened and mechanisms to ensure accountability must be enhanced.

5 The participation of people's organizations and NGOs at all levels must be strengthened and deepened.
6 International law must guarantee the right to food, ensuring that food sovereignty takes precedence over macroeconomic policies and trade liberalization. Food cannot be considered as a commodity, because of its social and cultural dimensions.

The declaration closed with a paragraph on follow-up, engaging civil society to monitor the implementation of the WFS commitments and participate in the 'Food for All Campaign'. In return, it called for an opening up of the intergovernmental Committee on World Food Security to include participation by all actors of civil society involved in the follow-up tasks assigned to the committee.

A major strength of the declaration was, quite simply, the fact that it was crafted inclusively and adopted by a wide variety of civil society actors, the majority coming from the South and a good proportion from people's organizations. 'For the first time since they started to hold forums in parallel to United Nations conferences', stated one of the journals published during the WFS, 'the NGOs have accomplished a remarkable task of dialogue which has resulted in a common position' (ENDA 1996:1). A second strength was the fact that this common position wove together a number of the networks that had separately accumulated considerable expertise on particular areas of the agro-food complex of issues and experience in interacting with the FAO and member governments. In these areas, taking off from a basis of previous work, the reflection went beyond denunciation of present abuses and telegraphic annunciation of alternatives using 'must' language. The workshops on sustainable agriculture started to actually map out the substance of the approaches being advocated. These ranged from the overtly political issue of agrarian reform to a reorientation of agricultural research and extension in the light of local knowledge and perceived problems, and also included the mainstreaming of agro-ecological food production based on family farming and the privileging of local and regional food systems. The proposals were not abstractions; they were based on extensive NGO-promoted field experience. The link between locally rooted action and global policy advocacy was beginning to be made.

The impact of international agricultural trade on food security was another area to which a growing number of NGOs and farmers' organizations were turning their attention, following the 1994 signing of the Marrakesh Agreement which established the World Trade Organization (WTO). Workshops on trade-related questions mushroomed in the NGO Forum programme.[64] The NGO Forum offered an occasion to initiate dialogue with the FAO on these issues, on which the secretariat itself was trying with some difficulty to define a role and a position in the charged political field that accompanied the birth of the WTO. The NGOs maintained that, far from offering the solution to food insecurity, international agricultural trade constituted a good part of the problem. A new term introduced into the lexicon by Via Campesina, that of 'food sovereignty', made its way into the text of the forum's statement. Not widely understood or used in civil society circles at the time, it was destined to emerge over the following years as the paradigm that civil society opposed to the neoliberal Washington consensus. Much of the force of this concept stemmed from its capacity to subject the elusive terrain of macroeconomic policy to a rights-based approach, offering the prospect that moral indignation could be incarnated in provisions of international law.[65] The forum statement noted that 'each nation must have the right to food sovereignty to achieve the level of food sufficiency and nutritional quality it considers appropriate without suffering retaliation of any kind' (UN-NGLS 1997:7). In consequence, it continued, the Uruguay Round agreements should be reviewed to reflect this right and to ensure that agriculture could fulfil its multiple functions, not limited to that of market-oriented production.

The food sovereignty imperative was coupled with the instrument of international law to introduce two of the most innovative proposals put forward by the NGOs. The voluntary Code of Conduct on the Right to Food would call on national governments to implement policies that would ensure access by their citizens to safe, adequate, nutritious food supplies. It had been developed by a group of specialized international NGOs, in particular the Foodfirst Information and Action Network (FIAN), the Jacques Maritain Institute and the World Alliance for Breastfeeding Action (WABA). A separate initiative, the Global Sustainable Food Security Convention, was born from NGO disappointment at the weakness of the official WFS texts. It aimed at creating a legally binding framework that would formally establish food security in the structures of international law. In an open letter dated 31 October 1996 a drafting group of nine NGOs from various regions[66] asked CSOs to sign on to a call for such a convention, a call that would be distributed at the WFS and the NGO Forum.

In wording that recalled the dashed proposals of the first Director-General of the FAO, the drafting group stated the primary goal of an internationally coordinated approach to food security as that of 'increasing stability in the food supply by reducing volatility in agricultural markets, and by making food production and distribution systems sustainable over the long term' (Italian Committee for the NGO Forum on Food Security 1997:62). Structural adjustment and the creation of the WTO had significantly reduced national control of agricultural policy. In compensation, the convention was intended to build a framework at international level that would allow governments to define and implement the specific packages of policies required to ensure that food security be given highest priority in the national context. Some of the actions proposed, whose implementation would be guided by a secretariat housed in the FAO, were constituent elements of the alternative platform on which a far broader coalition of CSOs and social movements is working more than a decade later: supply management to avoid surpluses that drive down agricultural commodity prices, exemption of staple foods from WTO rules when the latter undermine national food security, international commodity agreements among exporting and importing countries, an international network of food reserves accumulated from the local level up, funding of implementation of the convention from alternative financing mechanisms such as a tax on agricultural commodity trade. The Code of Conduct on the Right to Food and the Global Convention on Sustainable Food Security had been developed separately, but the groups backing them were able to bind the two initiatives together into a mutually reinforcing package.

A final aspect of the outcome of the NGO Forum that merits underlining was the careful attention paid to the actors of food security. The report of the forum included a paragraph distinguishing among the roles and responsibilities of different actors: governments, international institutions, private sector and multinational corporations, cooperation and solidarity NGOs. Pride of place went to organizations of peasants, women, indigenous peoples, fisherfolk, herders, consumers, considered to be the 'key actors in any food security strategy'(Italian Committee for the NGO Forum on Food Security 1997:18–19).

The impact on World Food Summit outcomes

The very large amount of effort that CSOs invested in attempting to influence the content and the wording of the official texts of the WFS was not rewarded to anything near a satisfactory degree. Civil society disagreement with the outcome of the WFS[67] was systemic and profound. The two most controversial and heavily bracketed sections of the Plan of Action, up to the last minute, were those dealing with models and policies of agriculture (Commitment Three) and international trade (Commitment Four). CSOs lobbied strongly to avoid language that would link attainment of world food security with the extension of international trade. These efforts did not succeed, and Commitment Four, as finally adopted, stressed in no uncertain terms that 'the progressive implementation of the Uruguay Round as a whole will generate increasing opportunities for trade expansion and economic growth to the benefit of all participants' (FAO 1996b: para. 38). In a related move, CLONG had proposed an amendment committing signatories to 'establish and enforce an effective international regulatory environment for transnational corporations trading in agricultural commodities' (CLONG 1996: 10). This language, sandwiched between brackets, actually made its way into the text of Commitment Four, which went before the CFS session in September 1996. As an NGO bulletin wryly commented, 'in the working group on international trade it took only 30 seconds for the three big regional blocks to delete this amendment, without the slightest bit of discussion' (*Les Brèves du CSA*, October 1996:3).

Divergences between regional blocks made it possible for the CSOs to make a bit more headway on Commitment Three. European NGO lobbying contributed to, but did not single-handedly determine, the determination of the European Union to maintain a reference to 'the multifunctional character of agriculture' in the title of the commitment in the face of trenchant opposition from the United States as a major food-exporting country. Other civil society successes included the recognition in the official text of the roles of indigenous peoples and women, and the need to strengthen the capacities of organizations representing peasant farmers, herders and fisherfolk. References to agrarian reform, triangular food exchanges and organic agriculture were also to a good degree the result of NGO lobbying. But, overall, the Plan of Action presented food insecurity as being a result of inadequate production, above all, and recommended trade- and technology-driven solutions to the perceived problem, in sharp contrast to the vision that underlay the comments and proposals that CSOs had introduced during the negotiation process. The concept of 'food security' had nothing to say about where food should be produced, how and by whom, nor about who has the right to make these decisions.

The area in which CSO lobbying made greatest headway in the intergovernmental process and opened up the most significant room for future negotiation and political manoeuvring was the identification of freedom from hunger as a fundamental human right. Objective 7.4 of the Plan of Action committed governments, in partnership with civil society actors, 'to clarify the content of the right to adequate food and the fundamental right of everyone to be free from hunger ... and to give particular attention to implementation and full and progressive realization of this right as a means of achieving food security for all' (FAO 1996b: para. 61), entrusting responsibility for coordinating these efforts to the UN Commissioner for Human Rights. NGO skill in building up an alliance with like-minded governments and staff of international organizations undoubtedly contributed to attaining this result and to the isolation of the US negotiating team.[68]

Commenting on the final draft of the Plan of Action, an English-language independent civil society bulletin, *The [Bread] Bracket* (1996:4), noted that identifiable targets, measurable goals and monitoring facilities 'evaporate at every negotiation'; it summed up its overall scorecard in these terms: 'it has all the right nouns but none of the right verbs'. Many other civil society observers felt that even the nouns were at fault. The French-language *Les Brèves du CSA* (December 1996:2) deplored the dominant role assigned to the liberalization and extension of international trade in what was otherwise 'a shopping list rather than a coherent and coordinated policy'. Most disturbing was the fact that arbitration of international agricultural policies had been ceded to the General Agreement on Tariffs and Trade/World Trade Organization (GATT/WTO), with no attempt to empower a world authority that would place food security concerns above the promotion of trade and with no attempt to discipline the food chain multinationals, whose impact on food security had gone unmentioned in the Plan of Action. *Les Brèves du CSA* (December 1996:2) closed its evaluation of the WFS with the prophetic comment that 'this last (?) of the great summits, thanks to its lack of results, may have contributed more than other conferences to convincing civil society to develop its own agenda'. In fact, as Alison Von Rooy points out in her study of NGO lobbying at the 1974 World Food Conference and the 1992 Earth Summit, longitudinal and comparative studies are necessary in order to assess influence in any meaningful way (Van Rooy 1997:1). Lessons learned and seeds sown at the 1996 WFS would start to bear fruit during the World Food Summit:*five years later* (WFS:*fyl*) process.

The impact on civil society networking

The experience of the WFS and the parallel forum gave impetus to CSOs in three major interrelated ways. One important outcome was broadened and more focused networking on the main issues that had emerged from the NGO Forum (Valente 1999). Preparations for the WTO revision of the GATT agreement in 1999 provided a focus for work on trade issues by a range of CSOs. Sustainable Agriculture and Rural Development (SARD) was due to come up at the 2000 session of the UNCED review mechanism, the Commission on Sustainable Development (CSD), and this prospect mobilized the attention of some – but not all – of the organizations concerned with this area at the NGO Forum. The interaction of these two UN family processes, as we will see, was to spark off dynamics that have interesting lessons to reveal in terms of civil society–UN relations.

The most linear and transparent issue-based follow-up action by civil society was in the area of the right to food. The lead organizations on this question had made a point of seeking and receiving a formal mandate from the NGO Forum to draft a text for discussion at a subsequent international NGO conference. They did so, and the NGOs' draft Code of Conduct on the Human Right to Adequate Food was made publicly available in September 1997, less than a year after the WFS. It served as a basis for lobbying government delegates both in the FAO's Committee on World Food Security and at the Commission on Human Rights, and for sensitization within the civil society movement itself (see Windfuhr 1998).

A second area of impact on civil society networking was the heightened attention the forum process generated to the need to go beyond the usual NGO circles and give priority to the involvement of people's organizations and social movements, a direct result of a determined policy orientation on the part of the forum organizers. This commitment tended to remain in the domain of rhetoric, however, for not only cultural and methodological but also political reasons. It constituted perhaps the most important bone of contention within the NGO world in follow-up to the forum, even more so than differing views on specific issues, although these too were not lacking. As we will see, several years were to go by before the people's organizations themselves gained sufficient strength to impose their protagonism on a largely ambivalent NGO universe at the time of the civil society Forum for Food Sovereignty of 2002.

A third area of impact was progress in strengthening networking in regions in which civil society interrelations were weakest, although here too the results were limited. The 270 African CSOs present at the 1996 forum, predominantly NGOs, agreed to establish a Coalition of African Organizations for Food Security and Sustainable Development (COASAD/Coalition des Organisations Africaines pour la Sécurité Alimentaire et le Développement Durable). The coalition did indeed meet in Tanzania in November 1998, but it was burdened with a highly complex formal constitution and a mode of operation that required substantial outside funding which did not materialize. The West African farmers' movement, which was supposed to be a main founding member, declined to join the organization and its legitimacy faded. Its Brussels-based secretary-general continued somehow to gain access to the ear and the funds of officials in the European Commission (EC), however, a minor example of the persistence of CSOs thanks to foreign funding rather than support from their putative bases. Regarding the two other regions where civil society networking was weakest, the forum managed to bring together some forty organizations from East and Central Europe and some eighty from the Middle East and North Africa, which met as a group and issued a joint statement to the forum. No continued networking on food and agriculture issues emerged in these two regions as a result of the forum, however, although the contacts made there did lay a basis for building future relations.

The NGO Forum did not give expression to a single overall mechanism of civil society networking on food and agriculture issues, and probably the time was not ripe for this to happen. The final plenary session of the forum did not dedicate focused attention to the formulating of a follow-up plan and mandate. A group of NGOs headed by the Rural Advancement Foundation International (RAFI)[69] had put forward a draft Eighth commitment intended to supplement the disappointing seven commitments of the official WFS Plan of Action. It was accompanied by a memorandum suggesting that 'we could imagine cobbling together the more attractive elements of the Plan of Action into a real campaign ... a truly grassroots approach that could be carried within the framework of the proposed Food for All Campaign'.[70] The same group advocated the establishment of a 'Global Forum on Food Security', or 'New Roman Forum', designed as a 'global, multi-stakeholder forum to forge a new relationship among public and private stakeholders in order to ensure strengthened international activity'. The forum would 'bring governments, industry, people's organisations and intergovernmental institutions together, on an equal basis, at regular intervals, to review progress on Food Summit commitments, report on their activities, and set agendas for further improvement and multi-party cooperation towards implementation of the Plan of Action to be adopted by the WFS'.[71] In contrast, other voices in the ISC opposed the idea of a permanent forum because, as they said:

1   It would create an underlying framework of powers of attorney that cannot be delegated: who appoints representatives? How? Where?
2   It would put an end, through co-option, to the best part of being non-governmental: the ability to represent specific, individual, original points of view in a global context.
3   Negotiations on problems should not be held at the UN – as is normally the case – but at all levels: local, national, regional and global; and to do this we do not need anything 'permanent', but merely the certainty of exercising one right, namely that of being respected as interlocutors.[72]

The ISC was not able to generate funding to continue its work and ceased to operate as a coordinating group. The Italian committee that had been set up to guide the organization of the NGO Forum gave way to a broadly based but not very active national food security coalition fancifully named PASTA. The most inclusive mechanism that did emerge was the Global Forum on Sustainable Food and Nutritional Security, set up in 1997 and headquartered in Brasilia. The nucleus of this network was essentially the membership of the Global Network on Food Security that had been established in Quebec in the run-up to the WFS. It incorporated other elements of the NGO Forum population as well, including the African COASAD, the NGOs working on SARD and on the right to food, and organizations with access to resources, such as the Fondation pour le Progrès de l'Homme and some of the Protestant development NGOs. At its height the Global Forum produced a newsletter in four languages that was diffused to a list of more than 3,000 member and partner organizations throughout the world. Divergences existed between the ISC and the Global Forum, mainly on issues of relations with social movements, but also over the FAO, with ISC members considering the Global Forum too accommodating and insufficiently critical of the FAO. Some members of the former ISC did participate in the coordinating committee of the Global Forum, however, with the hope of developing what could have been a 'federating' project: a proposed 'Food Watch' monitoring activity that could have equipped civil society with the capacity to engage autonomously and authoritatively in the WFS follow-up processes. Funding for this activity did not materialize, and in the end the Global Forum itself ran out of resources and closed shop.

The impact on FAO–civil society relations

Like the other final documents that emerged from the summits of the 1990s, the WFS Plan of Action was liberally laced with references to the indispensable role of civil society in attaining the plan's goals. Its final commitment contained two provisions regarding civil society participation in follow-up to the summit. One of these was the injunction to governments 'in collaboration with civil society, [to] formulate and launch national Food for All Campaigns [FFA] to mobilize all stakeholders at all levels of society and their resources in each country, in support of the implementation of the World Food Summit Plan of Action'.[73] This idea seemed to hark back to the National FFHC committees of the 1960s and 1970s but without bothering to learn from that past experience. The idea was dear to the heart of the Director-General of the FAO, who saw it as a tool for building worldwide, bottom-up support for the WFS agenda. It also appealed to the more campaign-oriented, less political wing of CSOs involved in the WFS and the NGO Forum. Applying the Director-General's vision of how such things should be done, the FFA concept was implemented in an unimaginative and bureaucratic fashion by asking Ministries of Agriculture to establish national campaign committees. There appeared to be a threat that this framework for civil society outreach would take the FAO's relations with civil society back several decades. In the end, however, the FFA initiative proved to have neither a soul nor a political programme nor substantial funding, and it simply failed to get off the ground.

The other specific operational mention of civil society, contained in the objective regarding monitoring of the WFS Plan of Action's implementation, committed governments to 'encourage the effective participation of relevant actors of civil society in the CFS monitoring process, recognizing their critical role in enhancing food security' (FAO 1996b: para. 60).[74] This provision potentially opened the door to engagement by civil society actors in debate and decision making in what had previously been practically an exclusively intergovernmental forum. The secretariat acted on this indication by inviting a wider range of CSOs than in the past to the subsequent session of the CFS. At a meeting held the following year, in June 1998, the Bureau of the CFS accepted some suggestions put forward by a delegation of NGO representatives. These included proposals for ongoing dialogue between NGOs and the CFS Bureau and secretariat and a face-to-face meeting before the opening of each CFS session. NGO collaboration in drafting CFS papers was also envisaged. The Bureau agreed to consider the NGOs' request to have designated spokespersons take the floor without having to wait until the end of agenda items, but was less receptive to the idea of NGO presence in the drafting committee. Other ideas were left open for exploration: the need to develop guidelines on the involvement of NGOs in the national reporting process; the proposal to create space in the CFS agenda for NGOs to present their own global analysis of the evolution of food security; and the proposal to find resources to ensure involvement of more developing-country NGOs.

'Broadened Participation of Civil Society and Other Partners in the Work of the CFS' was a main agenda item at the 1999 Committee on World Food Security session and it was agreed that the floor be given to civil society representatives without restriction during the discussions on this topic.[75] The session's report (FAO 1999b) was more cautious than the Bureau had been in its informal interaction. The CFS invited CSOs to report their activities and suggestions related to WFS follow-up to subsequent sessions of the CFS but made no commitments regarding enhanced conditions of participation in plenary debate. On a delicate issue related to the autonomy of civil society representatives, the CFS suggested that it be left to them to determine the method by which their spokespersons be selected.[76] It did, however, express its concern that there be balanced representation of all categories of CSOs on a regional and sectoral basis. The committee 'noted with interest' the suggestion to hold a broad consultation of NGOs/CSOs in 2006, within the framework of the mid-term review of follow-up to the WFS, and to hold civil society meetings in conjunction with the FAO Regional Conferences in 2000. All told, the CFS was taking no risk of revolutionizing its working habits.

It bears underscoring that the official process of monitoring and reporting on progress toward attainment of the WFS goals was, itself, weak and defective. At its 1998 session, the CFS had decided to undertake two full cycles of reviews, beginning in 2000, before the mid-term review scheduled for 2006. The monitoring task was to be carried out every other year, clustering the commitments into two groups, the 'people-centred' objectives[77] and the 'development-centred' objectives.[78] A format had been developed in 1997 to report on the first cluster and had been sent to governments, relevant UN agencies, international organizations and regional and subregional bodies, but not to CSOs. The results of this first exercise, reported to the 2000 session of CFS in a secretariat document, were found to be unsatisfactory.

> Few national reports provide information on the results of the actions taken or being taken, in terms of reducing the number of the undernourished. Most country reports also do not include information on actions taken on certain key recommendations contained in the reviewed Commitments of the POA [Plan of Action], notably actions related to advancing land reform and recognizing and protecting property rights, water and user rights to enhance access to resources by the poor (FAO 2000a: paras. 3–4).

Governments' reluctance to open up CFS debate to civil society input was only part of a broader political discretion.

But the most significant impact of the WFS process on the FAO's relations with civil society was not a product of the Plan of Action's recommendations. It resulted, rather, from a strategic decision by the staff of the NGO/CSO unit to take advantage of the summit momentum to obtain the institutional opening up to civil society that they had been advocating for years.[79] Already in 1995, the newly created unit had solicited and obtained the Director-General's instruction to carry out a thorough review of the FAO's experience in cooperation with NGOs and other CSOs on which to base new policy guidelines. Well aware of the resistance to change that characterizes large intergovernmental institutions such as the FAO, and the relatively low level of familiarity of many staff with the civil society world, the unit adopted a participatory approach. The objective was to take the time necessary to allow perplexities to emerge and be dealt with and to build a sense of corporate ownership of the review's results. The unit itself played a facilitating role, helping the persons appointed to act as focal points for civil society outreach in the various technical divisions and regional offices of the FAO to carry out their own reviews.[80] On the other side of the fence, a respected civil society figure[81] was asked to prepare a discussion paper presenting civil society expectations regarding the FAO, in broad consultation with organizations and networks in all regions of the world. This paper served as the kick-off for in-house discussions within the FAO, ensuring that civil society perspectives were at the heart of the review. Insights were also built into the review from a panel of experts on civil society involvement in the follow-up to the

WFS, organized at the instruction of the Director-General in January 1998 (FAO 1998). The final outcome of the review was a paper issued in December 1999 under the signature of the Director-General (FAO 1999a), which committed the FAO to a new policy and strategy of cooperation with CSOs. The document listed the expected benefits of increased engagement. It clarified the different nature and roles of various kinds of CSOs to which the FAO relates and indicated that, given its mandate, the FAO would attach priority to 'membership organizations representing important FAO constituencies, such as farmers and consumers'. Another key element was the distinction between subcontracting NGOs to carry out services for the FAO, and seeking partnership 'on the basis of shared objectives and resources and mutually agreed actions going beyond generic talk of *participation* in project formulation, implementation and evaluation to look at whether programmes are actually *negotiated* with civil society actors, resulting in clear responsibilities for all concerned' (FAO 1999a:16).[82] The document committed the FAO to improve the institutional environment for cooperation by revising procedures for granting formal status and for CSO participation in FAO meetings. Partnerships would be integrated into the FAO's programme planning and resource allocation, and a 'partnership culture' would be promoted within the FAO. The capacity of field offices to build relations with civil society would be strengthened. In-house responsibility for monitoring the implementation of the new strategy was entrusted to a network of representatives of FAO technical divisions and field offices, with the NGO/CSO unit serving as coordinator. A 'Director-General's Bulletin' brought the new policy to the desks of all FAO staff at headquarters and in the field, with an injunction to apply it.

The main lines of the new policy were incorporated into *The Strategic Framework for FAO: 2000–2015* (FAO 1999c), designed to recast FAO's work programme in the light of the World Food Summit's conclusions, which was adopted by the FAO Conference in November 1999. For the first time since the days of the FFHC, the FAO had a strong policy framework that gave support to staff that were already working with CSOs and prodded along those that were not. The legitimacy of the strategy in the eyes of civil society partners was further enhanced the following year, when civil society consultations were organized in conjunction with the FAO's biennial Regional Conferences. These meetings brought together many of the groups that had taken an active part in the NGO Forum, with an accent on people's organizations, to translate the strategic framework into action plans suited to different regional contexts. The chairpersons of these consultations attended the 2000 session of the CFS where they presented a summary of their conclusions in a plenary session and interacted with spokespersons of the regional groups of member countries in an innovative panel discussion on WFS follow-up. A basis had been laid for a regionally rooted, people's-organization–based infiltration into the citadel of intergovernmental decision making on food and agriculture.

From Commitments to Action: In Pursuit of Elusive Political Will[83]

The World Food Summit: five years later

The WFS Plan of Action did not foresee a +5 event as other summit processes did. It stipulated, instead, that a special mid-term review forum would be held in 2006 in the context of the Committee on World Food Security. But during the first years following the summit it became increasingly clear that progress toward halving the number of the world's hungry by 2015 was distressingly unsatisfactory. At the same time, the FAO had experienced the danger of the marginalization of food issues within the world development agenda during the formulation of the Millennium Development Goals (MDGs) adopted by the UN Millennium General Assembly in September 2000. The 'hunger goal' was not originally included in this complex cobbling-together of the results of a decade of summits,[84] and it took strong lobbying by the FAO to get it incorporated into the MDG Number One on poverty reduction.

The September 2000 session of the Committee on World Food Security had before it the first report on implementation of the WFS commitments, which indicated that 'In the majority of the developing countries, especially in Africa, the food security situation has deteriorated and the number of the undernourished has risen' (FAO 2000a:1). The Director-General consequently proposed that to review progress the FAO Conference should host a high-level forum on the fifth anniversary of the WFS, in November 2001. Reactions of the delegates were divided. The United States and other donor countries were reluctant to hold another meeting at the level of heads of state and government, particularly in view of the generally disappointing results of the +5 conferences that had taken place in the follow-up to other UN summits. The Director-General prevailed in the end. The report of the

November 2000 session of the FAO Council expressed support for the proposal, albeit less than unanimously enthusiastic, on the understanding that it would not reopen debate on the documents adopted by the WFS or entail significant incremental costs and that each member would be entitled to determine the level of its representation (FAO 2000b: para. 25). The reference to civil society participation was equally tepid: 'Some Members also emphasized the importance of civil society's participation in the review' (FAO 2000b: para. 24).

The subsequent 27th session of the CFS (28 May – 1 June 2001), just five months before the forum was scheduled to take place, deliberated on arrangements for the conference. It was agreed that observers from NGOs be invited to attend, applying the same criteria and procedures as for the WFS (FAO 2001b: para. 28).[85] In addition, the CFS agreed to a recommendation proposed by some European countries in favour of greater cooperation with civil society that a multistakeholder dialogue be held as a parallel event, with voluntary attendance by member country delegations, and that its report be communicated orally to the plenary (FAO 2001c: para. 42). This measure was intended to partially compensate civil society observers for the fact that they would not be allowed even to witness, let alone participate in, the major innovation foreseen at the summit: three roundtable discussions involving heads of delegations on the theme of mobilizing political will and resources to attain the WFS goal.[86] The FAO Council, meeting later in June, endorsed these conclusions. It sounded as though the process of intergovernmental deliberation was grinding along its bureaucratic way as usual, in blissful indifference to the expectations of non-state actors.

Behind this placid façade, however, the tone of civil society-intergovernmental relations had changed profoundly following the street demonstrations during the WTO ministerial meeting in Seattle in December 1999. Italy and the FAO might have seemed backwaters compared with the United States and the WTO, but just one month after the meeting of the FAO Council, confrontation in Genoa during the 20–22 July 2001 Group of Eight (G-8) summit led to the death of a demonstrator and widespread accusations of police brutality. The Italian government, under Silvio Berlusconi's administration, took this tragic incident as a reason to put the Rome summit on hold. An official proposal to postpone the conference until June of the following year and move it to a more easily protected venue reached the FAO in late September after weeks of frantic diplomatic negotiations and following the 11 September attack on the Twin Towers in New York. A few days later the FAO Council members acceded to the Italian government's request.[87]

The underlying threat of violence from real or imagined 'black blocks' like the masked protestors of Seattle and Genoa was one of the factors that characterized the evolution of the civil society interface with the World Food Summit:*five years later*. The supportive stance of the Italian civil society host committee and its skill in dealing with the hottest collars in the Italian social movements were highly appreciated by FAO top management and were instrumental in building up an unprecedented level of mutual trust. It was not, however, the only new factor within the FAO secretariat as compared with the WFS. The clearer it became that lack of political will was the major constraint to beating hunger, the more the FAO's politically aware Director-General became convinced that harnessing civil society lobbying power had to be an essential element in his strategy. Within the FAO, civil society cooperation had made important strides in terms of institutional legitimization. The NGO/CSO cooperation unit found itself in a far stronger position than in 1996 and could count on a network of focal points throughout the organization. The WFS:*fyl* secretariat, a leaner and lighter operation, ceded responsibility for handling civil society participation in the event to the FAO unit that had ongoing institutional responsibility for these relations. Finally, the post of Assistant Director-General of the department in which the unit was situated, the Technical Cooperation Department (TCD), had been taken up by a person who allied intelligence and political acumen with understanding of, and sympathy for, the world of civil society. At the same time, he had the confidence of the Director-General and was one of the few people in his entourage with the courage and the capacity to influence his views, at least on some occasions. For the first time since the early days of the Freedom from Hunger Campaign the FAO unit responsible for civil society cooperation had strong and capable backing at the top management level.[88] Since the TCD was responsible for the FAO's relations with donors, it also had improved chances of obtaining access to extrabudgetary resources to fund civil society activities in connection with the WFS:*fyl*. In these new circumstances, there was a far more organic link between preparations for the official summit and preperations for the parallel civil society components than in 1996.

On the civil society side, the period since the WFS had seen a radicalization of positions on food and agriculture issues in reaction to trends such as the intensified liberalization of agricultural trade that had followed the adoption of the WTO Agreement on Agriculture, increasingly aggressive marketing of biotechnology, and continued reluctance of governments to take action on issues such as agrarian reform. At the global level, the first World Social Forum held in Porto Alegre in January 2001 was an affirmation of a mature civil society's need for:

> an open meeting place for reflective thinking, democratic debate of ideas, formulation of proposals, free exchange of experiences and interlinking for effective action, by groups and movements of civil society that are opposed to neoliberalism and to domination of the world by capital and any form of imperialism, and are committed to building a planetary society directed towards fruitful relationships among Humankind and between it and the Earth (World Social Forum 2002).

Within the overall world of civil society, people's organizations related to food and agriculture had made particular progress in strengthening their networks and their lobbying capacity. Via Campesina had continued to build its position as the major international movement seeking to coordinate peasant organizations of small and middle-scale producers, agricultural workers, rural women and indigenous communities from all regions. The visionary and politically adept peasant movement in West Africa had established an independent and autonomous subregional network in June 2000.[89] In 1997, the first ever worldwide federation of fisherfolk was formed, the World Forum of Fish Harvesters and Fishworkers, followed in October 2000 by the World Forum of Fisher Peoples. Indigenous people's battles, originally situated on human rights territory, were moving slowly to other areas more closely related to food and agriculture, such as genetic resources and access to land.[90] Agricultural workers had their trade unions behind them,[91] although their highly hierarchical organizational mode differed considerably from the organization of other social movements. Under these circumstances, it was understandable that divergences within the civil society universe had deepened. The divide between people's organizations and NGOs did not by any means coincide with a neat categorization of more or less radical positions. The issue was more one of forms of legitimacy, with people's organizations increasingly contesting the right of NGOs to conduct lobbying 'on behalf of' sectors of the world's population from which they had received no mandate and to which they were in no way accountable. Underlying the legitimacy question, in the best of circumstances, was a contrast in approaches to defining positions and building consensus. People's organizations often invested time and resources in laborious grassroots consultation,[92] while NGOs could take a stand at the close of a telephone conference with the help of in-house or hired expertise.

Informal discussions between the FAO and CSOs had begun as soon as the proposal for a WFS:*fyl* was voiced. In early 2001 an in-house proposal was formulated coupling 'NGO/CSO participation in both the World Food Summit:*five years later* and FAO preparations for the World Summit on Sustainable Development' (WSSD).[93] A main feature of this proposal was the suggestion that the FAO should welcome the constitution of an autonomous civil society group which would be the organization's interface regarding the WFS:*fyl* and would also be invited to provide input into FAO preparations for the WSSD (FAO 2001a).[94] The first step in this direction was a meeting of a civil society planning group on 30–31 March 2001 in conjunction with the FAO Committee on Agriculture. The participants, some 25 in all, came from organizations representing indigenous peoples, rural women, farmers, development NGOs, and thematic and regional networks. The group reviewed developments since 1996. It reiterated civil society's critique of the WFS Plan of Action as a trade-driven shopping list lacking a coherent strategy, precise targets, and an effective monitoring mechanism. Participants proposed to focus civil society attention, instead, on a limited number of issues on which they believed governments had to take action if they were serious about ending hunger. These were identified in the following terms in a *Call for Action and Mobilisation at the World Food Summit: five years later* which was widely distributed through civil society networks over the following weeks (IPC 2001):

> In 1996 NGOs/CSOs formulated principles and concepts of food security – such as food sovereignty – that are now beginning to be accepted by some official policy makers. Today we want to go one step further and present successful demonstrations and alternative proposals. We have identified five strategic issues on which to focus because we feel they are the keys to attaining world food security:
>
> - *Right to Food* – in relationship to international arrangements (e.g. trade) and domestic social policies.
> - *Food Sovereignty* – the right of the people of each country to determine their own food policy.
> - *Agricultural Production Models* – agro-ecological, organic and other sustainable alternatives to the current industrial model.
> - *Access to Resources* – land, forests, water, credit and genetic resources; land reform and security of tenure.

- *Democracy* – international mechanisms should aim to support economic, social and political processes of democratization at the country level, rather than encouraging their marginalization.

The civil society strategy involved marrying the NGOs' technical expertise with the outreach of regional networks and the legitimacy of organizations representing major constituencies of rural producers. To this end, thematic background papers and a draft position paper would be prepared for discussion and enrichment at national and regional levels. The organizations present at the meeting agreed to establish a mechanism that came to be known as the International CSO Planning Committee for Food Soverignty (IPC), composed of focal points for the regions, for major constituencies and for key themes. It defined its role as one of mobilization and facilitation, not representation. A second meeting of the IPC during the May 2001 session of the CFS allowed the group to define its strategy and action plan further.[95] When the decision to postpone the summit was taken, an IPC meeting was scheduled during the FAO Conference, from 3 to 5 November 2001, to share experiences emerging from the regions and to readjust the civil society strategy to the new timing. Plans for the parallel CSO Forum were also firmed up, and in mid-November 2001 the FAO and the Italian host committee signed a letter of agreement covering the financial contribution that had been negotiated with the Italian government.

The FAO's NGO/CSO office and the IPC joined forces over the coming months to promote decentralized consultation in the run-up to the summit. FAO country representatives were requested to facilitate inclusion of CSOs in the national preparatory committees.[96] Drawing on extra-budgetary funds available to the FAO and with the support of the FAO's regional offices, the IPC organized a series of five regional consultations between June and October 2001. A second round of regional consultations took place in the first five months of 2002, this time in conjunction with the FAO biennial Regional Conferences which were used as 'stepping stones' to the rescheduled WFS:*fyl*.[97] Cooperation between the IPC regional focal points and the FAO regional offices in organizing these events helped to build mutual understanding and trust, although the quality of collaboration varied from region to region in function both of the political context and of the character and convictions of the regional directors. Participation in the FAO Regional Conferences themselves gave civil society representatives an opportunity to dialogue with governments at this level, a key level in view of the regional caucusing practices within the

UN system and the growing importance of regional economic organizations in an era of globalization.[98] Within the civil society world, the consultations strengthened regional networking and made it possible to interpret and contextualize, in very different situations, the strategic issues that the IPC had identified.[99] In addition to the five regional consultations, at the IPC's request the FAO supported the organization of an international consultation of indigenous peoples, judged to be the weakest of the constituencies, which brought together participants from 28 countries in all regions to build up a common platform on food security and sovereignty issues from their special viewpoint. By the end of these two rounds of meetings, preparations for the WFS:*fyl* – and the IPC itself – had built strong roots in the regions, with an accent on organizations representing rural producers of various kinds.

Over the same period, tensions built up in the fraught encounter between the IPC mechanism of interface with the FAO and the Major Group (MG) approach adopted by the Commission for Sustainable Development (CSD) in the follow-up to the Rio Conference and in preparation for the World Summit on Sustainable Development (WSSD) due to be held in Johannesburg just two months after the rescheduled WFS:*fyl*. Agenda 21, the action plan adopted by the Rio Conference in 1992, included a chapter defining and describing nine groups of social actors whose participation in implementation of the objectives and policies contained in the plan was felt to be critical: women, children and youth, indigenous peoples, NGOs, local authorities, workers and trade unions, business and industry, the scientific and technological community, and farmers. When it set about implementing this concept, the CSD secretariat took the initiative of identifying specific international organizations/networks within each MG to coordinate and facilitate the input of that group to the CSD processes. Multistakeholder Dialogues among various MGs, with government delegates in attendance, became the most visible and successful mechanism of civil society interaction with official CSD processes. They involved preparation of a consensus paper on the topic under discussion by each participating MG as a starting point for engaging in dialogue with the others.

This mechanism contrasted sharply in several important ways with the IPC approach. On the one hand, the MGs had been predefined by an intergovernmental forum, whereas the IPC emerged from an on-going civil society process of self-definition. Second, the MG approach assumed that broad categories like 'farmers' would be able to come up with consensus positions on issues in which, in reality, different components of the categories often had widely different interests. Third, the MG consultation process was orchestrated by global focal points, whereas the IPC process was strongly rooted in regional and local consultation. Fourth, the MGs included business and industry as one component within a single process of stakeholder dialogue, whereas the IPC definition of civil society excluded the private sector.

In a spirit of inclusiveness all of the organizations that were operating as MG focal points for Sustainable Agriculture and Rural Development (SARD) in the context of CSD preparations for the WSSD were incorporated in the IPC, with the exception of business and industry.[100] The initial encounter between the two processes at the March 2001 session of the FAO Committee on Agriculture (COAG) had gone relatively smoothly. Over the following months, however, their paths began to divide as some of the MG focal points and the unit of the FAO responsible for SARD began to formalize their relationship. An FAO–Major Group Committee was established with terms of reference that mentioned cooperation between civil society and the FAO on sustainable agriculture and rural development generally, not only in the specific context of the WSSD. The committee selected priority issues which overlapped with those that had been identified by the IPC and drafted thematic papers whose theses clashed on some important points with those of the IPC papers.[101] Finally, the committee determined to develop a 'SARD Initiative' as a 'Type 2 Partnership' to be launched at the WSSD, which would serve as a central and well-resourced mechanism for conducting multistakeholder action on sustainable agricultural and rural development in the future. Many IPC members viewed these steps as pre-empting their own efforts to develop an autonomous agenda for validation at the NGO/CSO Forum planned in parallel to the WFS:*fyl*. We will trace the evolution of this conflict when we discuss follow-up to the WFS:*fyl* and the NGO/CSO Forum.

The official summit and the NGO/CSO Forum for Food Sovereignty

The tense, confrontational climate that prevailed outside the walls of the FAO in the period after the 11 September attacks on the United States and the Genoa period translated into unprecedented levels of fears for security within the official planning group responsible for preparations for the World Food Summit:*five years later*. The threats of terrorist attacks and of protestors' violence were amplified by the unconfessed individual and collective fears and quests for control that animate members of security apparatuses and bureaucracies even in less threatening circumstances. Civil society was cast in the role of Subversivity *par excellence*. Part of the secretariat was working hard to weave links between the NGO/CSO Forum and the official summit, since the best way of helping the civil society organizers to keep the contesters in tow was to demonstrate that there was indeed room for democratic advocacy in the WFS:*fyl* deliberations. Working toward this objective, the NGO/CSO unit was making every effort to accredit to the official summit as many as possible of the delegates selected to attend the NGO/CSO Forum in order to enhance interaction between the two events. This was not facilitated by the fact that the civil society delegates were designated with great delay, whereas the official accreditation process was expected to be completed well in advance so that the host country secret services could check the identities and records of the individuals proposed for entrance into FAO premises. The NGO/CSO unit also sought to obtain direct transport connections between the two venues to allow interested delegates to visit the NGO/CSO Forum and vice versa. This was denied on grounds of security.

Even those lucky civil society mortals who were accredited and did attain access to the FAO headquarters were severely hampered in their movements. All of the areas where the major meetings were taking place, and most of those where the official delegates were congregating, were accessible only with a special day pass in addition to the normal WFS:*fyl* photo identity card. Limited amounts of the passes were available,[102] and FAO staff were obliged to hand them out directly to the individuals who would be using them on the morning of the day for which they were valid, noting down the names of those who received them. This restrictive procedure was difficult to justify on security grounds, given the fact that all of the recipients of the passes had already been subjected to security clearance in order to receive their accreditation and would not be allowed onto FAO premises without their photo identity cards. The result was that only a small proportion of the day passes were actually distributed and used, which greatly inhibited the presence of civil society actors at the WFS:*fyl*.[103]

In any event, relatively little happened at the WFS:*fyl* that merited civil society presence. The background papers on 'Fostering the Political Will to Fight Hunger' and 'New Challenges to the Achievement of the World Food Summit Goals' had been recognized by CFS delegates to be refreshingly sharp and eloquent,[104] but the same cannot be said of the draft declaration put to the summit and adopted on the opening day.

The latter was an uninspiring reaffirmation of the WFS commitments, with no more teeth in it than the original version. The only new initiative it contained, a product in good part of determined NGO lobbying, was an invitation to the FAO Council to establish 'an Inter-governmental Working Group, with the participation of stakeholders, in the context of the WFS follow-up, to elaborate, in a period of two years, a set of voluntary guidelines to support Member States' efforts to achieve the progressive realization of the right to adequate food in the context of national food security' (FAO 2002a: para. 10).[105] On the down side, the declaration plugged the outcome of the WTO Doha Conference, 'especially the commitments regarding the reform of the international agricultural trading system' (FAO 2002a: para. 12), and pledged to help developing countries, 'particularly their food producers, to make informed choices about, and to have access to, the necessary scientific and technical knowledge related to new technologies targeted at poverty and hunger reduction' (FAO 2002a: para. 24). The only mention of food producers in the entire text was thus linked to diffusion of biotechnology!

The Director-General of the FAO had championed two new initiatives. The first was an International Alliance against Hunger to replace the defunct Food for All Campaign as a framework for global mobilization of political will to fight hunger. In the declaration, this objective was reflected in the exhortation to 'all parties (governments, international organizations, civil society organizations and the private sector) to reinforce their efforts so as to act as an international alliance against hunger to achieve the WFS targets no later than 2015' (FAO 2002a: para. 2), a wording that studiously avoided any explicit suggestion that a new mechanism or institutional initiative should be established. The Director-General's second initiative, targeting the obstacle of insufficient resources, was the proposal to launch an Anti-Hunger Programme funded in part through an FAO trust fund. The final declaration provided only lukewarm endorsement for this idea. The extent and level of participation at the WFS:*fyl* itself was a disappointment for the FAO. A total of 173 delegations attended, 73 of which were led by heads of state or government or their deputies, down from the comparable figures – 185 and 112 – of the WFS. Most of the rich country leaders were absent, a significant void given the fact that – as the FAO round-up press release reported – 'OECD [Organisation for Economic Co-operation and Development] countries provide a billion dollars a day in support to their own agriculture sector, six times more than all development assistance' (FAO 2002b). The lack of political will to address the problem of insufficient political will was evident.

Nor was civil society offered much scope to redress or at least denounce the situation. The programme foresaw three moments for civil society communication to the plenary. One of these was the report of the Multistakeholder Dialogue held in the context of the summit.[106] The second opportunity was afforded by the four-minute slots reserved for the spokespersons of 12 civil society 'caucuses', sandwiched in at the end of the official declarations. The experience put a final nail in the coffin of this time-honoured, decorous and increasingly ineffectual mode of civil society intervention in intergovernmental deliberations. As one of the FAO respondents in an assessment of FAO–civil society interface during the summit put it:

> The civil society interventions in Plenary were scheduled late in the evening when the room was practically empty. This is a classic scenario and we know the reasons for it. But can't we think of another way to have the NGO/CSO voice heard by governments? Because this way, clearly nobody was listening (FAO 2002c:4).[107]

The only contribution the civil society slots made to history was a memorable scene that took place in a deserted plenary hall at 22:30 one evening, when an Indonesian member of Via Campesina arrived to present the statement of the peasant caucus accompanied by the French farmer leader José Bové, who had not managed – or bothered – to pick up one of the hard-to-procure daily plenary hall passes. Like a Maenad in a Greek tragedy, a tall, vigilant FAO guard rushed across the hall to swoop down on the offending presence, but was stopped in his tracks by the quick action of a member of the FAO secretariat who reached out and politely offered Bové a surplus pass just in time.

The third and most significant moment in which the summit programme foresaw that civil society would be able to make its voice heard to governments was the presentation of the final statement of the NGO/CSO Forum. We will return to the statement's content following an examination of the forum proceedings, but note here that the statement attracted considerable media attention and was received with applause by plenary delegates. In less formal fashion, civil society delegates took part in a number of the side events on FAO premises. They also organized encounters in the meeting room in the FAO put at the disposition of civil society. The overall assessment of civil society interaction with governments, which had been one objective of the IPC strategy, was negative. 'Interaction with government delegates was largely unsatisfying. The IPC was unable to obtain commitments of government officials to meet with civil society. Only a meeting with the German agricultural minister provided an opportunity for substantive interchange' (FAO 2002c:4).

The NGO/CSO Forum for Food Sovereignty itself, housed in the rather daunting premises of the Palazzo dei Congressi, took place from 9 to 13 June 2002. The host committee invited well over 700 civil society participants to attend the forum. They had been selected through the IPC network on the basis of the preparation process that had taken place in the regions, respecting criteria that ensured balance by regions, type of organization and gender.[108] A number of these people had difficulties obtaining visas.[109] In the end 570 participants were accredited to the plenary sessions with the right to participate in the forum's decision-making processes. All participants from Southern regions and from Eastern and Central Europe received support to cover their travel and living expenses. A far larger number of people were accredited to gain access to the building, where they could attend seminars in the afternoon and witness what was happening in the morning plenary sessions via an enormous video screen. Funding for the forum was provided through the FAO by the Italian government.[110]

The civil society events took off on Saturday, 8 June 2002, two days before the opening of the official summit, with a march that brought some 30,000 people from all parts of the world onto the streets of Rome to demonstrate for food sovereignty and to highlight the situation of the hundreds of leaders of people's organizations suffering imprisonment and torture. The press and many sections of the establishment were expecting violence, but the organizers kept control of the crowd and the end result was a colourful, peaceful and energizing event that added lustre to the summit process. The programme of the forum itself foresaw plenary sessions in the mornings of 9–13 June to discuss and adopt a position paper that had been drafted on the basis of the earlier IPC discussions and the regional consultations and to debate and decide on the content of the main components of the food sovereignty action plan that was expected to emerge from the forum. Plenary sessions in the afternoons of the opening and closing days were dedicated to encounters with FAO officials. The plenaries were complemented by regional meetings and a rich variety of thematic workshops proposed and organized by participating groups in the afternoons. The evening events were decentralized throughout Rome in an effort to break down the barriers that often exist between international forums and the citizens of the host city.

The dynamics of the forum were characterized above all by the dominance of people's organizations, in particular the numerous and well-organized delegations of Via Campesina members from Latin America, Asia and Europe. The style of Via Campesina advocacy, as compared with the mode of debate at the 1996 Forum, was over-whelming. Key positions, including the view of food sovereignty as the alternative civil society paradigm and 'WTO out of agriculture' as the necessary precondition for finding acceptable solutions to the govern-ance of world trade, were defended uncompromisingly. In plenary sessions, the disciplined behaviour of the Via Campesina delegates multiplied the effectiveness of their already significant numbers, as they burst into rhythmic chants to underline their points or carried thou-sands of signed postcards attacking the WTO up to the head table to deliver them to FAO officials. Alongside the habitual debate, Via Campesina introduced the dimension of the 'mistica': moving repre-sentations of the social and spiritual dimensions of the struggles in which peasant communities are engaged and of the bonds that link them with nature.

The reactions of other civil society actors to this unbeatable presence were varied. Via Campesina's positions were supported by a number of NGOs that were working closely with peasant movements in Asia and Latin America, shared its views, and advocated a protagonist role for social organizations in civil society decision-making processes on food and agriculture issues.[111] At the other extreme, Via Campesina's massive entry onto the scene was contested by those organizations whose hegemony in world forums dealing with food and agriculture was directly threatened by the emergence of this new style of rural social organization. Chief among these was the International Federation of Agricultural Producers (IFAP), which had claimed for decades to represent the interests of the farmers of the world but in fact had tended to privilege the larger, market-oriented producers, although it was making efforts to reach out to smallholders in the South. The trade unions also, with their highly hierarchical style of representing workers' interests, found it difficult to countenance the horizontal approach that had characterized the preparation for the forum, in which national trade union members allied with peasant organizations and others to develop positions on a national/regional basis.

In between these two extremes were several types of organization. Among the broad category of NGOs, the tendencies that had already operated at the 1996 Forum came to a head in 2002. Many NGOs felt marginalized by the language of a forum which constantly reiterated the hegemonic role of people's organizations; they felt ill at ease with some of the positions adopted by the plenary, and/or repelled by what they felt was an undemocratic piloting of the decision-making process. The issues at play were not only ones of power but also of culture. Many Westerners tend to identify democracy with a certain style and trappings to which they are accustomed. They may find it difficult to recognize that exclusion can be engendered even though these attributes are respected and, conversely, that other forms of democratic process are conceivable.[112] Within the broad category of NGOs, however, a range of positions could be found, with some organizations adamantly defensive of their traditional roles and others more sensitive to the process of change under way. In any event, the West-based NGOs which generally tended to dominate global forums were a minority in the Forum for Food Sovereignty, given the quota procedures, and many of the major actors did not bother to come since they were not admitted as plenary delegates with voting rights.[113]

Another category of the marginalized – however inadvertently – were people's organizations other than Via Campesina. Africa at that time was largely outside the Via Campesina network although dialogue with members of ROPPA (Réseau des Organisations Paysannes et des Producteurs Agricoles de l'Afrique de l'Ouest/ Network of Farmers' and Agricultural Producers' Organisations of West Africa) had begun several years earlier. The African small farmers' organizations, weakly structured and hampered by a language divide, felt unable to defend their specificities and their positions in the debate. African NGOs and people's organizations were looked down upon by some of their Latin American and Asian counterparts for what was judged to be a less radical political analysis and a more accommodating style of negotiation with government authorities. At the 2002 Forum the fact that the African farmers' organizations were investing time and effort in dialoguing with the New Partnership for Africa's Development (NEPAD) initiative was disapproved of by their counterparts in the other regions. NEPAD was denounced in the final Political Statement in the same breath as the FTAA (Free Trade Area of the Americas), in contradiction to the position of the people's organizations directly concerned.[114] In their self-evaluation at the end of the forum, the African farmers' organizations criticized the advocacy style of Via Campesina for not allowing space for others to represent themselves. Above all, however, they critiqued their own weaknesses and ineptness and took the experience as a stimulus to build the strength of their networks and their lobbying capacity. Representatives of indigenous people's organizations were more numerous than in 1996 and they were allocated space in several seminars to present their distinctive views and lifestyles. Their participation in forum decision making was minimal, however, a reflection of the scarce or poor relations between peasant and indigenous people's organizations existing in the real world outside the forum. The same could be said of fisherfolk's organizations, while pastoral peoples continued to be virtually absent.

Evaluations of the impact of the 2002 Forum on the construction of a strong autonomous civil society movement in defence of food sovereignty clearly vary according to the viewpoint from which they are formulated. A representative of one of the IPC members whose power was threatened by the emerging dynamic stated his view, during a round-up evaluation of the forum held the day after it closed, that 'the meeting results were hijacked'. He added, 'My organisation's membership cannot relate to the political stances taken. It was more of a political event for social movements than a dialogue and consensus on critical issues.'[115] In contrast, the forum's president, Sarojeni Regnam, judged that

> Our real success was in mobilising the participation and involvement of the people's movements … They shaped and gave direction and clarity to the proceedings. Hunger and malnutrition, struggles and human rights violations were no longer just academic exercises of reeling off of data and statistics, but the reality of the everyday lives of people articulated by the leaders of the people's movements living these realities (IPC 2002b:9).

In any event, the forum should be judged not in isolation, but as a moment in a process – and it is difficult to imagine a smoother transition to the emergence of people's organizations and social movements as the main protagonists in crafting the advocacy platform on food and agriculture issues. What was perhaps most important at this juncture was that the more radical social movements felt the process represented them, in sharp contrast to the WSSD in Johannesburg just two months later. The forum demonstrated clearly that people's organizations introduce different styles and languages to the process of debate. Peasant organizations around the world share the same overall objectives, but the methods of work and the forms of expression they adopt vary and can be complementary. In 2002 the voice of Via Campesina was dominant, but over the following years those of other peasant movements have emerged more strongly. The African movements, in particular, have brought to the strategic drawing board their adeptness at building dialogue with other sectors of society and alliances with their governments. A key task of the IPC in the follow-up to the forum would prove to be of managing relations and communication among disparate civil society components of the network, on the one hand, and the interface with intergovernmental institutions, on the other.

The 2002 Forum adopted two documents, the Political Statement of the NGO/CSO Forum for Food Sovereignty, *Food Sovereignty: A Right for All*, and an Action Agenda.[116] The Political Statement (ICP 2002b) was drafted by a five-person committee, adopted by the forum plenary on 13 June, and delivered on the same day to the plenary of the official summit. It rejected out of hand the official Declaration of the WFS:*fyl* which, in the forum's view, offered only 'more of the same failed medicine'. In contraposition to the dominant paradigm, the forum proclaimed the concept of 'food sovereignty', defined as the umbrella under which policies and actions to end hunger could be placed:

> Food Sovereignty is the RIGHT of peoples, communities, and countries to define their own agricultural, labor, fishing, food and land policies which are ecologically, socially, economically and culturally appropriate to their unique circumstances. It includes the true right to food and to produce food, which means that all people have the right to safe, nutritious and culturally appropriate food and to food-producing resources and the ability to sustain themselves and their societies (IPC 2002a:2).

A key aspect of this concept, already introduced at the 1996 Forum but now fully formulated, was the application of a rights-based approach, implying in particular 'the primacy of people's and community's rights to food and food production over trade concerns' (IPC 2002a:3). The Political Statement came down clearly on the side of removing agriculture from the WTO and promoting the adoption of a Convention on Food Sovereignty which would 'enshrine the principles of Food Sovereignty in international law and institute food sovereignty as the principal policy framework for addressing food and agriculture' (IPC 2002a:4). This was a defeat for those CSOs who felt there was scope for reform of the WTO; some of these, including some members of the IPC, concluded that the forum process did not offer room for their analyses and strategies. Recognition and defence of social movements was another dominant thread in the Political Statement, which closed with a celebration of diversity and 'a vision of one world with room for many worlds'.

The novelty of the 2002 Forum compared with its 1996 predecessor

– a measure of the road covered between the two events – was the adoption of a detailed Action Agenda aimed at translating into practice the principles enunciated in the Political Statement.[117] The plan incorporated the outcomes of the regional meetings and other proposals that had emerged from the discussions in the plenary and the workshops. It was a first effort to move from principles to action, but there was insufficient time during the forum to prepare a coherent strategic document. Nonetheless, the fact that the 2002 Forum did adopt a document of this nature undoubtedly conferred a legitimizing mandate on the IPC, which was called upon to carry the Action Agenda forward.

If interaction between CSOs and government delegates at the official summit was a weak point of the June 2002 experience, progress was made in terms of enhanced exchange with the FAO secretariat and this helped to build a basis for continued dialogue following the summit.[118] Some 40 FAO staff members, many of them divisional focal points and members of the internal NGO/CSO working group, volunteered to be part of a team working to facilitate interaction between the official summit, civil society participants, the NGO/CSO Forum and the FAO secretariat.[119] Members attended practically all of the civil society seminars held both at the forum and at FAO headquarters and produced brief reports highlighting the main issues treated, the positions expressed, and the implications for the FAO. These were sent to top management on a daily basis and circulated throughout the organization through the network of NGO/CSO focal points. A number of FAO staff were invited to participate as resource persons in civil society workshops. The three Rome-based food agencies, the FAO, IFAD and the World Food Programme (WFP), teamed up to operate an information stand and to organize a series of information sessions at the forum.

All in all, a good proportion of FAO staff came into direct or indirect contact with the reflection that was taking place at the civil society forum. Commenting afterwards on their impressions of the forum, staff noted that 'the voices of people from developing regions and of farmers and indigenous peoples were strong' and remarked that much ground had been covered since the 1996 Forum. 'Then they identified issues and denounced abuses; now they presented articulated alternatives. This opens greater scope for cooperation' (FAO 2002c:1). The challenges for the FAO were felt to be considerable:

> The themes … went to the heart of FAO's mandate. NGOs/CSOs are asking for few (although substantial) things, such as the adoption of a rights-based approach, in particular the right for each country to define its own

national policy and, more importantly for FAO, the systematic participation of small producers at FAO meetings, fora and conferences. FAO, in its neutrality, should assure that publications, papers, documents always include NGO/CSO perspectives. FAO needs to engage more systematically in activities which bring stakeholders together for policy dialogue and for tangible development activities. This implies that stakeholders must see FAO as a facilitator for all concerned, not only for governments (FAO 2002c:1).

As one experienced staff member noted, 'How to reconcile NGO/ CSO views with those of governments is a big challenge. There should be greater efforts to promote policy dialogue at the country level so that NGO/CSO concerns are heard and appreciated by the governments before they travel to an event like the Summit.'

At the level of top management, the Director-General of the FAO addressed the opening session of the 2002 Forum and three senior staff represented the organization and its chief at the final plenary.[120] In presenting them with the Action Agenda, the IPC Forum officers expressed their assessment that CSO discussion with the FAO had never been more dynamic and inclusive. The Forum proposed that the FAO study the Action Agenda, whose final section on 'Access to International Institutions' listed six pages of proposals aimed at improving the relationship in the context both of intergovernmental meetings and of field programmes. 'The FAO Secretariat should be able to indicate its position on each of these initiatives prior to the FAO Council at the end of October 2002', the Action Agenda suggested, while 'CSOs should be able to evaluate the change in the relationship at the World Social Forum in January 2003'.

In his response, the Assistant Director-General of the Technical Cooperation Department expressed the FAO's appreciation for the bottom-up methodology adopted by CSOs in preparation for the WFS:*fyl*. He agreed it was important for the FAO and CSOs to listen to one another on complex questions such as the WTO and genetically modified organisms (GMOs), and he recognized the limits of market-based regulatory instruments, given the special character of food and agriculture. In concluding, he noted that the FAO's general reaction to the proposals coming from the forum was positive, and that 'we should now sit down together and see what we can do and when'.

In contrast with the '+5' summits held elsewhere in the UN system, the experience of the WFS:*fyl* thus marked a decisive intensification in civil society interaction with multilateral governance, both quantitatively and qualitatively, creating the basis for the forging of an innovative relationship that could move beyond the global conference to influence the FAO's overall mode of conducting its business.

Outcome: a negotiated FAO–civil society relationship

The day after the summit ended, the Director-General of the FAO let it be known that, in his view, the civil society forum had been the most dynamic aspect of the entire show and that he wanted to meet with the IPC soon to plan for the future. Civil society expectations were also high. Assessing the results of interaction with the UN at the close of a year which had witnessed the Monterrey Summit on Financing Development, the World Food Summit:*fyl* and the World Summit on Sustainable Development, the authoritative ETC Group (Action Group on Erosion, Technology and Concentration) concluded that 'NGOs and social movements who were embroiled in the summits must end … the pitiful pageant of pep rallies that have pacified CSOs since 1972 – and develop a tough love strategy for our intergovernmental work' (ETC Group 2003:1). Within the desolate overall panorama, however,

> one area of progress in 2002 (perhaps the only area) was in the changing of the structural relationship between civil society and FAO as a result of the World Food Summit. Along with an extensive list of substantial issues and demands, the NGO/CSO Forum at the Food Summit produced an equally extensive list of technical and institutional proposals intended to strengthen the participation of social movements in intergovernmental committees and to create new spaces for national organizations and minority groups to interact with the FAO Secretariat and governments. Many of the proposed changes seem incredibly modest. Collectively, however, they amount to a major structural adjustment in the way in which a major UN agency will relate to civil society (ETC Group 2003:4–5).

The choice of when to hold the FAO/IPC encounter and how to prepare it was a delicate one. The Director-General suggested a date just a few weeks distant and would probably have been satisfied to rely largely on his own persuasive powers to bring civil society on board. On its side, the IPC was committed to respect the style and rhythm of consultation it had developed among its far-flung, grassroots-based multilingual membership, which made it unthinkable to throw together a major institutional encounter at short notice. In the middle, the FAO civil society office was painfully aware of how much work still needed to be done to bridge gaps between the two sides in terms of objectives, language, institutional mandates and working styles, and to create a propitious terrain for a dialogue that could lead to concerted action. In the end it was agreed to schedule the meeting in early November 2002, at the time of the FAO Council. An intermediary encounter with the Assistant Director-General of the Technical Cooperation Department was scheduled in mid–October to make sure there was a mutual political understanding of what was desired, negotiable and unacceptable to both sides. As the relationship moved from principles to practice, IPC members needed to refine their understanding of how the FAO worked, to distinguish between matters on which the secretariat could act autonomously and those on which it required an intergovernmental mandate, and to build its confidence that engagement did not necessarily imply cooption. Conversely, the FAO was challenged to look outside the boxes that institutions are so apt at constructing around their peepholes to reality and to relax procedures that, over time, had lost their rooting in anything other than bureaucratic familiarity. There were all the ingredients for a beautiful love affair, or a resounding flop.

The FAO took the important decision to adopt the four pillars of the NGO/CSO Forum's Action Plan as the point of departure, and to document how the FAO's current and planned activities related to these issues, rather than insisting that the dialogue be based on the official outcome of the WFS and the WFS:*fyl*. Preparations were undertaken through the mechanism of the internal NGO/CSO working group to ensure that the entire organization was involved. Many staff were generally positive about the prospects of stronger political support for civil society outreach on the part of top management and happy to be a part of making it happen. There was, however, a sense that relations with a global networking mechanism such as the IPC were taking the FAO onto a different terrain than had pertained so long as each technical unit or field office had cultivated its own interaction with specific sectors of civil society. Concerns existed in some parts of the FAO that this kind of interaction would be more difficult to manage politically. The issue of legitimacy was felt to be important by all: staff generally were concerned to see how the IPC would demonstrate the broad outreach and consultation capacity it claimed to exercise.

The FAO preparatory effort produced a unique background document (FAO 2002d), which identified opportunities for cooperation with NGOs/CSOs in the four main substantive themes of the civil society Action Agenda.[121] This 're-reading' of FAO activities according to a civil society agenda turned out to be a stimulating experience for the FAO itself even before the dialogue with the IPC was engaged. Staff working within the organization to promote such minority concerns as a rights-based approach to development, agro-ecological food production, or the prioritization of food security over market liberalization were pleasantly surprised to discover colleagues in other parts of the FAO with whom they could make common cause.[122] In an effort to keep the member countries informed about, and comfortable with, the ways in which the FAO's relations with civil society were evolving, a paper was prepared entitled *Information on NGO/CSO Participation in the WFS:fyl and Their Involvement in the Follow-up in Pursuit of the WFS Goal* (FAO 2002e) and distributed to delegates at the session of the FAO Council in late October.

The IPC's preparatory effort involved an iterative process of communication. It was necessary to clarify aspects of the network's functions on which a common understanding had not been reached during the heated discussions at the forum. Basic principles to be respected in the relationship between civil society and inter-governmental organizations had to be defined. The Action Agenda needed to be transformed into a more strategic and operational proposal. The communications were cumbersome and time-consuming, a practical illustration of the rhythm required for meaningful consultation to take place involving social organizations which, in their turn, have to respect their own internal consultation practices. In the end, the document[123] was finalized and adopted only on the eve of the meeting with the FAO Director-General. Recognizing that direct and systematic involvement with social movements and CSOs was a relatively new departure for the FAO, the paper started off by carefully defining what the IPC was and was not.

> The International Planning Committee advances principles, themes and values developed during the NGO/CSO Forum for Food Sovereignty in June, 2002 ... which was based on principles of self-organisation and auton-omy of civil society. For these reasons, the IPC is not centralized. Nor does it claim to represent organizations attending NGO/CSO fora. Instead, the IPC acts to enable discussions among NGOs, CSOs and social movements, as well as to facilitate dialogue with FAO. Each NGO/CSO, and all the diverse constituent groups they represent (fisherfolk, Indigenous Peoples, peasants/smallholder farmers, waged workers, and so on), continues to speak for itself and to manage its own relationship with FAO and its Members ... The IPC's current priorities and action agenda arise from a regional and global process of sustained discussions over many months ... and is not limited to the agenda of FAO (IPC 2002c:3).

On the institutional front, the IPC asked the FAO to respect the role of people's organizations and social movements and their effective participation in policy processes. The FAO was also urged to strengthen its independent role vis-à-vis the Bretton Woods institutions and to develop new ways of organizing its work so that emerging themes that cut through institutional boundaries could be dealt with systematically in collaboration with civil society. These general requests were followed by more specific proposals in the areas of information, policy debate and field work and in the IPC's four priority substantive themes. Short and readable, the IPC paper constituted an effective counterpart to the FAO background document.

The FAO/IPC meeting took place on 1 November 2002, with the participation of the Assistant Directors-General of the major departments of the FAO and its Legal Counsel. The Director-General was expected to be present throughout the three hours of its duration, since it had been billed as a face-to-face dialogue, but in the end he characteristically overbooked his time and underestimated the importance of dedicating more than an 'opening remarks' slot to his civil society interlocutors. His stock with the IPC dropped sharply, but it bounced up again the following morning, a Saturday, when he walked into the room in which the CSOs were assembling for a closed-door wrap-up meeting, unannounced and clad in such casual attire that no one recognized him. The purpose of this unexpected visit, he indicated as he chatted with the participants, was to underline the importance he attached to the FAO's collaboration with civil society and his conviction that only their advocacy could stimulate the political will that was so sorely lacking in rich-country capitals. The IPC reacted to this 'straight-from-the-heart' exchange, as much as to the more formal commitments they later received from the Director-General, by feeling that the institutional relationship with the FAO had been further bonded by a personal rapport of mutual confidence with its leader.

At the close of the meeting it was agreed that the main lines of future relations between the FAO and the IPC would be set out in writing in a formal Exchange of Letters.[124] The text stated the principles governing the FAO's relations – not only with the IPC but with NGOs/CSOs generally – in the following terms, specifying rights and responsibilities on both sides:

> FAO accepts the principles of civil society autonomy and self-organization on which the IPC bases its work and will apply them in all of its relations with NGOs/CSOs. FAO appreciates the IPC's decentralized method of work and the direct involvement of social movements and organizations representing the food insecure, rural people, food producers and consumers in its deliberations. FAO accepts the IPC's definition of its role as one of facilitating discussions among NGOs, CSOs and social movements and their

dialogue with FAO. FAO recognizes the IPC as its principal global civil society interlocutor on the initiatives and themes emerging from the WFS:*fyl* and the NGO/CSO Forum of June 2002. The IPC acknowledges its responsibility to ensure broad outreach to NGOs/CSOs and social movements in all regions and to demonstrate and document the transparency, inclusiveness and effectiveness of its methods of work. Both parties concur with the need to distinguish between the interests of social movements/non-profit NGOs and those of private sector associations, and to make separate interface arrangements for these two categories of organizations (FAO and IPC 2003a:1–2).

The FAO committed itself to undertake a certain number of steps to enhance the institutional environment for relations with NGOs/CSOs. The letter further established a framework for a programme of work in the four IPC priority areas, listing specific activities deriving from the IPC's Action Agenda and from the FAO's programme of work. The final section of the letter dealt with the implementation and monitoring of the agreement, including joint approaches to potential sources of extrabudgetary funding.

The letter was signed and dispatched to the international focal point of the IPC on 16 January 2003 and was returned, co-signed, a month later once approval of IPC members had been obtained. The following sections will document how it has been implemented and with what impact on the FAO in both its substantive and its institutional dimensions. Although these two dimensions are discussed sequentially, in fact they are very closely interrelated since dialogue on substance takes place within, and most often has an impact on, institutional space.

The impact on development discourse: chipping away at dominant paradigms

Three of the major paradigmatic shifts advocated in the civil society platform are the application of a rights-based approach to fighting hunger, the mainstreaming of family-based agro-ecological approaches to agricultural production as distinguished from industrial agriculture, and the overarching concept of food sovereignty seen as an alternative to the dominant paradigm of neoliberalism. Different degrees of impact on development discourse have been achieved with regard to these three principles.[125] Regarding another plank in the IPC platform, that of access to land and agrarian reform,[126] the issue was not one of introducing a new concept but rather of rescuing one with an honourable pedigree from the oblivion into which it had progressively fallen – for political reasons – in the years following the 1979 World Conference on Agrarian Reform and Rural Development.

The most decisive success story in terms of substantive impact on discourse within the FAO, accompanied by significant progress on the institutional front, has been in the area of the right to food. As we have seen, the official Declaration of the WFS:*fyl* invited the FAO Council to establish an Intergovernmental Working Group (IGWG) charged with elaborating voluntary guidelines to support member states' efforts to achieve the progressive realization of the right to adequate food. The inclusion of this provision in the declaration was, to a good degree, the product of determined civil society lobbying. Intense discussion within the secretariat during the preparation of the document on the basis of which the FAO Council would take its decision (FAO 2002f) culminated in the presentation to the governing bodies of two options for stakeholder participation.[127] The IGWG could simply practise business as usual, with observers intervening only after all members had spoken. Another option would be to adopt the innovative step of allowing stakeholders to participate fully during the IGWG's deliberations, while reserving decision making for the members in a second phase. The latter option won out.[128]

Despite the voluntary nature of the guidelines, the exercise was important since it was the first time that a legal interpretation of an economic, social and cultural right was being negotiated by states in an intergovernmental forum outside the UN human rights bodies. Lines of contrast within the FAO membership were well demarcated. In general terms, some countries, with the United States, Canada, Japan and Australia in the lead, denied the justiciability of economic, social and cultural rights and were prepared to resist any strong use of rights-based language in the guidelines which might create a precedent. The European Union was divided, with Sweden and the United Kingdom dragging their feet. On the other side, a number of developing countries,[129] Norway, Germany and Switzerland and the CSOs supported a full rights-based approach. The second conflict zone concerned whether the guidelines should include a chapter on international dimensions of the right to food or whether they should be limited to state duties within national borders. Whereas most of the industrialized countries opted for a national focus, maintaining that trade and other international issues should be discussed in other, 'more appropriate' forums, all of the developing countries and the CSOs favoured inclusion of an international chapter. Some of the developing countries made it clear that they would not accept guidelines that did not take account of the fact that national policies and programmes cannot suffice to ensure the right to food if a government's capacity to deliberate and act is strongly conditioned by outside influences.

The difficult negotiations were skilfully managed by the chairperson of the IGWG, Ambassador Noori of Iran. The IGWG held its start-up session on 26–28 March 2003, followed by a second session on 27–29 October 2003 when the negotiations began in earnest. The third session, 5–10 July 2004,[130] was decisive. The member states agreed on around 90 per cent of the text, leaving four main problem areas to be dealt with in a Friends of the Chair meeting conducted during the September 2004 session of the Committee on World Food Security. This group worked so well that the CFS was able to approve the guidelines on 23 September and send them on to the FAO Council for final adoption in November 2004.

The civil society stakeholders organized themselves very effectively to influence the political process of the IGWG. Michael Windfuhr of FIAN, the IPC focal point for the right to food, took the leadership role. The coalition of CSOs following the process brought together two groups of CSOs that had not previously been in close communication: the rural producer constituency and the regional networks of the IPC, most of which were not particularly knowledgeable about the legal dimensions of the right to food although they strongly supported the principle, and the FIAN network, which mobilized organizations – mostly NGOs – in all regions working in a focused way for the recognition and application of the right to food but not always well versed in agricultural policy issues. A conference held in Mulheim in November 2002, four months before the IGWG got under way, gave the CSOs an opportunity to frame the issues and agree on initial input to prepare for the first session of the IGWG. Once the official negotiations got under way, some 40 CSOs were mobilized to attend some or all of the sessions.[131] The CSO participants organized strategy meetings, designated their spokespersons, keeping geographical and gender balance in mind, and functioned as an effective lobbying mechanism during and between the sessions. Michael Windfuhr reported on the process to the annual general meeting of the IPC in November 2003; the regional NGO/CSO consultations that took place in the first half of 2004 in conjunction with the FAO Regional Conferences were used as an opportunity to inform regional people's organizations and NGOs about right-to-food issues.

Throughout the information-gathering phase of the IGWG's work, the CSOs were allowed to intervene in the discussions on the same footing as the governments. They used this privilege with discretion and intelligence, preparing joint positions which were delivered by recognized spokespersons, and made substantive contributions to the debate. From the third session in July 2003 the IGWG entered its negotiation phase. Thanks in good part to the general appreciation of the CSOs' behaviour and contributions, their spokespersons were allowed to take the floor and make a statement on each paragraph, moving beyond the space that had initially been allotted to them. Outside the meeting rooms, encounters were held with member delegations, many of whom were dealing with human rights issues for the first time. Without any doubt, the CSOs were better prepared than many or most of the governments. They knew what they wanted and they went for it. Point after point, as the negotiations proceeded, they managed to get their views incorporated into the text. As one of the CSOs put it ironically at a wind-up evaluation, 'the governments have been so concerned about the details of the text that they haven't noticed all our ideas are in it'. The final decisions taken in the Friends of the Chair meeting in September, to which the CSOs were allowed to send two 'silent observers', alongside the three government spokespersons per region, also went in the direction that the CSOs were championing. In particular, the section on international dimensions was included in the text as a separate section, Section III, not as a simple annex, and a guideline was added to the main text committing states 'to fulfil those measures, actions and commitments on the international dimension as described in Section III'.

The CSOs' overall assessment of the outcome of the process was positive. Although they termed their final evaluation report *No Masterpiece of Political Will* on account of the weakness of much of the language, in their view the legal substance was surprisingly good.[132]

> One of the main characteristics of the whole process surrounding the World Food Summit is the low commitment of states to change their policies in a way that would lead to a reduction of the number of hungry and malnourished world-wide ... It is therefore not surprising that the governments present tried a lot to avoid any formulation in the text of the guidelines that seemed to be binding to them and would require major policy changes ... Fortunately it was possible in the course of the last year to improve most of these weak formulations. The verb 'should' has become the standard verb ... It is the first time in the history of economic, social and cultural rights that one of these rights has been spelt out in detail by state parties. It is therefore an astonishing success that all the major standards of interpretation that were developed in the human rights community over the last decade are properly reflected in the document (Windfuhr 2005).

In particular, the text strengthens the legal interpretation of the right to food by extending it beyond simple access to food to include access of individuals and groups to productive resources. It reiterates the obligation of states to respect, protect and fulfil their citizens' right to food. It underlines that governments need to have a national strategy to do so and describes the necessary elements of such a strategy. It sets standards for use of food aid and prohibits the use of food as a weapon in conflicts. It addresses governments' responsibilities for the impact of their policies on other countries. Although the guidelines are voluntary, they provide both valuable support to governments that are interested in implementing the right to food and a powerful lobbying instrument for civil society actors in countries where the government is less proactive. The first focus for CSO follow-up action is at the national level, where the guidelines can be used as an educational tool and as a basis for monitoring government compliance, lobbying and denouncing violations. Internationally, a major concern is to lobby the FAO to undertake meaningful follow-up in support of implementation of the guidelines and to incorporate a rights-based approach into its work generally.

What were the major success factors in the process of promoting a paradigm shift within the FAO around the concept of the right to food? One was related to the subject matter itself. Human rights could be classed among the 'soft' issues on which civil society agendas can more easily be advanced than on 'hard' issues like trade and financial interests, although this case is borderline since the right under negotiation was an economic one. Nonetheless, the immediate impingement was on governments, not on the behaviour and profits of corporations. The agribusiness lobby, a common feature in many FAO policy forums, was conspicuous for its absence from the IGWG. Another factor was the consensus within the civil society community regarding the positive value of human rights discourse. There were no major disagreements on substance and strategy as there have been in the case of other issues such as international trade and the WTO. A third factor was the galvanizing effect of the fact that a specific policy negotiation process was in place. This gave focus to civil society efforts, directing them toward having an impact on a particular product to be produced within a given timeframe. A fourth 'plus' was the willingness of a serious and well-resourced NGO to take the issue up and provide leadership, since the voluntary guidelines process was at the heart of its 'core business'. The quality of this leadership was a fifth success factor. FIAN as an organization and Michael Windfuhr as an individual performed their focal point task in a democratic and transparent fashion, providing effective coordination without excessive centralization. Good use was made of Internet communications, with care taken to post messages not only in English but in Spanish and French as well. Meetings during the IGWG sessions were conducted with respect for the contributions of each member of the group and with a view to teasing out consensus and to building team work. A sixth, related factor was the intellectual excellence of the civil society input and the effectiveness of the strategy the group evolved for identifying key points and using the spaces accorded to CSOs by the IGWG to get them across. A seventh factor was the good relations and virtuous alliances that developed at various levels: within the FAO secretariat between the NGO/CSO office and the unit responsible for the IGWG process; among the FAO secretariat, the chair of the IGWG and the NGOs/CSOs; between the NGOs/CSOs and key 'like-minded governments'. This latter factor facilitated a solution to a problem that persistently dogs civil society lobby efforts, that of resource mobilization. Throughout the IGWG process the civil society stakeholders were able to count on the necessary resources to bring participants from developing countries and to help cover communication costs.

The civil society actors participating in the IGWG process formally functioned as an IPC working group on the right to food and respected the IPC concept of how such a group should function. Statements made during the intergovernmental meetings were not claimed to 'represent' the IPC but only those organizations that were present at the meeting and/or had underwritten the positions. All efforts were made to enable the presence of a balanced group of regions and constituencies, and to ensure transparency of decision making. It can be questioned, however, whether most of the individuals who attended the meetings considered themselves to be part of the IPC mechanism. Conversely, more effort would be required for the IPC regional and constituency networks to be fully enabled to use the voluntary guidelines in support of their efforts at national level.[133] These processes take time, and they are continuing within the ambit of the IPC.

IPC–FAO interaction around mainstreaming family-based agro-ecological approaches to food production, another pillar of the CSO Action Agenda, provides an interesting contrast to the work in the area of the right to food. A proposal for a specific programme in agroecology was tabled at the IPC's meeting with the FAO Director-General on 1 November 2002. It was promoted by one of the most authoritative civil society figures in the field of agroecology.[134] A detailed draft working plan was submitted to the FAO by the IPC shortly after the Exchange of Letters had been signed by both parties. The objective was to bring together accumulated civil society experience and the range of existing but fragmented relevant programmes in the FAO[135] in order to 'build a coherent and effective FAO capacity to provide member governments and other stakeholders with policy advice and technical support for agroecology as an approach to sustainable food production, especially for smallholder and marginal farms' (IPC 2003:4). Synergies would be sought between NGO expertise, social movements' lobbying capacity and FAO technical and political authority to tilt the balance of the FAO's work more toward seeking pro-poor alternatives to the dominant industrial agriculture approach to food production.

The IPC set up an agroecology working group to carry this proposal forward. It was the first operational mechanism to be established and as such it constituted a terrain of experimentation. The general idea was that working groups were expected to develop technical input and proposals which would facilitate political decisions by the IPC. The working group included a mixture of IPC members with expertise on the field in question and regionally based civil society experts who were not necessarily IPC members.[136] The questions of how the interaction between technical formulation and political deliberation should be conducted, who should be remunerated for what kind of contribution, and what role the IPC coordination office in Rome should play were not clearly addressed at the outset. On the FAO side, leadership was vested in the director of the highly successful Integrated Pest Management (IPM) programme and chairperson of an inter-departmental working group on biodiversity which had established good working relations with civil society actors. Some ten FAO staff from different units participated in the initiative with regularity, and some 50–60 constituted an informal core group of individuals who could be said to share the principles of an agro-ecological approach.

The two groups met for the first time just before the late March 2003 session of the FAO Committee on Agriculture (COAG) where the IPC organized a side event on agroecology, an auspicious beginning for the initiative. Lively and well attended, it drew positive reactions from governments as diverse as Brazil, Kenya, the Netherlands and Iran, and was reported on at the final plenary session of COAG. At the second meeting in mid-June a suggestion was made to form a single 'common working group' rather than two separate interfacing groups. FAO staff argued in favour of an action-oriented, demand-driven process in which the people's organizations would use their lobbying power to induce governments to request technical assistance with an agro-ecological slant from the FAO's Technical Cooperation Programme. The FAO technicians scattered throughout the organization could then justifiably be brought together, along with the civil society component of the common working group, as a task force to ensure that members' expressed needs were being met. Mainstreaming would take place by building up a critical mass of demand and response, with an effective information diffusion component, not through management decree. As one staff member put it, there had been a strong shift in paradigm over the previous ten years in the attitudes of many technicians but not yet in the institution, which tended to remain sectoralized. The joint agro-ecology initiative, it was agreed, had to facilitate the work of the already convinced FAO staff so that they could 'contaminate' others.

The group prepared a concept paper which laid out basic principles of agroecology, argued the benefits of the approach, and identified opportunities where it could be applied in practical ways (FAO and IPC 2003b). The paper, which described a win–win situation for all except agribusiness interests, was intended for comment and reaction from IPC members worldwide and to be used as a background paper for a joint IPC/FAO seminar to be held in late November 2003, just before the FAO Conference. IPC members were asked to identify countries in each region in which the civil society actors could prevail on government to send official expressions of interest to the FAO. Funds were sought and found within programmes managed by the FAO to cover the costs of the seminar, where 12 national case studies were presented by civil society, government and FAO experts. Despite the wide variety of situations, a number of common principles emerged. All the experiences involved what the group was terming 'agroecology' even if this word was not always used. In all cases the dimensions of participation, empowerment and enhancing local initiative were central. Farmer innovation played an important role and efforts were made to match traditional and scientific knowledge. All the experiences took a systemic approach, even though one or more specific entry points were targeted. The areas in which technical advice was sought to overcome constraints that had been encountered included technology, methodology, research, local market development and supportive policies.

What would be required to enable the FAO to react to such a demand? The flagship Special Programme for Food Security, in the process of transformation under enlightened management and with input from the IPM programme, was indicated by FAO staff as a promising entry point for field work, with the Technical Cooperation Programme[137] picking up at least some of the tab. The biodiversity Priority Area for Interdisciplinary Action (PAIA)[138] could provide technical support. For this to happen would require political endorsement by senior management, who would need to identify a coordinator within the FAO with whom civil society could interface and to allow individual staff to free up time to work in a common task force. It was agreed that the IPC would advance this request to the FAO Director-General. The results of the seminar were reported to government delegates to the FAO Conference in a side event on 1 December 2003, bringing this first phase of the initiative to a successful conclusion (FAO and IPC 2003c).

By the end of 2003 the common agroecology portfolio had grown to include some 16 existing or potential programmes. IPC members had induced the ministries of agriculture of eight member countries covering all Southern regions[139] to write to the FAO Director-General expressing interest in the initiative and in six cases explicitly requesting technical assistance and/or a formulation mission. Yet the momentum that had been created was not maintained in 2004. A draft letter from the IPC to the FAO Director-General was prepared immediately after the side event. In the end, however, it was decided to integrate the agroecology requests into a more general letter covering all IPC activities. This letter was sent only in May 2004, on the eve of a major crisis in FAO–IPC relations provoked by the publication of a controversial report on biotechnology, which will be discussed in the following section. One formulation mission was sent to Niger and Mali in October 2004,[140] but follow-up was sluggish and ten months later no concrete field action had been engaged. The other requests were allowed to lapse.[141]

What accounts for this relative lack of impact? The FAO had long-standing relations with CSOs in specific programme areas related to agroecology, such as biodiversity, natural pest control and organic agriculture, much more so than was the case for the right to food. Yet the attempt to mainstream agro-ecological approaches was less successful. A major issue at play is the fact that the conflict between agroecology and industrial agriculture strikes at the very heart of agribusiness interests. This has impacted on the agroecology initiative in at least two ways. On the one hand, FAO staff working to promote approaches that contrast with the dominant industrial agriculture model have tended to feel that they were operating in a threatened position of weakness and marginality. Understandably, some have reacted by feeling both self-defensive about whatever activities they were able to develop and diffident about joining forces with others to seek greater visibility. The strongest FAO programmes, like the IPM, politically savy, managing their own resources, and already successfully conducting strategic action to bring about changes in FAO orientations, were unlikely to go out on a limb in the name of civil society partnership unless the alliance brought clear advantages and the civil society actors were effectively shouldering their part of the bargain. But it has not always been clear that the IPC was doing so. The leading figure on the IPC side became highly absorbed in fighting for agroecology and against biotechnology on his home front in Brazil and did not dedicate much time to the global agroecology initiative he had fathered. The IPC coordinating office in Rome was overworked and lacked a clearly defined role regarding working groups. The biotechnology report crisis – itself in part a product of the weight of agribusiness interests – did the rest. The IPC declared a temporary block on cooperation with the FAO when the contested document was published, suspending the action of the person who had done the most to coordinate the IPC's agroecology efforts.[142] The agroecology agenda was a self-propelled one, not tied to an official process as in the case of the Voluntary Guidelines on Application of the Right to Food. As such, it was bound to flounder in the face of institutional sectoralization and bureaucratic constraints if it was not buoyed up by a determined effort on the part of the promoters to keep the momentum alive.

The economic interests behind the clash between agroecology and industrial agriculture were also reflected in the persistent tension, referred to in an earlier section, between the FAO's work with the IPC on agro-ecological approaches to agriculture and its collaboration with the Major Groups on SARD in the context of the WSSD. The aftermath to the WFS:*fyl* witnessed two cross-fired letters. Via Campesina wrote to the Assistant Director-General of the Technical Cooperation Department on 16 July 2002 denouncing the Major Group–SARD initiative.

> A process which assumes that all actors – governments, international institutions, global industrial and financial interests and social movements – are essentially all playing equal and complementary roles on a 'level playing field' of negotiations and dialogue misrepresents reality and further marginalizes the less powerful actors in very harmful ways (La Via Campesina, 2008).

Ten days later the International Fertilizer Industry Association, focal point of an international coalition of agribusiness associations established to interface with the FAO, wrote to the Director-General praising the constructiveness of the FAO's SARD initiative as one in which 'all of the defined groups have a place at the table and all of the groups are treated equally'. The fact that both the FAO secretariat and the non-profit civil society community were divided certainly weakened the attempt in 2003 to mount a strong alternative to the industrial agriculture complex and the dominant agricultural development paradigm which it champions. As we will see, the issue of whether promoting sustainable improvements in food production by the many smallholders of this world is a more effective strategy for fighting hunger than pumping use of 'green revolution' technology by the few who can afford it hit the headlines in 2008 with the eruption of the global food crisis, offering civil society a more politically significant opportunity to challenge the dominant industrial agriculture model.

The impact of the overall principle of food sovereignty on development discourse within the FAO is yet another story. As we have seen, food sovereignty was proposed by participants at the June 2002 CSO Forum as the alternative paradigm to the neoliberal, technology-driven analysis that had dominated development discourse and action for over two decades. It was the concept that overarched and unified the four pillars of the 2002 Forum's Action Agenda. The Political Statement delivered to the plenary of the WFS:*fyl* spelled out the ground that the paradigm was understood to cover in the following broad terms:

Food sovereignty requires:
- *Placing priority* on food production for domestic and local markets based on peasant and family farmer diversified and agro-ecologically based production systems.
- *Ensuring fair* prices for farmers, which means the power to protect internal markets from low-priced, dumped imports.
- *Access* to land, water, forests, fishing areas and other productive resources through genuine redistribution, not by market forces and World Bank-sponsored 'market-assisted land reforms'.
- *Recognition and promotion of women's role* in food production and equitable access and control over productive resources.
- *Community control over productive resources*, as opposed to corporate ownership of land, water, and genetic and other resources.
- *Protecting seeds*, the basis of food and life itself, for the free exchange and use of farmers, which means no patents on life and a moratorium on the

genetically modified crops which lead to the genetic pollution of essential genetic diversity of plants and animals.

- *Public investment* in support for the productive activities of families and communities geared toward empowerment, local control and production of food for people and local markets.

Food sovereignty means the primacy of people's and communities' rights to food and food production, over trade concerns. This entails the support and promotion of local markets and producers over production for export and food imports (IPC 2002a:2–3).

An acute editorial in the April 2005 issue of *Seedling* noted that 'food sovereignty implies that the global food system should be turned upside down'. Putting the accent on nutritious locally produced food, it attacks the restrictive mainstream definitions of food security that allow 'food exporters – North and South – to argue that the best way for poor countries to achieve food security is to import cheap food from them, rather than trying to produce it themselves' (*Seedling* 2005:2).

Food sovereignty is in the first instance a political principle rather than a policy guide. It attacks the economic interests of the global agribusiness food chains. It advocates restitution of policy space and regulatory power to conditionality-ridden developing country governments. It unmasks the false dichotomy that has pitched North and South against each other for years. The conflict, it clarifies, is between opposing models of agriculture. Small producers and family farmers all over the world are fighting the same battle against industrial food production, processing and retailing. It provides a terrain on which different social movements – farmers, pastoralists, landless workers, fisherfolk, indigenous peoples – can recompose the differences that the 'development' of the past decades has helped to engender among them, and to reach out to consumers and other actors in their societies. It is not surprising that so all-encompassing and politically charged a concept should take time to permeate the marble walls of UN palaces.

The process of discussion and appropriation of the food sovereignty framework by social movements and NGOs, on the contrary, is well under way.[143] Launched by Via Campesina at its international conference in Tlaxcala, Mexico in April 1996, it was taken forward – as we have seen – to the NGO/CSO Forums in Rome in June 1996 and in 2002. Since then it has been picked up and developed in a wide range of national and regional contexts and thematic campaigns. It is worth underlining that, however complex a concept it may seem, food sovereignty is meaningful to small producers around the world, who easily relate it to the struggles they conduct in their local spaces. The

Seedling editorial cited above quotes women farmers in Bangladesh for whom food sovereignty is incarnated in their 'community seed wealth centre' (see also Ayres and Bosia 2008). Examples from other parts of the world abound. In Mexico farmers have grounded their fight against GMO contamination of maize in food sovereignty discourse. In West Africa, farmers' platforms are conducting a food-sovereignty-inspired 'Africa can feed itself' campaign under the banner of their subregional organization ROPPA. Food sovereignty is a leitmotif for Canadian producers' organizations defending their successful supply management system from attack within the WTO, for the People's Caravan that toured Asia in 2004 visiting villages throughout the region where local people are defending their right to decide what food to produce, for the national Food Sovereignty platforms in Europe which have joined up in a regional network to lobby for changes in the European Common Agricultural Policy. At the global level, food sovereignty has been high on the agenda at the World Social Forum since the 2002 Porto Alegre edition and has been propagated by Via Campesina and by the IPC and its other members in their statements and publications. Thematically, the food sovereignty framework has made greatest headway in civil society opposition to the WTO agenda in food and agriculture, although biodiversity and agrarian reform are two other areas in which the concept is increasingly invoked.[144] Already in 2002, in the run-up to Cancun, food sovereignty was taken on as the battle cry of the broad 'Our World Is Not for Sale' coalition.

Social movement mobilization has led to the introduction of the principle of food sovereignty in official policy documents at national and regional levels, above all in the South.[145] Not surprisingly given the strength of Via Campesina in the continent in which it first saw the light, Latin America has been seen as a particularly fertile terrain for efforts to construct alliances with progressive governments. In Venezuela President Chávez has taken food sovereignty as a basic tenet of his programme and alliances with social movements as a founding strategy, followed by Bolivia under Evo Morales, but there have been disappointments as well, above all in the case of Lula's Brazil. In Asia, the new constitution drafted following the fall of the monarchy in Nepal makes specific reference to food sovereignty, and people's organizations are negotiating with the government to ensure that this principle is applied in practice. The All Nepal Peasants Federation called on other IPC members for input into a 'food sovereignty law making workshop' held in Kathmandu in August 2007, a good example of the kind of horizontal social movement 'technical assistance' that facilitating mechanisms such as the IPC can promote.

In Africa, West Africa has been the theatre of the greatest gains for the alternative paradigm thanks to the political strength of the peasant farmer movement mobilized by ROPPA,[146] which has been negotiating with national governments and regional intergovernmental organizations on a food sovereignty platform since its establishment in 2000.[147] As a result of an intensive process of consultation with farmers' associations and rural communities throughout the country organized by the national peasant farmer platform of Mali, the agricultural framework law put before parliament in 2006 refers to food sovereignty as its overarching principle. At the regional level the Common Agricultural Policy of the Economic Community of West African States (ECOWAS), adopted by the heads of state of the 15 countries that composed it in January 2005, states that its first objective is 'ensuring the food security of the West African rural and urban populations and the sanitary quality of the products within the framework of approaches that guarantee the food sovereignty of the region'. Moreover, the overall orientation of ECOWAS policy was heavily influenced by the farmer consultation process supervised by ROPPA at ECOWAS's request. And here too, as in Mali, the battle has now shifted to defence of the implementation of the policy against conditionalities imposed by outside actors.

In November 2006, ROPPA organized a regional Food Sovereignty Forum in Niamey. Held under the patronage of the president of the Republic of Niger, at that time president of ECOWAS, the forum was billed as 'an occasion for reflection on the right to food sovereignty and the implementation of the agricultural policy of ECOWAS (ECOWAP) in a period of multilateral (WTO) and bilateral (EPAs) [Economic Partnership Agreements] trade negotiations'.[148] The objective was twofold: sensitization of national farmer leaders in order to increase the effectiveness of their national advocacy efforts and lobbying, and alliance building with the political leaders of the ECOWAS region. A major outcome was the undertaking by ECOWAS to oversee the formulation of a subregional Food Sovereignty Charter spelling out the policy implications of the principle and the roles, responsibilities and commitment of all of the actors, as well as a mechanism for collective monitoring of the application of the charter's provisions (see ROPPA 2006). Since early 2006, ROPPA has concentrated a good deal of its lobbying efforts on the EPAs that the European Union is negotiating with six regional blocks of its members' former colonies. In the West African context, this free trade agreement would open the regional market to European exports and subject local farmers to unsustainable competition with the subsidized products of European industrial agriculture. Thanks in good part to ROPPA's advocacy and mobilization, ECOWAS refused to sign the agreement on the stated deadline of 31 December 2007 and the farmers' network is now pushing the regional economic organization to formulate its own detailed food-sovereignty-oriented development strategy rather than taking the EC proposals as the basis for negotiation.[149]

Far less progress has been made in accrediting the concept within the UN system in general – and the FAO in particular – than with Southern governments, despite the fact that food sovereignty made its appearance on the global scene in the context of a UN world summit. The term 'food sovereignty' figures in a few documents published by the FAO, the United Nations Conference on Trade and Development (UNCTAD) and IFAD but only in contexts in which it has been introduced by civil society actors. The rare non-civil-society references to 'food sovereignty' in UN documents – perhaps the only ones – are the work of the Special Rapporteur of the Commission on Human Rights on the Right to Food.[150] Academic studies of how the UN system functions, or fails to function, generally place greater emphasis on intergovernmental politics than on the less flamboyant role of the secretariat. In an exception to this tendency, a French researcher who spent two years in the FAO's policy assistance division as an out-posted academic has analysed what she considers to be the FAO's failure to exploit its potential normative role in the field of agriculture and trade policy (Fouilleux 2008). She highlights a number of weaknesses in the FAO's discourse about 'food security', the concept that the organization has adopted as a synthetic description of its mission.[151] These are attributable, in her view, to three major factors. Bureaucratic dysfunctions plague the organization in the form of sectoralism, insufficient internal communication and coordination, and weak linkages between normative work and field experience. The strong political control exercised by the developed countries which hold the strings of the FAO budget is another handicap, insufficiently contested by the developing country members who are less interested in policy issues than in the possibility of obtaining funding. Finally, in her assessment, the FAO has failed to develop effective procedures for associating its reflections on agricultural policy in a systematic and concrete fashion with people's organizations and NGOs. The case of the food sovereignty paradigm illustrate these weaknesses.

The institutional difficulties inherent in dealing with so politically charged a concept have been compounded by the fact that the dimension of food sovereignty that has received most attention thus far is that of its implications for international agricultural trade. This is a field in which the FAO is under very strong pressure from some of its most powerful member countries to stay out of the WTO's space and to avoid excessive critiquing of the neoliberal agenda. The intense conflict engendered in 1999 by the FAO's attempt to highlight the multi-functionality of agriculture with the support of the Netherlands and other governments[152] taught the organization a lesson it was not likely to override in the name of reinforcing its collaboration with civil society. Individual technical staff of the FAO have been forthcoming and helpful in their dialogue with the IPC and its members on trade issues. Institutionally, however, occasions for formal exchange have been few and not highly productive.

The Exchange of Letters between the IPC and the FAO foresaw the organization of a joint FAO–IPC 'side event' on the trade-related dimensions of the concept of food sovereignty in conjunction with the 2003 session of the FAO technical body that deals with trade issues – the Committee on Commodity Problems. The rationale for such a dialogue was to give the FAO secretariat and member governments a better understanding of civil society concerns while assisting the IPC in exploring some of the dimensions of the concept of food sovereignty on which further thought was required for it to be applicable to analytical work and policy guidance. Preparation for the event was difficult on both sides, a good illustration of the complications involved in sitting such different actors around the same table. The IPC had undertaken to produce a 'state of the art' synthesis of civil society thinking on the topic but in the end did not move far beyond restating the principles underlying food sovereignty. On its side, many of the FAO staff involved were diffident about dealing with such a hot issue in the limelight moment of the run-up to the WTO Cancun Ministerial Meeting. They also had some real conceptual and methodological problems in dealing with the issue. In the end the presentations to the event[153] were of good quality, however, and the discussion between IPC members and FAO staff was animated and interesting. As a first step it could have gone worse, and the few government delegates who attended found it stimulating.

The outcome of the Cancun WTO session six months later heightened the IPC members' expectations of the FAO and their hopes that a major change in global institutional responsibilities for agricultural trade could be in the offing. The IPC general meeting on 26–29 November 2003 took trade and food sovereignty in the context of the post-Cancun situation as its central political and strategic point for discussion. A consensus emerged that the FAO, based on its mandate of fighting hunger, was the best-placed global institution to take charge of issues of food and agricultural trade. When an officer of the division responsible for trade issues joined the meeting for a dialogue session, he noted that the IPC's high expectations were unlikely to be fulfilled and urged participants to produce a clear and well-reasoned action proposal for discussion with top management. The outcome of the IPC deliberations, mediating between hotter and cooler heads, was a letter[154] addressing the FAO Director-General in strong and impassioned language, urging him to return to the FAO's original mandate and to ensure its freedom from subjection to the dominant neoliberal paradigm and the will of a few powerful countries. The tone and content of the letter were felt by senior FAO management supportive of the IPC to be inappropriate and unhelpful. The reply, which came under the signature of the Assistant Director-General of the FAO's Technical Cooperation Department rather than the Director-General himself, was dignified, institutional and noncommittal. The contrast between these two missives is illustrative of the difficulties of finding a mutually acceptable and productive mode of negotiation on hotly contested terrains between subjects as different as an international institution and a variegated civil society network.

At the heart of the problem was the technical/political divide that had plagued the FAO since its foundation and led to the resignation of its first Director-General. Admitted that more or less drastic correctives to liberalization were required to attain the goals of the WFS, was the organization already doing what it could by providing developing countries with training and strategic information to strengthen their negotiation capacity, by undertaking analyses and case studies, and by providing a neutral forum for discussion of trade issues? Or did the FAO's mandate of fighting hunger have a political as well as a technical dimension, as maintained by the IPC?

A further occasion for a meeting of minds on the topic occurred in the context of the negotiation of the voluntary guidelines for the right to food. The term had been cited frequently in the interventions of the civil society participants in the IGWG, and the FAO secretariat decided that it could be useful to include a document on this concept in the series of information notes on selected key themes that it was preparing in support of the negotiation process. The exercise got off to an unfortunately unilateral start when a draft paper was prepared in the FAO and only subsequently shared with the IPC and FIAN. The draft was found to suffer from weaknesses of coverage (too exclusive a focus on the trade-related aspects of food sovereignty), analytical approach (too squarely in the neoliberal camp), tone (ironically critical in an academic mode), and process (lack of exchange with civil society actors to reach a shared view of how best to frame and conduct the analysis). During an informal discussion between FAO staff and IPC members, it was agreed that the FAO should not put the concept on the table without properly discussing it with the civil society actors who were most engaged in developing it. The meeting proposed the preparation of an information paper in order to facilitate a continual dialogue between the FAO and civil society. Resources would be needed to enable the IPC to delegate someone to work with the FAO on this project. The proposal to develop a common paper was accepted by the IPC annual general meeting in October 2004. In the end, however, the proposed process was overtaken by the successful conclusion of the IGWG's work and the limitations of the IPC's follow-up capacity.[155] Since then food sovereignty has been cited in discussions in FAO technical committee and council meetings but has encountered the opposition of member countries that do not wish to see the concept accredited in FAO parlance.[156]

The vicissitudes of the FAO–IPC encounter around the concept of food sovereignty are far from casual. They are substantive and significant. They highlight a deep – and often ignored – problem involved in building a dialectic between governmental negotiating spaces and the social spaces in which the most meaningful alternative approaches are born. Despite the acclaimed introduction into UN forums of multistakeholder dialogues and other techniques that apparently open breaches in normal intergovernmental practice, in fact the vast majority of the encounters between the two worlds take place in inter-governmental spaces and are orchestrated according to the rhythms, procedures and language that prevail there. Yet, as the *Seedling* (2005:3) editorial already referred to points out, 'food sovereignty is a process of people's resistance and its conceptualisation cannot be carried out outside the dynamics of the social movements that are central in these struggles'. Up to now, civil society actors have been shouldering more of the burden of bridging the gap between spaces than have the intergovernmental organizations. An Institute of Development Studies working paper looking at civil society participation in trade policy negotiations in the United Kingdom and East Africa notes that 'many of the Southern actors interviewed for this research make sense of impenetrable complexity by constantly referring what they are learning to their own experiences … asking themselves or others key questions: "how are the peasants going to benefit from this?" ' (Brock and McGee 2004:51). The West African farmers' network ROPPA, a strong participant in global trade policy forums, gives priority to training a nucleus of farmer leaders in each country in agricultural and trade policy issues; it takes this approach in order to fight against the danger that a handful of farmer cadres might hegemonize knowledge of such complex issues. It is likely that processes like these will need to move ahead and bear their fruits locally for a real paradigm change to be promoted at the global level.

This, indeed, was the kind of process envisaged by the proposal for a carefully prepared world forum on food sovereignty launched by Via Campesina and adopted by the IPC general meeting in November 2005.[157] Guided by a steering committee composed predominantly of people's organizations,[158] the forum was intended as an occasion for reflection by some 500 delegates representing farmers, fisherfolk, indigenous peoples, pastoralists, women's groups, workers, environmentalists, consumers, NGOs, and youth groups from around the world, all of whom had subscribed to the concept of food sovereignty and were taking action to put it into practice in their different settings.[159] The objective was to build up a common understanding of what food sovereignty entails, starting from the concrete practices of the participants, and to develop collective strategies and action plans. Building alliances among various sectors of civil society and with sympathetic governments and intergovernmental organizations was part of the agenda, but care was taken to guard against co-optation of local movements. The thematic discussions were prepared by a 'methodology group' that drew on NGO and academic expertise, subjected to the political control of people's organizations. The coherence between the topic of the forum and the style of organization was just as important as the content, in sharp contrast with intergovernmental modes of deliberation. The venue was a village in southern Mali where huts for accommodation and areas for meeting and eating had been constructed to house the forum and would afterwards serve as a training facility for the West Africa farmers' movement.[160] The staff – including interpreters, cooks and a medical team – were all volunteer activists. The meals were prepared using exclusively local products. The different food-producing constituencies from regions around the world built up a shared understanding of their identities and interests not only through formal discussions, but equally by collectively preparing *misticas*[161] and presenting them to the rest of the assembly. The only two international agencies invited to participate in the forum as observers were the FAO and IFAD, testimony to the fact that they were perceived to be more sensitive to social movements than other parts of the UN system. Indeed, as the IFAD representative stated at the closing ceremony, encountering the social movements in their own space made their aspirations and discourse far more understandable than they were in the 'normal' mode in which the UN and social organizations meet.

The dominant thrust toward paradigm change – particularly in so politically charged an area as that of winning acceptance for an alternative to the neoliberal approach to development – is clearly more likely to come from outside UN institutions than from within, although alliances with motivated UN staff and like-minded governments are an important part of the process. The global food crisis which mobilized international attention in early 2008, to which we will turn at the end of this chapter, is providing an occasion to observe what can happen when a decade of gradual civil society paradigm construction encounters a significant political opportunity.

The impact on institutional interaction: opening up political space

The preceding section has provided considerable insight into how institutional interaction between the FAO and civil society has progressed since 2002. In this section we undertake a more systematic look at, though not a fully comprehensive review of, some key developments in the areas of normative work and policy dialogue and in how these two domains are linked with action at country level.

A major crisis in relations between the IPC and the FAO, which exploded in May 2004, illustrates the complexities of fostering collaboration in the area of work which is at the very heart of the FAO's identity and authority as a specialized technical agency of the UN. 'Normative work', as it is termed in the intergovernmental world, involves the collection, analysis and diffusion of information, data and research findings regarding food and agriculture and the identification and exploration of new issues as they emerge. It is a fundamental part of the FAO's mandate. FAO documents and yearbooks serve as authoritative sources of information and interpretation the world over. Normative work also underlies the FAO's capacity to serve as a quality global policy forum. It sets the stage for policy debate, through the production of secretariat papers on the basis of which governments deliberate, by defining the issues, assembling and interpreting the evidence, outlining the options among which governments can choose and illustrating the probable consequences of each option. The corporate enhancement of technical expertise which normative activity is expected to result in is the main justification for maintaining an FAO-operated field programme. Many of the FAO's industrialized country member governments have been pushing in recent years for a realignment of the organization's programme of work to focus more strongly on its activities as a normative 'centre of excellence'.[162] Harnessing more effectively – some would say domesticating – the normative capacity of the specialized agencies, which are not directly accountable to the UN secretariat and the General Assembly, is also a recurrent theme of the UN reform process, as we shall see in Chapter 3.

How are the scoping and the content of FAO's normative work determined? The organization's governing bodies exercise considerable oversight over the FAO's normative activities through the technical committees, the Committees of Programme and of Finance and, ultimately, the FAO Council and Conference. But what takes place behind the scenes? According to the game plan of positivistic science and Western representative democracy, the experts should produce objective and neutral analysis on the basis of which governments would proceed to take enlightened political decisions, and civil society would proceed to exercise its monitoring function. What is more, the two kinds of activities should be distinct and sited in different arenas. In fact, credence in the neutrality and objectivity of scientific inquiry is no longer as entrenched as it once was, although its longevity is astounding. On the one hand, it has become evident that the objectivity of schools of thought and of individual scientists is affected by assumptions – in some cases outright dogmas – which restrict their capacity to entertain and evaluate evidence and can even impact on how they define the problems to be researched. On the other hand, the idea that a 'safe space' for independent scientific activity can be delimited and defended has proved to be illusory. The scope of the normative activity of institutions such as the FAO is affected by political decisions of the governing bodies that approve their programmes of work and budget. Even the content of normative efforts, or at least the way in which it is presented, is sometimes influenced by self-censorship influenced by what the secretariat feels the most powerful governments are, or are not, likely to find acceptable. Nor are the governments the only actors that wield an influence on FAO's normative activities. CSOs, as we have seen, want to have an input. So do the corporate interests of the agrifood business complex, and they have infinitely more resources at their disposal. To complicate matters further, individual member countries may promote the input of one or another interest group vis-à-vis the FAO secretariat. Or the influence can take place upstream. NGOs have contested for years the dominance of the Consultative Group on International Agricultural Research (CGIAR) system,[163] authors of the Green Revolution of the 1970s and now defenders of biotechnology applied to agriculture, and its close relations with the FAO.

Managing such a complex scenario is clearly no easy job. It becomes increasingly difficult the more strongly particular economic interests impinge on an issue in ways that may clash with the common good or with the interests of the poor and the hungry which the FAO is expected to defend. In some cases the situation is relatively straight-forward. No controversy, for example, has been engendered by the collaboration of the FAO secretariat with knowledgeable NGOs in the development of a UN system-wide mechanism for better targeting the hungry.[164] Individual units have, over the years, built up relations with NGOs whose technical competence they appreciate and whose input they seek on an ongoing basis.[165] Even on more delicate terrain the FAO's experience demonstrates that sensitive and transparent manage-ment of external input to normative work can turn potentially explosive situations into win–win engagements.[166]

This was not the case with the 2003 edition of FAO's flagship publication, *The State of Food and Agriculture* (*SOFA*). Preparation of this authoritative yearbook got under way shortly after the close of the WFS:*fyl*. A junior staff member of the unit responsible for *SOFA*, who had served on the FAO volunteer team at the 2002 NGO/CSO Forum and had taken careful note of civil society's interest in the issue of biotechnology, came forward with a suggestion that dialogue be engaged with the IPC in the course of preparation of the 2003 thematic section, provocatively entitled 'Agricultural biotechnology: Meeting the needs of the poor?' This idea was welcomed by the NGO/CSO unit, and a proposal went forward to the editors of *SOFA* that input to the 2003 edition of the publication should be sought not only from the IPC but also from representatives of the corporations producing biotechnology products and any other significant stakeholder groups. The idea was to allow stakeholders to present and underwrite their views, rather than assuming that the FAO secretariat could, and should, subsume them all into its own objective and neutral meta-position. The proposal was not accepted by the editors. Instead, they decided to organize an email conference on the topic 'What should be the role and focus of biotechnology in the agricultural research agendas of developing countries?', despite the NGO/CSO unit's advice that a moderated monolingual electronic conference would not be likely to attract IPC members, a number of whom operate only in Spanish or French and had neither the time for nor the practice of engaging in e-conferences.

The 2003 *SOFA* issue was officially released on 17 May 2004 at the Regional Conference for Asia and the Pacific, hosted by China, a strong supporter and practitioner of agricultural biotechnology. Civil society reaction to the publication, which they felt validated the use of biotechnology as a solution to the problem of hunger, was immediate and strong. The organizations attending the parallel NGO/CSO consultation issued a denunciatory press release. The IPC network was alerted and action was taken to prepare and post an open letter to the Director-General of the FAO (IPC 2004a). The letter criticized both the process and the content of the 2003 *SOFA*. Regarding process, CSOs felt that the 'FAO has breached its commitment to consult and maintain an open dialogue with smallholder farmers' organizations and civil society'. In fact, the Exchange of Letters between the FAO and the IPC foresaw the establishment of a joint FAO–IPC working group on the impact of biotechnology on agrarian and food production systems. Instead, the content of the *SOFA* issue had been prepared by the FAO interdepartmental working group on biotechnology without consultation with civil society although, the open letter maintained, 'there appears to have been extensive discussion with industry'. Regarding the content of the report, the CSOs found that although the document 'struggles to appear neutral, it is highly biased and ignores available evidence of the adverse ecological, economic and health impacts of genetically engineered crops'. Targeting the role and mission of the FAO, the letter stated that 'with the advent of genetic engineering the threat of genetic erosion has increased. As the normative intergovernmental institution for genetic resources, FAO should be developing policies to prevent genetic erosion and take action to address the negative global implications'. By 16 June, more than 850 CSOs and 650 individuals had signed the letter, which was delivered by hand to the Deputy Director-General of the FAO by the international coordinator of the IPC.

The *SOFA* incident sparked off extremely interesting discussions within the FAO. The fact that a prestige publication taking a controversial position on a delicate topic with a preface signed by the Director-General could reach publication without whistles being blown[167] raised issues of process and quality control. The eventuality that corporate interests might weigh on FAO normative activities was preoccupying. The question of whether or not the FAO was empowered to have a position on a given issue other than that adopted by its members was subject to debate. If it was so empowered, should this position be based on neutral scientific weighing of the facts? Or should the FAO itself act as a stakeholder on behalf of the world's hungry, as it had opted to do during the IGWG negotiations on the application of the right to food?

The Director-General met with a delegation of the IPC on 14 October 2004. He expressed his unhappiness with the process by which the *SOFA* issue had been prepared and reiterated his own view that biotechnology would not solve the problem of hunger. The *SOFA* issue, he indicated, was to be considered a technical report prepared by an expert committee and not an FAO policy paper. He committed the FAO to facilitating the preparation and publication of a civil society report presenting other views on biotechnology. The IPC would also be fully involved in the preparation of the upcoming *SOFA* issue which would focus on the equally hot issue of trade and food security. The delegation reported back to the IPC annual general meeting two days later. The results of the latter's discussions were conveyed to the FAO Director-General in a letter dated 19 October 2004 that accepted his proposals and raised issues of process and resources. In the end, resources were not made available to support preparation of a civil society document on biotechnology. IPC members concluded that it would be counter-productive to devote considerable amounts of their scarce time and attention to rebutting the already published FAO document rather than forging ahead with their own agenda. On the trade issue the IPC was unable to produce a substantive input at short notice without dedicated resources, and it limited itself to putting together a collection of existing social movement declarations on trade. On this occasion, as on others, the people's organizations and the IPC mechanism, as a whole, proved more effective in mobilizing a far-reaching and credible denunciation than in following through rapidly to document alternative positions. All told, the incident constituted a salutary shake-up of the 'neutral scientific-technical' identity often adopted by the secretariats of intergovernmental agencies. Seeking stakeholder contributions has now become a standard procedure in the preparation of SOFA. The clash contributed to clarifying the issues involved in normative cooperation between the FAO and civil society, although it did not solve them on a corporate basis. They must be addressed if a qualitative step is to be taken toward the adoption of transparent and reasonably resourced procedures for stakeholder participation throughout the range of FAO's normative work.[168]

In the closely related area of policy dialogue and decision making, what new ground has been broken in civil society participation in FAO forums? At regional level, as we have seen, preparations for the WFS:*fyl* provided an occasion to build relations between the FAO's offices and regional civil society networks and to solidify the practice of holding civil society consultations feeding into the intergovernmental FAO Regional Conferences. In late 2003 these precedents were institution-alized in the form of a document entitled 'Guidelines for FAO Regional NGO/CSO Consultations',[169] which put them on the official map of the governing bodies. The guidelines clarified the FAO regional offices' responsibilities for making the consultations happen, for enabling their output to be presented to the official sessions, and for covering some of the meeting costs. Key to the process – at regional as at global level – was to get the right balance: ensuring a good degree of CSO autonomy to set the agenda, choose the participants and plan the programme while maintaining a link with, and consequently a right to report to, the official proceedings.

The existence of the guidelines undoubtedly facilitated the organization of the 2004 round of regional consultations and their interface with official events. Some 300 CSOs from 100 countries participated in the five meetings, with the accent on people's organiza-tions. In many cases national and subregional discussions prepared for the regional dialogue, giving greater legitimacy to the consultations' declarations. Some innovative practices, including side events, were introduced into what have traditionally been highly formal events. The civil society participants generally strengthened their interaction with government delegates, particularly in those regions where they have less lobbying experience. The consultations' conclusions were presented to plenary sessions in all five regions and were referred to in the reports of the official conferences. All told, the 2004 consultations were a virtuous example of building from precedent to institutional change, but a fragile innovation nonetheless. The major limitations of such consultations are the continued dependence on extrabudgetary funds to cover participants' travel costs[170] and the uncertain political clout of the regional conferences themselves, a potentially important but presently neglected level of intergovernmental dialogue within the FAO governing body system.

So far as global policy forums are concerned, the discussion of the guidelines on the right to food has highlighted one of the most important innovations introduced since the WFS:*fyl*. This is the distinction between the discussion and the decision-taking phases of the work of policy forums, facilitating full stakeholder participation in the former while reserving the latter for governments. In the context of the IGWG, stakeholders were allowed to take part in the discussion phase on the same footing as governments and were requested, in return, to adopt a disciplined and responsible approach to their participation through the preparation of caucus positions and the designation of spokespersons. The IGWG experience also validated the important precedent of allowing silent civil society observers to be present even in the more restricted Friends of the Chair meetings, a significant step toward ensuring transparency in negotiation processes.

Efforts to create more space for civil society input have also been made in the sessions of the FAO's technical committees. Exchanges among the secretaries of the committees, promoted by the NGO/CSO unit, have generalized a series of basic practices. These include briefing sessions, provision of equipped offices and meeting rooms, and wrap-up meetings between CSO participants and the FAO secretariat to discuss how to build ongoing cooperation from one session to the next. Different committees have experimented with different ways of improving communication of civil society views to government delegates without subverting the procedures of the formal plenary sessions. In some cases the results of civil-society-organized side events have been presented to plenary sessions. In others the rapporteur of a preparatory meeting of civil society observers on an agenda item of particular interest to them has been enabled to speak to the plenary session at the opening of debate rather than at the end. The chair of the drafting committee of the International Treaty on Plant Genetic Resources for Food and Agriculture, adopted by the FAO Conference in November 2003, asked one representative each from civil society and the private sector to participate in the committee's work, traditionally off limits for observers. All told, intergovernmental policy processes held under FAO auspices have opened up to civil society voices steadily and in small but cumulatively significant ways in the years since the WFS.

The World Food Summit +10 Special Forum, held in the context of the Committee on World Food Security session in September 2006, could have provided an occasion to consolidate this progress. The forum was conducted in the form of a multistakeholder dialogue, with the usual provision that decision-making power continued to be vested exclusively in governments.[171] In the end, however, the event was far from earth-shaking. The +10 process was overshadowed by the eruption of serious controversy about FAO reform (see below). Keeping the civil society component of the forum in focus would have required a proactive stance on the part of at least one of the actors, and this was not forthcoming. The NGO/CSO unit, along with many other parts of the FAO, had been plunged by the reform process into a debilitating state of flux and budget reductions. The astute and capable Assistant Director-General to whom the unit had reported for six years left the FAO at the end of 2005.[172] The IPC itself was reluctant to invest scarce human resources in an event whose political significance was doubtful. The members of the rump bureau of the CFS, whose mandate would expire shortly before the September 2006 session, were not likely to champion the cause of civil society participation on their own steam, nor was the FAO secretariat responsible for the CFS.[173] While the WFS +5 event demonstrated how institutional change can be promoted when a determined internal change agent is able to take advantage of a series of positive environmental factors, the +10 event illustrated the opposite. Nonetheless, the forum did reinforce the practice of promoting dialogue between civil society stakeholders and governments on determined occasions and reporting the results to the intergovernmental plenary.[174] In the follow-up to the +10 Special Forum, the Committee on World Food Security put on the agenda for its October 2008 session consideration of a full menu of options to strengthen participation in its work by civil society.

During approximately the same time frame the International Conference on Agrarian Reform and Rural Development (ICARRD), held in Porto Alegre from 7 to 10 March 2006, proved to be a far more significant terrain for experimentation with civil society participation in FAO global policy forums. The context was more favourable for several reasons. The issue was a top priority for rural people's organizations and social movements, and the agenda was more politically focused than that of the +10 Special Forum. The IPC was able to use to good advantage the synergies its membership afforded between strong rural people's movements and NGOs with expertise on agrarian reform issues. An alliance was established between the CSOs and the sponsoring Brazilian government, which counted on the IPC to facilitate its communication with radical Brazilian social movements. The fact that the conference was a special, one-off event and not a session of the FAO's governing bodies gave it greater flexibility. Dissenting powers, such as the United States and the European Union, were members of the steering committee but opted to adopt a low profile rather than attempting to scuttle the initiative. Relations between the IPC and the FAO secretariat office responsible for the conference were facilitated by the support of the Brazilian government and the institutional basis for cooperation that had been built up since the WFS:*fyl*, in particular the IPC–FAO Exchange of Letters. The head of the secretariat[175] was an experienced, intelligent and diplomatically skilful person who sincerely believed in the added value of civil society input, particularly by rural stakeholders, and he was assisted by a collaborator who had a long history of relations with Latin American peasant organizations. Finally, the resource problem was addressed by seeking the assistance of the FAO's sister organization, IFAD, which was then well advanced in developing its own innovative interface with rural people's organizations, many of which were IPC members. In short, the ICARRD scenario included many of the same success factors as had operated in the case of the voluntary guidelines on the right to food, with the notable exception that agrarian reform is hardly a soft issue.

In the run-up to the conference, the IPC declined an invitation to participate in the official steering committee in order to avoid co-optation. It decided instead to organize a parallel autonomous civil society conference that would have meaningful and well-defined opportunities to interact with the official conference.[176] In the end, the IPC obtained for CSOs the right to prepare one of the basic issue papers and several case studies, to name one of the speakers at the inaugural ceremony, and to engage in dialogue on an equal footing with governments in roundtable discussions, with seven civil society representatives pitted against seven ministers or other high government officials in what they dubbed 'gladiator style'. The conclusions of the parallel civil society forum were presented to ICARRD and included in its report. The people's organizations and social movements had a meaningful impact on the final statement of the official conference itself, whose vision is that 'rural development policies, including those on agrarian reforms, should be more focused on the poor and their organizations, socially-driven, participatory, and respectful of gender equality, in the context of economic, social and environmentally sound sustainable development' (FAO 2006b: para. 28). Victories won by the IPC included the recognition of collective rights to land as well as individual and communal rights; acknowledgement that land is a cultural, social and historical in addition to an economic asset; and the reference to 'control of' land, a more forceful concept than that of 'access to' land. The final conference declaration requested the FAO to include ICARRD follow-up in the agenda of the FAO Council, bringing the results of the conference to bear on FAO's regular programme of work.

Both the IPC and the FAO secretariat were pleased that the conference managed to rescue the issue of agrarian reform from the oblivion into which it had fallen in the decades following the 1979 World Conference on Agricultural Reform and Rural Development (WCARRD) and to link it to the emerging theme of the right to food. For CSOs the marginalization of market-assisted land reform, free trade and export-oriented agriculture as recipes for development was an important political victory.[177] Powerful FAO members, such as the United States and the European Union, were less satisfied and have done their best to slow-pedal follow-up. But the conference has stimulated a number of Southern governments and intergovernmental organizations to seek the FAO's technical assistance in applying the principles enunciated by ICARRD to their particular contexts, with stakeholder participation.[178] In terms of opening up meaningful political space for civil society, the conference set a new standard for the FAO, a standard which, however, has not yet been recognized as corporate practice.

Turning, finally, to the field programme component of the FAO's mandate, how is the global evolution of relations between the FAO and civil society translating into action at the country level, where the issues dealt with in global policy forums and normative work impact concretely on people's lives? Because of its strong anchorage in social movements and regionally based networks, the IPC has consistently been very clear about giving priority to local empowerment. The value-added of interfacing with the FAO, in the first instance, should be that of helping to open up political space for engagement between people's organizations and national governments, particularly in those countries in which such space is limited. Instead, as an eloquent IPC focal point in West Africa put it in late 2004, 'the persistent issue of what I may term "the Weak Periphery – Strong Center" profile of the partnership between IPC and FAO keeps making a sort of mockery of the energies invested in Rome'. Periodic joint FAO–IPC assessments of the relationship have corroborated this judgement.[179]

In consequence, in 2005 the civil society unit conducted a review of country-level FAO–civil society cooperation as a basis for developing a strategy and specific proposals to improve relations (FAO 2005a).[180] On the positive side of the balance sheet, the report of the review indicated that field-level respondents felt that dialogue with civil society

> can help FAO representatives to build up a comprehensive understanding of the complex development issues related to hunger and food security; a sounder basis for identifying priority areas and sequencing activities; fuller national/local ownership of and participation in initiatives; more effective coordination, implementation, monitoring, feedback; in short, greater likelihood of success of activities and initiatives (FAO 2005a:2).

Regarding government attitudes, a wind of change was felt to be blowing. 'In some countries there is awareness of the ineffectiveness of past or current approaches, with resulting willingness to try new ideas. FAO support to build government capacity to engage with civil society can be appreciated' (FAO 2005a:3).

The obstacles, however, were not underestimated. The institutional culture of the FAO was recognized to be dominantly oriented toward governments. Insufficient human and financial resources and communication capacity on the part of country offices constituted blockages, along with weak coordination among UN agencies in civil society outreach. On the civil society side, the proliferation and weak organization, capacities and accountability of national CSOs were seen to be the main obstacles. Many were looking essentially for financial assistance, which the FAO was not in a position to provide. The political agendas of some organizations were also problematic. Finally, many governments continued to resist opening up to CSOs and even viewed them as competitors.

The 42 FAO representatives who responded to the review questionnaire were asked to rate the degree to which CSOs were engaged in various types of activities in their countries of assignment. The results, tabulated in Table 2.1, document the degree to which CSOs tend to be stuck in the traditional roles of service and information providers.[181]

Table 2.1 Areas of FAO–Civil Society Cooperation at Country Level,
and Levels of CSO Involvement

Activity	None	Weak	Medium	Strong
Programme/project implementation	2	6	14	11
Public information	2	6	16	9
National policy/strategy formulation	6	7	12	6
Programme coordination	8	16	3	4
Programme/project formulation	5	7	19	3
National programme decision-making mechanisms	10	8	11	3
Early warning/preparedness	6	14	7	3
Programme/project monitoring/evaluation	6	14	12	2
Monitoring/reporting on government commitments	7	11	8	2
Developing FAO field programme framework	9	10	8	2

Table 2.2 Types of CSOs with Which the FAO Cooperates at Country Level

Type of CSO	None	Weak	Medium	Strong
Community-based organizations (CBOs)	2	2	13	13
National NGOs	1	3	21	10
International NGOs	3	10	13	8
National civil society umbrella organizations	4	5	13	5
National people's organizations/social movements	6	6	8	5

FAO representatives were also asked to differentiate the degree of involvement by type of CSO. Not surprisingly, rural people's membership organizations structured above the community level are at the bottom of the basket (see Table 2.2).

The package of proposals that emerged from the review was predicated on the need to clarify some basic principles, chiefly the need to identify the different forms of cooperation that are appropriate for different kinds of CSOs and to specify the roles/responsibilities of different actors:

- FAO as a source of information, technical advice, capacity building and as a neutral facilitator of civil society–government dialogue.
- 'intermediary' or 'service' NGOs as potential partners in implementation of programme activities.
- social movements (farmers' organisations, trade unions, Indigenous People's organisations, etc.) as mobilisers, advocates, participants in policy dialogue, and as service providers for their membership (FAO 2005a:4).

Based on suggestions from the field, the review proposed a package of institutional, communication and programme tools. It recommended adopting a strategic and progressive approach, targeting a certain number of countries initially. On a pilot basis, CSO focal points would be identified in these FAO offices, work plans would be developed and resourced and capacity-building would be provided for CSOs, for FAO staff and for key government services and officers to prepare them for a partnership mode of work.

During the same time frame, an independent evaluation was carried out of the FAO's progress in implementing the 'Cross-Organizational Strategy of Broadening Partnerships and Alliances' which forms part of its Strategic Framework and Programme of Work and Budget. The final evaluation report, published in July 2005, gave a positive overall assessment of the FAO's partnerships with CSOs but it too pinpointed the country level as an area for improvement. The results of these reviews were overtaken by the reform proposals to which we will turn in the following section, leaving the gap between global discourse and local action still largely to be addressed institutionally. Not surprisingly, the geographical areas where most progress has been made are South America, where the political mood is more amenable to social movements than elsewhere in the South, and West Africa, where the peasant farmers' network ROPPA has proved particularly skilful in building cooperation with the better-disposed FAO country representatives.

An instrument that had been intended to assist in bridging the global–local gap was the International Alliance against Hunger (IAAH), as well as the multistakeholder National Alliances against Hunger it was expected to promote. The IAAH constituted the major institutional and advocacy proposal emerging from the official WFS:*fyl*.[182] Within the civil society world, the Alliance has won support from a number of INGOs and faith-based organizations, such as Caritas Internationalis and the World Association of Girl Guides and Girl Scouts. The IPC has eyed it with greater perplexity. The possibility that the National Alliances might be a useful advocacy tool for social movements at country level was not excluded, and some of the IPC members have experimented with this hypothesis. For others, however, the fear of co-option or simply of investing precious energy in a politically insignificant endeavour has been dominant. On the other hand, the FAO has not consistently supported the initiative it spawned. At the outset the Director-General enticed the morally inspiring and politically astute former head of the US Congress Black Caucus, Eva Clayton, to Rome to head the IAAH Secretariat,[183] but in the long run she did not receive the political and financial backing she needed to get the Alliance off the ground. The fate of the IAAH, like that of the defunct Food for All Campaign launched by the WFS, illustrates the difficulties the UN system encounters in seeking to be supportive of tripartite cooperation between CSOs, governments and intergovernmental organizations in ways that inspire the confidence and engagement of all parties.

The Global Food Crisis: A Political Opportunity for Civil Society?

Calls for reform were echoing throughout the UN system as the twenty-first century got under way in earnest, both globally, as we will see in Chapter 3, and at the level of individual agencies and programmes. Braving the ire of member governments who had called for an Independent External Evaluation of the FAO, Jacques Diouf put forward his own reform proposals in autumn 2005 on the eve of elections to the post of Director-General in which he was standing unopposed for a third term. The reform aimed at redefining the organization's programmes to adapt to a changing global context, of which one aspect, in Diouf's view, was the emergence of new institutions and capacities.

> The changes ... in the respective roles of the state, the private sector and civil society call for FAO to broaden and deepen its links beyond its traditional

partners in the public sector and to engage more effectively with NGOs, the private sector, parliamentarians, chambers of agriculture and commerce, local government entities, professional associations and religious leaders (FAO 2005b: para. 31).

In this regard, he proposed to create an entire new department devoted to 'Alliances and Rural Livelihoods', bringing together the scattered units in the organization dealing with CSOs, rural people's institutions, other partners such as parliamentarians and decentralized authorities, indigenous peoples, gender issues, implementation of the right to food, national alliances against hunger, and promotional advocacy activities like World Food Day. Some aspects of the logic of this assemblage could be critiqued and many questions were left open, but there was no doubt that the proposal represented a validation of the thrust of four and a half decades of work with NGOs/CSOs and farmers' organizations.

In November 2005, the FAO Conference re-elected Diouf to a third mandate, but failed to provide resounding support or additional resources for his reform proposals. In the months that followed, six of the organization's major donors[184] made it clear that they intended to have a decisive say regarding the direction of FAO reform. The Independent External Evaluation (IEE) started its work in March 2006 and delivered its report in September 2007. The debilitating intervening period was one of staff insecurity and uneasiness and a disgruntled 'wait and see' attitude on the part of many member governments. In the end, however, the evaluation report was more constructive than many had expected. The team came down strongly in favour of a continued central role for the FAO in world governance of food and agriculture. It placed a good deal of the blame for the progressive decline in its effectiveness on low levels of trust and mutual understanding between member countries and the secretariat, and a resulting lack of support for the FAO's work. 'Reform with growth' was the report's dominant message. Tracing the institutional proliferation that had taken place over the past decades, the report noted that:

> By the beginning of the 21st century, the international development architecture had become anything but 'systemic', resembling more closely a collection of rather inarticulate components, efforts and initiatives. New institutional arrangements are now regularly created in order to bypass or rectify perceived deficiencies in existing institutions. But inertial forces remain dominant, and reform efforts have been typically frustrated by the pervasiveness and magnitude of structural factors and institutional inertias (FAO 2007:62).

In language not dissimilar to that of the declarations of the civil society forums held in parallel to the world food summits, the team insisted that, to counter this situation,

> FAO must strengthen its global governance role, as a convener, a facilitator and a source of reference for global policy coherence and in the development of global codes, conventions and agreements. The Organization's strategic objective must be to rebuild an authoritative and effective voice on behalf of rural people, the hungry and all those who can benefit from agriculture playing its role in the economy, including consumers. FAO is the only global organization to speak for this constituency (FAO 2007:14).

It could have been expected that this pronouncement would be accompanied by an injunction to build closer dialogue with the organizations that these constituencies themselves have established to defend their interests, but the report's recommendations on civil society partnerships are distractedly piecemeal and appear to equate civil society with NGOs (FAO 2007:219).

The IEE report was examined in November 2007 by the FAO Conference, which agreed to establish a Conference Committee to develop an 'immediate action plan' that would be put to a special conference a year later. Whatever the final output of the process may be, as the work of the committee proceeded, it did indeed seem to be fulfilling the IEE's hope of regenerating a sense of engagement and commitment on the part of the FAO's member governments. In the meantime, the IEE's emphasis on the need to strengthen global food and agriculture governance received dramatic confirmation when the 'world food crisis' erupted in the media, catching public attention in consequence of the clamorous riots in low-income countries and the fact that even consumers in the industrialized North were feeling the pinch. The social movements and CSOs tracking food and agriculture issues were expecting the crisis. Thanks to a decade of progressively solid networking since the 1996 World Food Summit, they were far better prepared than before to take advantage of what could prove to be an important political opportunity to address both the paradigmatic and the institutional aspects of world food governance. Already at its 2005 annual meeting, in the run-up to the WTO Hong Kong Ministerial, IPC members had taken good note of the renewed centrality of food and agriculture as a world problem area. This development, in their view, validated the hypothesis that it was strategically important to invest in the FAO. The UN system – and the FAO in particular – appeared indeed to constitute the only alternative to the WTO/Bretton Woods institutions as a multilateral locus for addressing these issues according to a logic in which human rights and equity take precedence over the liberalization of markets.

By the time of the IPC's 2006 and 2007 meetings, the trends that had continued to dominate over the intervening months seemed to corroborate this analysis. Powerful players, which had tended to ignore the FAO as an international forum over past years, had returned in force to bring their interests to bear on the decision-making processes of the organization. They had done so both in formal intergovernmental sessions and in less public ways, such as the letter cited above in which major donor countries strongly suggested to the Director-General what they felt the FAO should, and should not, do. Nor was the team of new and old entries in the agriculture playing field limited to FAO member governments. It was no coincidence that the World Bank was dedicating its 2008 annual report to the theme of agriculture and development for the first time in almost a quarter of a century. Nor that the Gates and Rockefeller Foundations had joined hands to form an Alliance for a Green Revolution in Africa (AGRA). Nor that a Global Donor Platform for Rural Development was reaching out to bring together OECD bilateral aid programmes, the EU and UN family multilateral funders with a vision of 'achieving increased development assistance impact and more effective investment in rural development and agriculture'.[185]

In the IPC's analysis the strategy of the OECD countries and agrifood corporations for addressing food and agriculture questions that could no longer be ignored was to reroute attention from structural and political issues toward renewed faith in the two planks of the dominant paradigm: free trade and technology-driven agriculture. The capacity of markets to generate 'development for all' was being refurbished through 'aid for trade' discourse and by promoting bilateral trade agreements as a tool to jump-start the stalled WTO Doha round. Technology as a tool to generate food for all was being reinvented through the new green revolution with its accent on technology transfer – including a strong push for GMOs – which would reinforce the control of agrifood business over the food chain at all levels. With the crisis of the WTO, the situation had become more acute and the offensive of the pro-liberalization interests more aggressive. If the WTO were to be discredited as a world trade forum, would agricultural trade oversight be brought to the FAO? Not if the pro-liberalization forces had a say in the matter. On the contrary, the role they envisaged for the FAO was a reduced one, privileging global 'normative' activities at the expense of presence in the regions and capacity to provide policy advice and technical support for developing country members. The IPC members felt this vision was only part of an overall strategy for reform of the UN system that would tend toward reinforcing the power of the central UN secretariat and the New York-based intergovernmental bodies, 'demoting' the autonomous technical agencies to the status of technical advisory bodies and further enhancing the role of the 'more effective' Bretton Woods institutions.

In such a context it was felt to be even more important than ever to take a systemic approach to strategizing about global food governance. And, more than ever, rural people's organizations and social movements needed the kind of analytical support the IPC could provide. It was to be expected that space for lobbying within the UN institutions would be progressively reduced the stronger the conflict became. Hence it was important to achieve an effective balance between mobilizing outside the institutions and maintaining hard-won political space inside. The success of mobilization, clearly, depended not only on numbers but also on capacity to formulate alternatives.

Developments during the first half of 2008 seemed to validate this reading. On the institutional front all of the players positioned themselves in reaction to the crisis. The FAO launched a 'soaring food prices initiative' aimed at providing farmers in low-income food-deficient countries with inputs in time for the coming production season. At the policy level it retooled an already scheduled High Level Conference on 'World Food Security: The Challenges of Climate Change and Bio-energy' to headline the global food crisis as well. Breaking with a consolidated practice of negotiating civil society involvement with CSO networks, the secretariat of the High Level Conference decided to maintain control of participant selection and programme planning for a 'preparatory civil society consultation' held in February and a 'civil society side event' organized during the High Level Conference itself in early June. When a delegation of rural producer organization leaders attempted to flag their concern about the lack of dialogue, they received scant attention from the Director-General's Chef de Cabinet. It was not until the eve of the High Level Conference and of the parallel autonomous civil society forum that they managed to get a letter directly to the Director-General himself and received a conciliatory response. Institutional space for people's organizations did, indeed, appear to be under attack from some quarters, although not from FAO's chief.

On the broader UN scene the scenario that developed recalled that of the previous major world food crisis of 1974. At that time the UN-sponsored World Food Congress made a decisive contribution to multiplying the international institutions dealing with food and agriculture and dismantling the focal responsibility of the FAO (see ETC Group 2008). On 29 April 2008 UN Secretary-General Ban Ki-moon announced that he would lead a task force to address the current global food crisis. The announcement came after a two-day meeting of the Chief Executive Board (CEB) which brings together 27 heads of UN agencies, funds and programmes, the International Monetary Fund (IMF), the World Bank and the WTO. Made up of CEB members, the High Level Task Force (HLTF) on the Global Food Crisis was slated to have two coordinators: Under-Secretary-General for Humanitarian Affairs John Holmes in New York and Senior UN System Influenza Coordinator David Nabarro in Geneva. Only in a second moment was the Director-General of the FAO added to the line-up as Vice-Chair. In mid-July the task force released a Comprehensive Framework for Action (CFA), a draft of which had already circulated at the FAO High Level Conference in early June and had received the endorsement of the General Council of the European Union on 20 June and that of the G-8 in its 8 July 'Statement on Global Food Security'.

The CFA is light on governance discourse. The HLTF is 'not envisaged as a permanent fixture, or as a reason for creating new mechanisms'. It will aim at 'catalyzing and supporting the CFA's overall objective of improving food and nutrition security and resilience in a sustainable way'. To do so, it 'will work at global, regional and country levels to track progress ... [and] will address some of the underlying policy issues at the global level ... (trade, export subsidies and restrictions, biofuels etc.)' (United Nations High Level Task Force 2008:41). The accountability of this mechanism to governments is close to nonexistent. All that is envisaged is 'regular consultation' ... through 'high-level briefings with the General Assembly, ECOSOC and UN regional groups, governing bodies and management committees of individual UN system agencies' (United Nations High Level Task Force 2008:42). The OECD countries hit the drawing board as soon as the CFA was released to sketch in the missing pieces. Who should be the members and the 'owners' of the 'global partnership for food' that the HLTF was expected to facilitate? How would the essential component of international policy coordination be exercised and what role could be foreseen in this context for a 'reformed' FAO? Who should be responsible for naming and supervising the international group of experts on food security that both the HLTF and the G-8 were calling for and, again, what would be the role of the FAO in this normative exercise? And what about the aid component, beyond the emergency assistance channelled through the World Food Programme that was receiving immediate priority? Was it best to favour the World Bank, which had jumped the gun by announcing the creation of a $1.2 billion fast-track facility for the food crisis on 29 May? Or was IFAD, the IFI with a special mandate to address rural poverty and rural development, a better bet? There was no doubt that OECD countries would have their say in determining the responses to these open questions. How the developing countries most affected by the food crisis were going to get a word in edgewise was less evident.

What about the paradigmatic component of the intergovernmental community's response to the food crisis? The declaration of the FAO High Level Conference, undersigned by representatives of 180 countries, avoided analysing the causes of the crisis and moved straight to the remedies. The short-term measures recommended took the form of food assistance and safety nets and 'immediate support for agricultural production and trade'.[186] Medium- and longer-term measures placed the accent on investment in technology and trade liberalization as instruments for promoting resilient food production systems and maintaining biodiversity under conditions of climate change, an improbable recipe in the view of civil society readers. The hotly debated topic of biofuel production, which President Lula of Brazil had travelled to Rome to defend in an unholy alliance with the United States, got off the hook with a call for in-depth studies and exchange of experiences. As for the UN Comprehensive Framework for Action, it discusses causes in the following terms, which cite trends but avoid reference to the policies that have helped to determine them:

> The dramatic rise in global food prices is not the result of any specific climatic shock or other emergency, but rather the cumulative effects of long-term trends and more recent factors, including supply and demand dynamics and responses which have caused further price increases and higher price volatility.
>
> During the past two decades, demand for food has been increasing steadily with the growth in the world's population, improvements in incomes and the diversification of diets. Until 2000, food prices were declining, with record harvests and the draw-down of food stocks. Simultaneously, public and private investment in agriculture (especially in staple food production) had been declining and led to stagnant or declining

crop yield growth in most developing countries. Rapid urbanization has led to the conversion of much farmland to non-agricultural uses. In addition, low prices encouraged farmers to shift to alternative food and non-food crops, or to transfer land to non-agricultural uses. Long-term unstable land and resource use has also caused land degradation, soil erosion, nutrient depletion, water scarcity, desertification, and the disruption of biological cycles (United Nations High Level Task Force 2008:8).

The key outcomes that can be expected to contribute to global food security in the longer term, in the CFA's analysis, are an investment-led menu of social protection systems, sustained smallholder-led food availability growth (although 'the majority of agricultural production will continue to come from larger farms' – United Nations High Level Task Force 2008:10), improved international food markets, and an international biofuel consensus (United Nations High Level Task Force 2008:5).

In framing their own analysis of causes and remedies, the people's organizations, social movements and NGOs associated with the IPC were well aware of the fact that the stall in the WTO process had combined with the media-magnified food crisis to produce an unhoped-for political opportunity to challenge the dominant neoliberal paradigm.[187] 'No More "Failures-as-Usual"!' was the title of a civil society statement drafted by IPC members and signed by some 900 CSOs in the run-up to the FAO High Level Conference.[188] Small farmers' organizations trace the roots of the current crisis to three decades of wrong policies.

> For over 30 years policy makers, national governments and international institutions like the World Bank, the International Monetary Fund and the World Trade Organization pushed the fundamental restructuring of national economies while chanting the mantra of liberalization, privatization and deregulation. In agriculture this led to dramatic shifts from production for domestic consumption to production for export ... Consequently, many developing countries that used to be self-sufficient in basic grains are now net importers of food.
>
> The restructuring of agriculture also facilitated the corporatization of agriculture. While peasants and small-scale farmers have been systematically driven from the land in the North and the South, corporations increased their control over the food chain...
>
> It is this neoliberal, industrial and corporate-driven model of agriculture that has been globalized over the past 30 years ... Agriculture has moved away from its primary function – that of feeding humans. Today, less than half of the world's grains are eaten by humans. Instead, grains are used

primarily to feed animals, and more recently, these grains are now being converted into agro-fuels to feed cars. This is manufactured scarcity par excellence.

The structural adjustment programs … combined with the World Trade Organization's trade agreements meant that agriculture and food policies are now controlled only by a faceless international market. National policies, such as price controls, tariffs, and marketing boards, designed to ensure the viability of small-scale farmers and an adequate supply of culturally appropriate food through support for domestic agriculture have been replaced by the voracious demands of the 'market' (La Via Campesina 2008).[189]

Small farmers of the South look to their own governments, in the first instance, to defend their citizens' interests by supporting local food production and promoting local and regional food markets (see ROPPA 2008). At global level the more than 100 CSOs from five continents attending the civil society 'Terra Preta' forum held in parallel with the FAO High Level Conference called for a paradigm shift toward food sovereignty and small-scale sustainable food production which, unlike industrial agriculture, can feed the world while making a positive contribution to 'cooling' the climate. Regarding global governance, echoing the 'No More "Failures-as-Usual"!' statement, the Terra Preta participants called for a fundamental restructuring of the multilateral organizations involved in food and agriculture under the auspices of a UN commission that would reach beyond the 'failed institutions whose negligence and neoliberal policies created the crisis' to include strong representation of 'those we must feed and those who must feed us' (IPC, no date, page 2), excluded from the present UN task force.

The lines were drawn. The coming months would show whether the IPC and the networks it reaches would be able to mount a sufficiently powerful campaign to, at the very least, forestall 'more of the same medicine'.

By Way of Conclusion

What does the experience of civil society engagement with the FAO during and after the World Food Summits have to teach us about the openings and the obstacles to interaction, on both sides of the fence? How can we situate the IPC within current thinking about transnational civil society networks? What characteristics distinguish it from other global advocacy initiatives, and what impact have these characteristics had on its effectiveness?

Let us listen to the IPC itself, in the first instance.[190] Reflecting on expectations and accomplishments during a self-evaluation exercise conducted in 2005, members judged that the IPC had effectively built links between social movements and the FAO and had opened up spaces for people's organizations independently of the big NGOs which tend to dominate the scene. The IPC was judged to have succeeded in maintaining its autonomy and to have contributed to the articulation of food sovereignty as an alternative paradigm to neoliberalism. On the weak side, it lacked effective mechanisms of communication and exchange, the key level of regional work did not receive enough support, financial dependence on the FAO's help to mobilize funds was a problem. A fundamental lesson was that, at the outset, the IPC had underestimated the difficulty of changing the FAO and had over-estimated its own capacity for action and that of the people's organizations that compose it. The latter, experience had demonstrated, simply did not have time and resources to invest in interaction with the FAO above and beyond the activities in which they were already engaged following their own agendas and the evolution of the situations in which they were grounded. This had become clear in the incident of the *SOFA* issue on biotechnology. The accent, it was determined, should be shifted more decisively away from the FAO's agenda toward the struggles and negotiations in which the social movements themselves are directly engaged. From that starting point the IPC should identify a few political priorities on which to interact with the FAO and other institutions, seeking to open spaces and exploit contradictions within the intergovernmental system. If it tried to cover the entire FAO scene, on the contrary, it would inevitably be dispersive and ineffective and would risk co-optation.

The civil society consultation held in parallel to the FAO High Level Conference in June 2008, in the midst of the food crisis, offered an occasion to take the analysis a step further following three years of efforts to apply the insights that had emerged from the earlier self-evaluation. The fact that the IPC functions not as a hierarchical, repre-sentative organization but as an autonomous facilitating mechanism was confirmed to be a fundamental success factor. 'Each sector can speak for itself, with no forced consensus as in other UN processes.' At the same time, the IPC is not a neutral space. 'The political statement of food sovereignty is what we have in common. This allows us to develop common strategies while respecting the voice of each component.' Although civil society interaction with the FAO pre-dated the creation of the IPC, members judged that the advent of this mechanism has enabled them to move beyond particular technical questions and tackle systemic policy issues.[191] The new global political space it has opened up for people's organizations has proved important for all, but particularly so for weaker movements such as those of indigenous peoples and pastoralists and those who are not part of a bigger family. The global mobilization and advocacy capacity of the IPC is felt to be reflected in the broad diffusion of the sign-on letter it launched on the eve of the June 2008 Conference, the recognition it has received from international institutions such as the FAO, and the success it has obtained on issues including the right to food and agrarian reform. But the greatest strength of the IPC lies in its capacity to network, synergize and support the separate struggles of its members in the regions and in the manifold policy forums in which it is on the front line of the battle for food sovereignty.

Diversity is a recurring term. In terms of the quality of analysis conducted within the IPC the high points are judged to come from bringing together the different regions and rural producer constituencies. 'Then we get interesting analysis that's not taking place anywhere else.' This diversity has also stimulated virtuous behaviour changes. NGOs have learned to put their expertise at the service of people's organizations. Indigenous peoples have understood the importance of learning from the struggles of other sectors such as pastoralists. Strong organizations, including Via Campesina, cite the IPC as a space which has helped them to learn to listen to the voices of other social actors.

The weaknesses of the IPC are felt, to some degree, to be the mirror image of its strengths. 'We are a very flat and heterogeneous coalition. Decision making is difficult. The IPC can't be top-heavy, and a flat coalition needs resources of communication, facilitation, alliance building.' And resource mobilization has not been an area of success. The political opportunity offered by the food crisis and the need to move beyond the FAO and take a more systemic view make it urgent to address these organizational issues. 'We can't ask the people's organizations to do more than what they are already doing. We have to avoid creating a "technical corps" that's not controlled by the people's organizations. But we also need to avoid the mistake we are making now of being less effective than we should be.' The very fact that the overall context has become more politically charged is viewed as a result to which the IPC itself has contributed, through its contestation of the dominant neoliberal paradigm. The current context constitutes a stimulus to strengthen and sharpen the IPC's capacity for action. There are, however, no illusions about the power of opposing interests and the restriction of political space within global institutions that is likely to apply while the battle is on.

Current analysis of transnational civil society networks and their interaction with international institutions is exploring a series of issues that are pertinent to the IPC experience. Under what conditions are sustained transnational networking and advocacy possible, and how are the global and the national/local levels linked? What organizational forms are proving most effective for transnational collective action? Do international institutions offer significant political opportunities for civil society advocacy? Tarrow (2005:159) tends to weight the balance to the domestic front, both highlighting the difficulties of diffusion and scale shift involved in reaching up to the international level and minimizing the extent to which Southern actors reach out horizontally to others with similar claims. He proposes a typology of transnational coalitions and suggests that issue-focused campaigns with low institutionalization 'may be the wave of the transnational future'. Tarrow concludes that 'transnational activism will be episodic and contradictory, and it will have its most visible impact on domestic politics'. International institutions will continue to be state-controlled, he foresees, but transnational activists will continue to frequent them to engage in lobbying, networking and alliance building, 'and, from time to time, to put together successful global–national coalitions' (Tarrow 2005:218).

Khagram et al. (2002) take the existence of effective transnational collective action as their starting point and suggest that certain aspects of social movement theory may need to be modified to help explain the emergence of this phenomenon despite the relative lack of favourable conditions normally present in national collective action scenarios, such as homogenous participants and informal mobilizing structures. Organizationally, they pinpoint issues of asymmetries and power within networks as important challenges to be addressed, and they identify a potential conflict between increased deliberation/ representativeness and effectiveness. 'Efforts to enhance representation and deliberation will slow down networks and make it more difficult for them to respond quickly to global problems and crises' (Khagram et al. 2002:312). They identify the process of the creation and enforcement of international norms as an important terrain for transnational collective action and argue that 'international institutions indeed present clear political opportunity structures for transnational advocacy' (Khagram et al. 2002:18). Smith (2008:228) concurs, arguing that 'those hoping to bring about a more just, peaceful and equitable world must work at many levels not the least of which is within existing *global* institutions', most importantly 'to make the UN Charter and international legal instruments such as the Universal Declaration of Human Rights the key principles around which our world is organized'. Like Tarrow, she expects that the future will see 'less energy devoted to the creation and maintenance of formal transnational organizations and more focused on cultivating more expansive and densely linked networks of activists pursuing common agendas' (Smith 2008:220).

On the basis of considerable previous empirical and statistical analysis – much of it focusing on civil society–UN interfaces – Marchetti and Pianta (2007) suggest a theoretical formulation of the key features of transnational social movements, contesting the interpretation of them as simply the internationalization of domestic experiences. Citing the experience of networks, such as Our World is not for Sale, ATTAC, Jubilee 2000 and Jubilee South Forum, that have been formed around global processes such as the WTO negotiations or the debt issue, they argue that the novelty of transnational networks consists in three factors:

> First, they constitute the organizational backbone of a new political agency that it is openly global, thus different from traditional contentious agency at the national level; second, they show a degree of political maturation of political issues and themes from local and national protest to global proposal; and finally, they have developed a specific strategic-political skill in both challenging and implementing institutional policy-making at the state and international level (Marchetti and Pianta 2007:2).

The IPC experience confirms a number of elements that emerge from this brief review. It provides decisive evidence of the possibility – however laborious – of building shared values and messages across a very broad range of diversities of all kinds. Indeed, as we have seen, these diversities are cited by IPC members as a major source of richness. It also confirms the significance of the norm-setting function of international institutions such as the FAO as a political opportunity for transnational advocacy and a goal-oriented focus for action. The fact that the IPC's advocacy moves it off the more travelled terrain of political and individual or communal rights and onto the more problematic turf of collective economic and social rights invests this experience with particular interest, since norm construction in this area is at the very heart of efforts to liberate global governance from domination by markets and corporate interests.

Organizationally, the IPC does not fit neatly into the categories described in social movement literature. In Tarrow's terminology (Tarrow 2005:167) it is not a short-term coalition. But neither is it a federation or a campaign, although it does contribute to campaigns conducted by its members and by other broader coalitions. Perhaps the description that comes closest to capturing its nature is the suggestion of Marchetti and Pianta that transnational networks 'provide political innovation in terms of conceptualisation, organisational forms, communication, political skills, and concrete projects to the broader archipelago of social movements' (Marchetti and Pianta 2007:3).

The major innovation of the IPC, compared with the experiences documented in existing literature, is its identity as a horizontal mechanism that has made a deliberate and successful effort to reach out to people's organizations in the South – peasant farmers, artisanal fisherfolk, indigenous peoples, pastoralists and agricultural workers – and to place them at the centre of reflection and decision making. The IPC is a rare, if not unique, example of an autonomous global civil society advocacy mechanism in which political direction rests with these organizations rather than with the NGOs which, often with the best of intentions, normally dominate decision-making processes in transnational collective action. In this sense, it responds to the concerns about asymmetries and power expressed by Sikkink in Khagram et al. (2002) and illustrates the experimentation with 'novel forms of transnational links involving popular organisations from the south' which, according to Marchetti and Pianta, is attracting interest as awareness of the risks of asymmetry increases. On the down side, it also confirms the consideration cited above that increased representation and deliberation, in this case involving multiple languages and cultures, can slow down the decision-making process.

The fact that the IPC groups major regional and global networks of small-scale rural producers, mandated to speak for a good proportion of the world's poor,[192] gives it a more compelling legitimacy than that of other civil society actors, whose legitimacy is based rather on the values they defend, the cogency of their arguments, the effectiveness of the services they provide. It also gives it far more political punch in the South, since in many cases these organizations represent the majority of the electorate. This is illustrated by the successful efforts of the West African peasant farmers' network, ROPPA, to bring food sovereignty concerns to bear on the West African regional economic organization ECOWAS. In contrast with Tarrow's reading, networking of this nature places strong emphasis on building South–South links among actors who have similar claims and not only, or primarily, reaching upward to international forums. Government accountability at national and regional levels in the South is likely to be a prerequisite to building accountable global governance. If this is the case, the IPC, with its focus on supporting and networking the struggles of Southern rural people's organizations and social movements, is on the front line of the battle.

Turning to the other side of the fence, 12 years after the World Food Summit there was no doubt that the FAO had been strongly affected by its interaction with civil society and social movements. As we have seen, the stall in the WTO talks and the food crisis seemed to many observers to confirm the thesis that resistance to, and contradictions within, neoliberal policies might be opening up some space for alternatives. The FAO clearly constituted a prime candidate, and for this very reason conflict had intensified concerning the role that the FAO should play. On one side, major donor countries were determined to privilege the organization's normative work and restrict its functions as a policy forum and as a development actor. On the other, social organizations were urging the FAO to play a more proactive and autonomous role in the fight against hunger and to call governments and intergovernmental institutions to account. Such contrasts are mirrored within the secretariat. Some staff attach great value to the IPC as a mechanism that makes it possible to reach the disenfranchised of the South and are essentially in sympathy with its political positions. At the opposite extreme, others regard it as an ideological bandwagon which, in their view, has gained too much attention on the FAO scene as compared with other currents of civil society and private sector partnerships. Whatever the outcome of these external and internal contrasts, the dynamic and contested nature of the FAO's situation testifies to its potential political significance as a governance terrain, in part a result of interaction with civil society.

From 1996 to 2008, practices of civil society participation in the FAO's policy formulation and governance had advanced considerably, although they had not been formally institutionalized. Significant civil society successes had been achieved in introducing paradigmatic change and formulating normative mechanisms to apply new concepts, as in the case of the right to food, or rehabilitate existing concepts such as agrarian reform. Links between national, regional and global policy spaces had been built up by social actors such as the West African small farmers' movement promoting family farming (see McKeon et al. 2004; McKeon 2008), South American and Asian artisanal fisherfolk fighting against corporate overexploitation of the seas,[193] and pastoralists defending the animal genetic resources on which their livelihoods depend.[194] The level of debate had deepened on basic questions that had dogged the FAO from its foundation: the lack of political will on the part of powerful member governments to address the problems inscribed in the organization's mission, and the ambiguity of the technical–political divide that bedevils the secretariat. The very fact that the walls of the organization had been shaken from the ground floor up by civil society outrage on the occasion of the release of the allegedly pro-GMO 2003 *State of Food and Agriculture*, was, in itself, an important sign of the de-impermeabilization of the FAO as compared with the dictatorial, arms-distance reaction of an earlier Director-General to an offending 1991 issue of the *Ecologist*. The defensive reaction of some Western governments – traditional proponents of civil society participation in public affairs as a key component of democracy – who now questioned the priority of FAO's civil society liaison and advocacy work,[195] could be taken as a disturbing sign of backlash. On the other hand, it could be read as a promising symptom of heightened recognition of the political character of FAO governance, itself a result both of the increased political significance of food and agriculture issues on the world scene and of the greater capacity of civil society actors to question the neoliberal agenda.

In the final chapter, conclusions will be drawn bringing the FAO experience together with evidence emerging from a cross-system analysis. For the moment we can limit ourselves to underlining the qualitative leap in the FAO's engagement with non-state actors that resulted from its entering into negotiation with the autonomous, people's-organization-dominated mechanism that emerged from the two summits of 1996 and 2002. Success factors on the civil society side have included the IPC's skill in defending its autonomy and in validating its legitimacy by effectively bringing the voices of Southern people's organizations to policy forums to which they had previously had no access. On the FAO side, in the best of circumstances the success factors have included the secretariat's recognition of civil society's autonomy and right to self-organization, willingness to valorize the IPC's efforts to involve organizations of the rural poor in policy dialogue, and engagement to facilitate their access to political space in which to defend their agendas. These factors, however, have not been institutionalized and the relation of the FAO to civil society is very much a work in progress.

3
UN–Civil Society Relations: A Comparative Look

How does the experience of the Food and Agriculture Organization of the United Nations (FAO) in interacting with civil society compare with that of other parts of the United Nations (UN) system? This chapter will set the FAO case study into a broader context by reviewing how the practices and procedures of the UN system as a whole are evolving in response in a changing political context in which the summit processes constitute valuable observation posts. The added value of adopting a comparative approach of this nature is highlighted throughout the literature of both institutional and social movement studies.[1] Most of the existing comparative studies of civil society involvement in global conferences take a civil society perspective. They are interested above all in looking at how the interaction has affected the growth of global civil society networking and advocacy and the degree to which civil society organizations (CSOs) have impacted on the outcomes of official events.[2] Here we will look at the encounter from the viewpoint of the UN system, through the eyes of the UN secretariats responsible for organizing the summits and implementing their outcome. As indicated in Chapter 1, this review is based on several sources of evidence, underpinned by three decades of direct experience. It draws on the testimony of UN system practitioners themselves through a survey which asked them to discuss how their organizations were handling civil society involvement in global policy dialogue and in country-level action, and what links existed between the two levels. This inquiry is supplemented by the insights emerging from a series of interagency exchanges organized recently by the United Nations Non-Governmental Liaison Service (UN-NGLS) (see UN-NGLS 2003a, 2004, 2005a).

The chapter also takes a look at system-wide efforts to ensure integrated implementation of summit outcomes through the Millennium Development Goals (MDGs) and at approaches being adopted to involve civil society in these efforts through the Millennium Campaign. Finally, it reviews the outcome and implications of steps taken by the UN since the early 1990s to reform rules, procedures and practices governing relations with civil society, culminating with the report of the Panel of Eminent Persons on United Nations–Civil Society Relations appointed by the previous UN Secretary-General Kofi Annan (United Nations 2004a) and the fate of its recommendations under his successor Ban Ki-moon.

The system-wide survey was conducted in late 2004–05 through a questionnaire sent to the network of civil society liaison offices of UN system agencies and programmes and international financial institutions (IFIs) which revolves around the UN-NGLS.[3] Although the IFIs were not directly involved in organizing the world summits, they were included in the survey because of their impact on global and national policy environments and their important role in the implementation of conference goals. The limitations of questionnaire surveys are well known. They include problems of sampling, response rate, the tendency of respondents to provide socially desirable answers, and the inevitably superficial nature of the information requested.[4] In this case the disadvantages of the questionnaire methodology weighed relatively lightly. The sample covered a good part of the universe of UN civil society liaison units. The response rate was very high (over 80 per cent) because the study was discussed and agreed upon with the respondents who saw it as something that would help them in their work. Veracity of replies was encouraged by following the established practice within the UN-NGLS network of preserving the respondents' anonymity.[5] Finally, questionnaire responses and the resulting analysis were validated in a UN-NGLS meeting that discussed a draft report on the survey (UN-NGLS 2005a). It is worth noting that, despite the importance accorded to networking in the literature on global governance, very little attention has been paid to the nature and the impact of the formal and informal exchange that takes place among those responsible for civil society outreach, a sensitive area of the UN system's efforts to adapt to a changing world. The present study makes a contribution to filling this gap.

In Chapter 1 we underlined the importance of taking a nuanced view of the UN system, distinguishing among different institutions and offices and among various levels of work, in particular headquarters and region or country-based work. The intent of this section is not to establish a tight interagency analysis of which variables produce what effects in terms of civil society relations, although some hypotheses regarding the most significant factors at play are advanced in the conclusions. The purpose of this chapter, rather, is to establish a practitioner's scoreboard of where the UN system is now in various areas of its efforts to engage with civil society and where the most acute challenges for the future lie. The chapter will end by looking at the extent to which steps being taken or contemplated in the context of the reform of the UN system currently under way appear to address the challenges identified by those who are on the front line of the interface between the UN and civil society.

The entities whose civil society units responded to the cross-system survey questionnaire can be divided into three large groups.[6] The first and most heterogeneous consists of offices within the UN secretariat (five) and programmes and funds (six), all accountable to the United Nations Economic and Social Council (ECOSOC) and the UN General Assembly. Some of these are primarily responsible for servicing ECOSOC's thematic work, organizing summits and monitoring follow-up. Others handle field-level policy advice and action, overall civil society accreditation and access, information diffusion, and different mixes of policy, normative and operational activities within the thematic areas of their mandates. The second category, that of specialized UN agencies reporting to their own separate governing bodies (four), typically encompass all of these various functions in their work and in their outreach to civil society. The third group is that of IFIs, also with their own governance structures (seven) and other relevant multilateral organizations (two).[7] The IFIs are generally more field-oriented than the other structures, although their influence in the policy arena – particularly that of the World Bank and the International Monetary Fund (IMF) – is considerable. They tend to be sited more decidedly on the CSO firing line, both because of the impact of their programmes – these being of neoliberal inspiration – and because of what is deemed to be insufficiently transparent and democratic governance.[8]

All of the UN entities and specialized agencies have established variously denominated units responsible for relations with non-governmental organizations (NGOs) and other civil society actors. The International Labour Organization (ILO), of course, is in a category of its own with its tripartite structure in which representatives of workers and employers enjoy equal status with representatives of governments. The IFIs report situations ranging from a single staff member and/or no dedicated unit for civil society to the highly articulated team approach adopted by the World Bank in 2002 involving more than 120 civil society engagement staff working across the institution, with a global Civil Society Team, a network of civil society specialists working in various units at World Bank headquarters, and civil society staff in some 70 country offices. Information regarding the various entities and their NGO/CSO interfaces at their headquarters and in the field is presented in the Annex.

Civil Society Participation in Global Policy Forums

The respondents are responsible for managing civil society involvement in a variety of global intergovernmental forums, as shown in the Annex. The following paragraphs compare the experience of these various bodies on six points that are key to interaction with civil society in global policy forums: access and accreditation, availability of resources, issues and practices of participation, civil society impact on global forum outcomes, civil society participation in summit follow-up, and the overall governance of the UN–civil society relation.

Who has access to policy forums? The issue of accreditation

There is no single standard approach within the UN system to granting NGOs accreditation or formal relations. Indeed, the confusing array of accreditation procedures was among the issues addressed by the Panel of Eminent Persons on United Nations–Civil Society Relations established by Kofi Annan.[9] An ECOSOC review of consultative status procedures was launched in the aftermath of the United Nations Conference on Environment and Development (UNCED) in Rio with a view to updating them to take account of the broader panoply of CSOs that had populated the conference. It came to a close in 1996 with a recommendation that extended the possibility of obtaining accreditation to regional and national NGOs as well as international NGOs (INGOs) (United Nations 1996a). This measure had been expected to democratize access, particularly for national developing-country NGOs. In retrospect, some observers judge that the result has been rather to open up the United Nations to national government-operated NGOs (GONGOs), organizations sponsored by governments to defend their positions in hot forums such as the UN Commission on Human Rights. Genuine developing-country NGOs, on the contrary, have benefited less since they most often lack the resources to attend international meetings.[10] The ECOSOC review did not, as many pro-civil-society observers hoped it would, extend accreditation to the General Assembly itself. Since many of the summit reviews (the so-called +5 and +10 conferences) have taken the form of General Assembly special sessions, the access of CSOs to these has practically evaporated in dramatic contrast with the summits themselves.

Most of the UN secretariat respondents in the survey rely on the ECOSOC accreditation process as their basic tool for determining which organizations to invite to intergovernmental policy forums.[11] In addition, the Preparatory Committee (PrepCom) or bureau of a specific event most often establishes specific rules appropriate for that particular case. For example, in 1992, under an ad hoc arrangement, out of the 1,378 NGOs that were accredited to the UNCED conference, a list of 539 organizations without ECOSOC status was placed on a Commission on Sustainable Development (CSD) Roster to enable them to participate subsequently in the work of the commission without necessarily obtaining ECOSOC status.[12] All specialized agencies have their own procedures for establishing formal relations with NGOs that are not subject to those of ECOSOC, although they take them into account. These procedures stipulate the criteria applicants must meet and the steps by which applications are vetted and processed. There is an important institutional distinction to make here. While the ECOSOC accreditation process refers primarily to participation in UN intergovernmental meetings, the granting of formal relations by specialized agencies typically covers a wider range of potential forms of collaboration including normative and operational activities as well as participation in policy forums. On the other hand, having formal relations with a specialized agency is often not a necessary condition for attending its policy forums. As we have seen, in the case of the World Food Summit:*five years later* (WFS:*fyl*) the secretariat made a particular effort to accredit those organizations that were invited to attend the parallel CSO forum – in order to encourage interaction between the two events – despite the fact that many of them were national people's organizations and newcomers to global forums.

None of the IFIs adopt a formal accreditation process with explicit criteria and vetting procedures. In most cases the secretariat takes the initiative to invite CSOs whose input to a particular meeting is desired. One respondent reports that invitations to meetings are issued 'on a rotating basis, with an attempt to balance representation between service-delivery and advocacy CSOs'. When CSOs themselves seek invitations, these requests are vetted by internal divisions or task forces. One respondent notes that government concurrence is required in the

Box 3.1 Accreditation: Difficulties Encountered

- Insufficient proactive outreach to appropriate NGOs by the secretariat.
- Applications often incomplete.
- Lack of specific procedures and criteria, leaving NGOs subject to the whims of secretariat members.
- The process is cumbersome and out of pace with modern trends of informal networking.
- What to do about business associations, which are formally not-for-profit but in fact often further the for-profit interests of their members?
- Difficulties in accrediting national NGOs and/or delays in obtaining government concurrence.
- Insufficient ability of NGOs to submit reports related to review of their status.

case of national NGOs. Another indicates that steps are being taken to streamline the process of application for invitations to attend annual meetings by putting them online.

What happens once accreditation or formal relations has been granted? How are NGOs held to the commitments they make in return for formal recognition? The ECOSOC accreditation process provides for periodic submission of reports by accredited NGOs and review of their status, a cumbersome and time-consuming operation. Most respondents in the UN secretariat report that no formal process is in place to review relations with ad hoc accredited CSOs that do not have ECOSOC status. In one case the secretariat 'reviews conduct and relevance of accredited NGOs to the process on a continuous basis to ensure effective engagement'. Specialized agency respondents are divided on the question, with half indicating that they follow formal review processes by which NGOs are obliged to submit periodic reports, while the other half do not.

Responding entities report a variety of difficulties encountered in the area of accreditation and invitation to intergovernmental meetings (Box 3.1). On the other hand, they point to some good practices that have evolved over the past years (Box 3.2).

Weiss and Gordenker (1996:220), in their study of NGOs, the UN and global governance midway through the summits decade, puzzled over the fact that officials from governmental, intergovernmental and non-governmental organizations have invested a seemingly dispro-

---

Box 3.2 Accreditation: Good Practices

- Provide CSOs with information in good time and clarify expectations.
- Ask CSOs to describe how their work is of relevance to the issues of the forum to ensure appropriate participation.
- Give governments 30 days to react and apply the rule of 'silence means assent'.
- Accredit umbrella organizations which can 'house' representatives of national CSOs within their delegations.
- Online registration.
- Develop a database to monitor relations with NGOs and maintain up-to-date information on them.
- Periodically review relationships with NGOs enjoying formal relations on the basis of agreed joint work plans.
- It is up to us to pilot an inclusive accreditation/invitation process through the meanders of bureaucracy. We have to be 'on the side' of civil society.

---

portionate amount of energy in determining which NGOs qualify for official 'consultative status', whereas informal relations are often more important in terms of impact. In highly formal institutions such as those of the UN, the granting of official status does tend to take on disproportionate interest, particularly where intergovernmental deliberations are concerned. The fact that the expansion of UN relations with civil society during the 1990s was located predominantly on the terrain of global policy forums has helped to engender a fixation, on the part of many UN officials and government representatives, with the requirement of formal accreditation or consultative status. It has also reinforced the automatic mental link between this requirement (understandable in the case of authorizing participation in intergovernmental summits) and the broader and more diversified terrain of UN–civil society engagement for which such formal status need not be a necessary precondition.[13] The effort to get the procedures right, to build credible barriers against the real or imagined threat of invasion by hordes of undisciplined or ill-intentioned non-state actors and to categorize them into neat boxes, can tend to substitute for grappling with the more substantive issues of UN–civil society engagement that we will examine in the section below on governance of the UN–civil society relationship. The global, formal context of the summits has reinforced this tendency. At the same time, it has tended to privilege international NGOs – the majority of which are based in the North – since they more easily satisfy the requirements for accreditation, are accustomed and equipped to dealing with bureaucratic procedures, and are present on the spot in the capital cities where UN organizations are headquartered and where most summits and post-summit reviews have been held.

Appropriate accreditation practices can enhance the transparency of the relationship and enforce respective rights and responsibilities, some UN officials feel.[14] But they are only a minor part of the answer at best, and the present practices leave a good deal to be desired in terms of insufficient transparency (particularly in the case of IFIs), political interference, limited inclusiveness, and incapacity to deal effectively with categories such as the private sector and parliamentarians, which do not easily fit into the traditional NGO mould.

Beyond accreditation: who picks up the tab for civil society engagement?

Insufficient resources to cover the costs of civil society engagement with intergovernmental deliberations remains a serious problem for most UN family entities. Lack of resources penalizes developing-country CSOs in particular. With the exception of a few IFIs that have been able to access existing funds managed by the secretariat, most UN family organizations are dependent on mobilization of external funding to support civil-society-related activities. This issue was another of those targeted by Kofi Annan's Panel of Eminent Persons. It is a question not only of equity in the civil society world, but also of intergovernmental politics, since Southern governments see the domination of Northern NGOs in global policy forums as a prolongation of the long arm of Northern conditionalities.

Respondents in the cross-system survey were asked to rank their success in mobilizing resources, directly or indirectly, for five activities pertinent to civil society engagement: translation and diffusion of civil society documents, travel to attend global forums, preparation and networking, and participation in national and regional follow-up. The three activities topping the list are translation and diffusion of documents (for which 14 respondents report medium or strong success), travel to attend global forums, and participation in summit follow-up at global level. On the contrary, resource mobilization for civil society preparation and networking is weak, despite the fact that both CSOs and UN respondents attach high priority to this activity (see Krut 1997:42 and Schechter 2001:189). Participation in regional and national follow-up also suffers from underfunding. The waning of the conferences process is generally leading to a decrease in resources for civil society engagement (Friedlander 2003), although the need is arguably even greater in the follow-up phase. Ideally the ball should be picked up by regional and country offices and programmes but, as we will see, this is not the case.

Once you get there: issues and practices of participation

Over the past decade UN family entities have experimented with a wide variety of practices in an attempt to enhance civil society engagement with the global intergovernmental forums for which they have been responsible. The summit mode has tended, of course, to focus attention on generating participation practices suited to global meetings and has skewed the experimentation in the direction of protecting inter-governmental decision-making prerogatives.

Respondents in the cross-system survey were asked to rank a list of 21 practices in terms of how successful they have proved.[15] The results provide an instructive photograph of the furore of invention in this area since the advent of the world summits and of the kinds of innovations that have gained easier acceptance. Topping the list are 'good practices', such as briefings for CSOs and side events that enhance participation without impinging on intergovernmental routine. Support for civil society networking and the preparation of position papers are also top rankers, despite the fact that, as we have seen, mobilization of resources to facilitate these processes is unsatisfactory. Parallel civil society forums and multistakeholder dialogues have become widely adopted practices, although some question their impact on the outcome of official forums. Respondents report less experience with practices that introduce changes into the way business is conducted in the intergovernmental sessions themselves, nibbling away at the rule whereby observers are given the floor only once government delegates have ended their debate. These practices include allowing civil society representatives to intervene freely on selected agenda items, enabling identified spokes-persons of selected caucuses to intervene throughout the debate, or separating periods of deliberation – with free civil society intervention – from those of decision making.

Beyond specific practices aimed at enhancing participation, respon-dents were asked to reflect on some of the quality issues related to civil society involvement in intergovernmental policy forums. One issue of particular significance to the problem of linking global and national engagement is that of achieving *balanced participation by Northern and*

Southern CSOs. Three respondents report no or weak success in this area, lack of funds being a major limiting factor. Thirteen feel they have achieved medium success, while six record strong success. Some respondents in the latter group specify the factors to which they attribute this success. Two emphasize the importance of using regional forums as a stepping stone to global meetings since they allow for broader participation and preparatory reflection on the part of Southern CSOs who have more difficulty in travelling to global events. One of these also credits the ability of the autonomous civil society mechanism with which it interfaces to privilege Southern organizations in its consultation practices.

An even lower rate of success is reported in another key area, that of reaching out beyond traditional NGOs (with which the UN has maintained relations for years) to the *social movements* and *people's organizations*[16] that represent those sectors of the population most directly affected by the issues on the UN agenda. Twelve respondents score no or weak success on this account. Two of these indicate that it is not their intention to interact with this part of the civil society universe, considered to be fundamentally hostile to the work of their organizations. Another states, on the contrary, that broadened outreach of this nature is necessary and desired. Seven respondents record medium success. Only three claim strong success.[17]

Fifteen respondents judge that they have achieved medium success in *balancing governments' concern to maintain the intergovernmental nature of decision making with civil society desire for meaningful input.* Four report strong success. Two agencies indicate that NGOs are allowed only one statement per agenda item. One respondent reports a trend toward more fruitful participation, thanks in part to peer pressure by some member governments. In one respondent's agency, interaction with civil society tends now to be limited to the secretariat. Attempts are being made to include government representatives in these dialogue sessions, but there is some resistance on both sides to making them tripartite. One respondent laments the lack of political will at senior level to establish a clear strategy for CSO participation. Another remarks that, although the rhetoric of civil society participation continues to sound loud and clear, in fact the priority of the concerned UN entity has shifted strongly towards the private sector.

Overall, the respondents' replies confirm that civil society participation in intergovernmental forums is a well-worked area for UN system entities. A whole panoply of practices has been experimented with over the years. The gap between the UN system and IFIs is striking in this regard, with IFIs lagging considerably behind the UN. This may be explained in part by their more limited experience, but it is due above all to structural issues of limited civil society access to official meetings, which the IFIs will need to address in order to achieve a substantial improvement in their engagement with civil society.

A core package of practices of participation is consolidated and operating effectively. These include the various forms of information diffusion and briefing that have become standard operations and are appreciated by all. Other traditional practices would seem to be wending their way toward a merited retirement, such as NGO speaking slots at the close of agenda items in formal intergovernmental sessions which themselves are characterized by the boredom they generate. Cutting-edge areas of participation practice, on the contrary, include those that support civil society networking and preparation, particularly when they build links between national/regional and global levels of consultation, and those that explore ways of enhancing interactive dialogue between civil society and government while preserving a space in which governments assume the right and the responsibility to take policy decisions for which they will be held accountable.

Broader issues relating to participation, and equally to governance and interface mechanisms, as we will see in a following section, include that of strengthening the UN family's generally weak capacity to relate to social movements, particularly people's organizations mobilizing the disenfranchised in the South. Another important area for exploration is that of enhancing civil society input into the setting of the agendas for intergovernmental policy forums. This is closely related to the need to define and distinguish clearly between the respective roles of secretariat and government membership in conducting policy negotiations, and to develop appropriate civil society engagement with both realms. Going beyond relations with UN secretariats to build dialogue with conference bureaux and alliances with like-minded governments are clearly two success factors in effective civil society participation. On the other hand, the comment by one respondent that civil society input to secretariat papers is important since secretariat papers are the basis of inter-governmental discussion is a refreshing admission, given the frequent tendency of UN secretariats to hide behind the membership's shoulders. The same position is echoed from the CSO viewpoint in the review of relationships of the United Nations Department of Economic and Social

Affairs (UNDESA) and civil society undertaken by Eva Friedlander in 2003:

> Information and analysis provide the underpinning for government negotiating positions ... The need to open up to different types of expertise in order to benefit from differing perspectives is considered particularly critical with regard to the fundamental questions asked and to measuring the ways in which progress is measured or impact evaluated.[18]

Why bother? Civil society impact on outcomes of forums

To what degree does the effort invested by CSOs in interface with UN family policy forums achieve an impact on the outcome of these processes? This question is important, given the growing phenomenon of consultation fatigue and the risk that civil society actors may lose interest in the UN as a terrain of engagement. The survey posed three queries in this regard, assessing civil society impact on the content of the final forum document, on policy positions of governments regarding the issues dealt with at the forum and, finally, on the way in which these issues are conceptualized. Respondents note that systematic reviews of impact have not been conducted but that it seems to vary considerably according to such factors as theme, region, and civil society access to the drafting process. There is a relatively high degree of consensus in literature on civil society and global summits that 'civil society has been more successful in gaining international attention and setting agendas than in getting results',[19] and that the impact of civil society is stronger on what Van Rooy (1997) terms highly salient low policy issues than on hardcore economic questions. Participants at the 2005 meeting of NGO/CSO focal points of international and regional organizations noted that 'NGOs have high expectations of impacting when they are invited to consult but often end up asking themselves: "We are being listened to but are we being heard?"' Yet there are occasions, like the negotiations on guidelines for the application of the right to food and the International Conference on Agrarian Reform and Rural Development analysed in the previous chapter, where civil society impact on outcomes has been high.

We will return to these issues in the concluding section. It can be noted here that there is room for improvement in methodologies of and approaches to assessing civil society impact on specific negotiation processes, bringing together the academics' capacity to construct theoretical frameworks with the practitioners and the activists understanding of the real world. Unless these different viewpoints are combined the results can be misleading, as in Corell and Betsill (2001), which assesses positively civil society impact on the United Nations Convention to Combat Desertification (UNCCD) and attributes this result in part to the nature of the desertification NGOs, most of whom were grassroots and community-based organizations. This analysis disregards the fact that the civil society interface mechanism established in the context of UNCCD, Réseau International des ONG sur la Désertification (RIOD/International NGO Network on Desertification and Drought), was in fact captured early on by intermediary NGOs who resisted subsequent attempts to participate in the process by structured social organizations directly representing the rural populations affected by desertification, particularly in West Africa. In this they were supported by the UNCCD secretariat, which perhaps found it easier to deal with NGOs than with the potentially more politically problematic people's organizations. In the end, the West African small farmers and herders organizations, strong actors in other important policy forums, simply disinvested from the UNCCD because they did not consider it to be a priority arena in which to work toward their political objectives.

Civil Society and Summit Follow-up: Linking Global Commitments and Local Action

Civil society engagement in follow-up to global forums is another important area that has received far less attention than it merits. Riva Krut's generally excellent study of NGO influence in international decision making devotes only half a page to the topic, although she observes that 'NGOs themselves frequently note that monitoring and follow-up are much needed and inadequately pursued' (Krut 1997:42). Indeed, the conference on Civil Society and the Democratization of Global Governance (GO2) organized by the Montreal International Forum (MIF) in 2002 identified 22 major successes of transnational civil society in global policy decision making but recognized that these had not been followed through adequately in implementation (MIF 2002:3). This inadequacy on the part of civil society is mirrored within the UN itself. As a well-informed UN officer in New York put it, 'The Department of Economic and Social Affairs[20] prepares policy background papers and assessments of implementation, but is not operational in supporting follow-up. When an issue moves to other parts of the UN involved in operations it drops off the map'.[21]

Academics and practitioners concur on the need to build a better understanding of what happens once the curtain falls on a summit. In Michael Schechter's introduction to the collection of essays he edited on the impact of, and follow-up to, the UN-sponsored world conferences, he notes that 'scholars of international relations ... have long called for more attention to the implementation phase of the policy-making process' (Schechter 2001:7). It is significant that an entire section of this work is devoted to the role of non-state actors in conference follow-up and implementation. Indeed, in Schechter's view, 'the success of the 1990s conferences and the future of UN-sponsored world conferences in the twenty-first century are to a considerable extent in the hands of NGOs' (Schechter 2001:185).

The role of civil society in attaining goals set by global conferences and in monitoring government action to meet commitments is highlighted emphatically in all of the declarations and action plans, without exception, yet implementation of this role has most often left a great deal to be desired. The Millennium Campaign, to which we will return in a following section, has sought to address this problem. However, the very process by which the MDGs themselves were formulated illustrates the hiccupy nature of civil society involvement in the world of what remains an essentially intergovernmental institution. CSOs participated actively in the summits which, as exceptional events on the outskirts of day-to-day business, were allowed some degree of freedom from the full range of international bureaucratic procedure. The follow-up dossiers, however, shifted to the General Assembly, a citadel of intergovernmental resistance to non-state interference. The very CSOs whose participation in implementation was so eloquently wooed in the summit declarations were completely excluded from the deliberations of the General Assembly working group on 'The Integrated and Coordinated Implementation of and Follow-up to the Outcomes of the Major United Nations Conferences and Summits in the Economic and Social Fields' which gave birth to the MDGs (see Friedlander 2003:23).

The cross-system survey asked respondents to assess the degree to which CSOs were participating in five important dimensions of follow-up to the global forums for which their entities were responsible: monitoring of progress toward attaining agreed forum goals, at both global and national levels; further global normative work and policy negotiation on issues discussed at the forum; design of policy changes and formulation of programmes at national and regional levels to facilitate implementation. A high proportion of the respondents indicated that they lacked the necessary information to reply. This reaction corroborates the hypothesis of a disconnect, in many entities, between global policy discussion and follow-up action, particularly at regional and national levels. In all areas of follow-up listed in the questionnaire the combination of no information and no or weak civil society involvement outweighed the combination of medium and strong involvement in proportions ranging from 54 per cent for the former, as contrasted with 46 per cent for the latter (in the case of global monitoring of progress toward attaining forum goals), to 70 per cent for the former, as compared with 29 per cent for the latter (in the case of national monitoring of progress).

Respondents were asked to describe what action their organizations are taking to facilitate civil society involvement in follow-up to global intergovernmental forums. They were also invited to identify difficulties encountered and instances of success. No single strategy emerges from the replies. Regular information dissemination and briefings are the preferred instruments of two respondents. Another cites efforts to organize strategic and technical workshops throughout the year and to promote continuous involvement of CSOs in governance, 'which encourages them to advocate on our behalf', but notes there are 'difficulties in convincing managers this is important'. One respondent reports that CSOs are invited to prepare action plans in follow-up to policy forums but that they often fail to do so. Another acutely notes that the success of CSO participation in follow-up depends to a good degree on the effectiveness of the intergovernmental processes themselves and suggests that there is considerable room for improvement in this regard. As Schechter observes in his assessment of what he terms the 'spotty' record of policy and procedural implementation, 'only part of that, of course, can be credited to the actions of the NGOs' (Schechter 2001:185).

One respondent reports an interesting practice: CSOs are explicitly authorized by the intergovernmental organization in question to signal breaches in implementation of guidelines and to act as watchdogs. Indeed the need for explicit definition and formal recognition of a role for civil society in the monitoring and reporting process has been highlighted by various students and practitioners of global governance. In assessing requirements for implementation of the Convention on Biological Diversity in the new millennium, for example, Thomas Yongo notes that CSOs need to be provided with direct and legitimate channels for providing reports to secretariats and having those reports considered in evaluating implementation and compliance.[22]

Ensuring a continuum between global adoption of policy commitments and operational follow-up is undoubtedly easier in the case of those entities that deal with both spheres of activities. The experience of the FAO, for example, indicates that CSOs that have tracked the negotiation of a particular convention or treaty frequently remain strongly involved in follow-up at various levels. In fact, they often become strong allies of the secretariat in promoting implementation and monitoring. For this to happen, of course, requires a sense of ownership on the part of the civil society actors. As we have seen in Chapter 2, an FAO secretariat good practice in follow-up to the WFS:*fyl* consisted in agreeing to collaborate with the autonomous CSO interface mechanism on the basis of the priorities expressed by the parallel civil society forum, rather than imposing the official summit outcome as the only agenda in town.

Of all the aspects of summit follow-up, the one on which there is the greatest consensus is the imperative of linking global commitments and local action. As we will see in the following section, this issue is at the heart of current efforts to reform the way the UN relates to civil society and it figures prominently in the recommendations of the Panel of Eminent Persons appointed by Kofi Annan to review UN–civil society relations (United Nations 2004a:9). Civil society's role in building these bridges has been recognized since the early days of the summit decade. In one of the first authoritative studies of NGOs and world conferences, the authors concluded that a crucial function of NGOs was to 'politicise the previously unpoliticised and connect the local and the global'.[23] Keck and Sikkink's thoughtful study of advocacy networks in international politics points out that 'individuals and groups may influence not only the preferences of their own states via representation, but also the preferences of individuals and groups elsewhere, and even of states elsewhere, through a combination of persuasion, socialization, and pressure' (1998:215–16).

The civil society actors involved in building North–South and advocacy– implementation linkages and the ways in which they relate to each other and to the UN have changed enormously over the past few decades. The history of the UN-NGLS is one interesting terrain on which to track this evolution. When it was established in 1975, the UN-NGLS focused on information, education and advocacy to the exclusion of operational activities, and the developed world was its main if not exclusive arena. NGOs were weak or nonexistent in many areas of the

South and, in any event, the UN's mission in that part of the world was assumed to be more of an operational nature. The geographical division blurred over the years as the universe of civil society expanded. At the same time, awareness spread that the problems the world faced stemmed from structural and political causes that afflicted both the South and the North in equal measure, although most often in different ways. The summits of the 1990s were instrumental in this process of sensitization. In 1997, the UN-NGLS joined forces with the more operationally inclined United Nations Consultative Committee on Programme and Operational Questions (UNCCPOQ) for an interagency look at operational collaboration with NGOs/CSOs. The consultation report emphasized the importance of involving CSOs in the country policy/ programme framework-setting stage, including world conference national follow-up plans (UN-NGLS 1998:7). The Common Country Assessments (CCA) and United Nations Development Assistance Frameworks (UNDAF), which had been launched in 1997 under the supervision of the UN Resident Coordinators as an instrument for improved UN system-wide coordination of analysis and programming, were felt to be an obvious focus for an effort of this nature.[24] In follow-up to the consultation, updated guidelines for UN system cooperation with NGOs/CSOs were produced, but their operational impact was limited. A desk review of 'Civil Society Engagement in the CCA and UNDAF Process' commissioned by the United Nations Development Programme (UNDP) in 2001 found that 'the Guidelines on CCA and UNDAF clearly state the importance of civil society engagement in these processes but do not provide any more detailed direction on how this might be implemented'. The country framework documents that had been produced thus far made scant reference to civil society participation. What CSO engagement there had been 'has largely taken the form of consultation and information provision rather than full and empowering participation of civic groups' (UNDP 2001:5). The gap between rhetorical references to civil society involvement and actual practice that characterized the declarations of the world conferences was being replicated at country level.

Replies to the cross-system survey allow us to take a closer look at how various parts of the UN system are coping with civil society outreach at country level. Respondents were asked to provide basic quantitative information on how they are equipped to interact with civil society at country level – the number of field offices they have and how many of these have formal or informal civil society focal points – and on the kinds of activities they undertake.[25] Situations vary widely, as shown in the Annex, from five with no field offices at all to one with 220 field offices, each of which has a civil society focal point. Several respondents without country offices indicated that the UNDP is their main channel for national-level backstopping. Others backstop their country-level activities through national committees linked to their organizations and/or through civil society focal points based in their regional offices. Functions undertaken at country level by the responding entities include policy advice (18), formulation of country frameworks (15), investment programmes (10), technical assistance programmes (17), humanitarian/ emergency programmes (10), and capacity building (20).

How much civil society involvement is there and in what activities?

Respondents were asked to rate the overall degree to which their organizations ensure civil society involvement in a range of activities for which their entities provide support at country level: monitoring and reporting on government action toward the achievement of global commitments, formulation of national policies and framework documents, formulation of programmes, programme implementation, programme monitoring and evaluation, and public information.

The differences in scores on various activities are significant. As in the case of the FAO review reported in Chapter 2, the top-of-the-list position across the system is accorded to CSO involvement in public information work, cementing them in a traditional, harmless role. Comments regarding CSO involvement in programme formulation and implementation, second- and third-ranking activities in the survey, point to a perpetuation of the use of CSOs as contractual service-providers rather than considering them stakeholders and partners.[26] The relatively high marks given to civil society involvement in formulation of national policies may be misleading since, as the comments under-line, the quality of such participation often leaves a great deal to be desired.[27] The Poverty Reduction Strategy Papers (PRSPs) receive particular attention because of the central role they play in setting policy frameworks in poor countries. The assessments of civil society participation in these exercises carried out thus far are generally critical (see, for example, Waites 2002; McKeon 2005). As the report of the World Bank–Civil Society Global Policy Dialogue Forum, held in April 2005, states:

> CSOs invited to consultation meetings were those who were easily accessible and approving of the government and the Bank's preferred strategies.

Moreover, CSOs who were invited often did not get enough timely and appropriate information about the issues at stake, the options being considered, and how the PRSP process works, thus limiting their ability to effectively participate in the process (World Bank 2005:2).

Finally, it bears noting that monitoring government fulfilment of commitments, an important area of country-level summit follow-up, has the lowest score of all (only eight respondents report medium or strong civil society involvement as compared with 13 for public information).

What types of CSOs are involved and how are they selected?

Equally revealing is the range of CSOs with which the UN system agencies interact. The survey asked respondents to rate the degree of involvement by type of CSO: INGOs, national NGOs, national people's organizations/social movements, community-based organizations (CBOs). The responses reveal that national NGOs have ousted INGOs as the preferred partners of UN agencies, an interesting evolution from the earlier days of civil society cooperation in which the outposted offices of well-known Western NGOs operating in the country were by far the most attractive choice for the UN.[28] At the same time, however, the feedback confirms the global tendency toward weak engagement with national people's organizations as compared with NGOs – both national and international – and with community-based organizations (CBOs).[29] This failure to interact with organizations that directly represent the end beneficiaries of UN programmes and policies is even less justifiable at country level than it is in the context of global forums. On the one hand, it is easier to identify and contact people's organizations the closer one is to their homes. On the other, they are the civil society actors most strongly legitimated to call their national governments to account and to negotiate with other development stakeholders on behalf of their constituencies. The two-pronged focus on CBOs at local level accessed through national service NGOs ignores the fact that rural people's organizations in most parts of the developing world are themselves structuring up to national level to represent the interests of the base with far more political clout than local associations alone or unrepresentative national NGOs can muster. The tendency to ignore structured rural people's organizations translates into operational terms the depoliticization of development that, as we will see, is a major thrust of what has been termed the 'post-Washington consensus'.[30]

UN field offices consistently lament the difficulty of identifying the 'right' partners within the mushrooming civil society universe. Respondents were asked to report on the tools they adopt to assist in selecting civil society partners at country level – adopting and publicizing clear selection criteria, peer review of potential civil society partners, CSO databases, more complex mapping exercises of civil society in the country – and to rate their effectiveness. The high proportion of 'no reply/no experience' reported, ranging from 28 per cent (for adopting clear selection criteria) to 52 per cent (for mapping exercises), would seem to indicate a generally low level of concrete country-level experience with civil society outreach tools which, in turn, hints at a generally ad hoc and non proactive approach to engagement with civil society.

Overcoming hindrances to country-level cooperation

Respondents were asked to identify the biggest hindrances to country-level cooperation with civil society, selecting from a list of nine potential obstacles.[31] At the top of the ranking are the lack of an enabling environment (a diplomatic way of getting at negative attitudes on the part of government), insufficient capacity of CSOs, and lack of human and financial resources to support UN offices' civil society outreach efforts. One respondent noted, however, that although insufficient CSO capacity is indeed a problem, it is often used as a pretext for non-cooperation. On the issue of lack of resources, several respondents felt that it was not as crucial a factor as it is made out to be and that funds could be found if civil society outreach were given higher priority by the agency. One respondent specified that his/her agency could play a bigger role than it is as a coordinator, mediator, troubleshooter between government and civil society and in providing training for CSOs. Generally speaking, the replies testify to thoughtful consideration of the problem.

Respondents were also asked to rate measures with which they had experimented in terms of their effectiveness in overcoming hindrances and strengthening cooperation with CSOs at country level. A relatively high proportion lack experience with many actions suggested in the questionnaire,[32] thus providing a further confirmation of the relatively low levels of current engagement. Among the inward-looking measures listed in the questionnaire, preparing guidelines for staff and including civil society cooperation in staff training and briefings receive high ratings (10 report medium/strong success for the former and 13 for the latter). Among the outward-looking measures, support for CSO capacity building and for regional networking top the list (12 for each), pointing to an awareness of the significant interplay between regional and national dynamics in the civil society world today.

A participant in the 2004 meeting on NGO/CSO focal points summarized reflection from a practitioner's viewpoint on bridging the global–national gap in these terms:

> The fact that we are all so concerned now about bridging the gap between global policy deliberations and meaningful change at the national level is incredibly important. A lot of us have seen this coming for a number of years now, but I think we have to be really careful that we do not clomp in like elephants onto the national level and bring the UN agenda and the UN criteria for selecting civil society partners, and UN coordination mechanisms, but really take the time to see what is out there and see how one can facilitate a process whereby civil society actors are empowered to engage ... and there is going to be a tendency very often for the NGOs in capital cities to be easier to engage with than the diffuse rural people throughout the country (UN-NGLS 2004:3).

As Keck and Sikkink point out, one goal of social actors in the complex local–global advocacy networking that is the object of their analysis is to try to transform state understandings of their national interests, and alter their calculations of the costs or benefits of particular policies (Keck and Sikkink 1998:203). Pianta concurs that 'a recovery of national political processes remains a major way to affect global outcomes ... Especially in some countries of the South, the opportunities to influence national politics and the policies of progressive governments increasingly attract civil society energies' (Pianta 2005: 28). For better or for worse, UN-family-promoted policy forums at national level are an important locus for this kind of negotiation. The power of UN agencies and IFIs to influence who sits around the table is not to be wielded unwittingly. And it is being wielded, more or less innocently, as we will see when we move on to look at the UN reform process.

Governance of UN–Civil Society Relations: Interface Mechanisms and the Issues of Representativity, Legitimacy and Accountability

With the pressure to extend participation in governance to a growing range of non-state actors, the question of how to articulate the collective interface between UN entities and the universe of civil society beyond simply accrediting or collaborating with individual organizations – has become a key one for both parties. Governance of the UN itself is formally grounded in the nation-state, in some cases acting as a member of regional groupings, on a one-state-one-vote basis.[33] The governments sitting around the table are assumed to represent the citizens of their respective nations, despite the fact that this is known not always to be the case. But how to deal with the variegated world of civil society that began to seek access to the UN as the wave of global conferences swelled? Who, beyond the member states, should have the right to participate in global intergovernmental deliberations and on what grounds?

Questions began to emerge with insistence in the mid-1990s. At a stocktaking conference in 1995 sponsored by UN-NGLS (UN-NGLS 1996), while the ECOSOC review of consultative relations was under way, some participants asked themselves 'are definitional issues being imposed on NGOs by bureaucratic requirements?' and suggested that 'the legitimacy of NGOs derives from their being true to their own goals and principles and from acting in an open and transparent way'. Others, however, wondered, 'is the NGO world any less oligopolistic than the world of governments?' A basic question underlies this debate. Is it useful or appropriate to apply to CSOs the same requirements of representativity that are assumed, sometimes erroneously, to pertain to governments? Krut's 1997 study notes that many NGOs make broad claims to speak on behalf of a human or natural 'constituency' like 'children' or 'the excluded', although in fact the representation is purely virtual. She recalls, however, that the credibility of CSOs has always stemmed from their moral authority as well as their membership base and concludes that 'while it may be fair to criticize some CSOs as "unrepresentative", as with national governments, this complaint may not be an appropriate basis for deciding on their rights of access to global governance or to the UN' (Krut 1997:27).

The criteria for what legitimizes civil society presence in global decision-making forums obviously vary according to the role they play. If they are to participate directly in decision making, it is reasonable to expect that CSOs should have mandates to represent the views of clearly defined sectors of civil society. If their role is rather one of informing and enriching an intergovernmental process, such a requirement of representation is inappropriate and other criteria need to be examined. A thoughtful session of reflection by UN practitioners clarified this issue by distinguishing between legitimacy, accountability and representativity and emphasizing that 'the notion that NGOs have similar or competing functions with respect to governments would be conceptually, organizationally and politically misguided … The governance role of NGOs does not include the objective of taking over the decision-making power of governments, but is rather to enrich their deliberations, mobilize communities of interest around issues of public concern, and contribute to holding decision-makers accountable for their actions and/or omissions' (UN-NGLS 2003a:8). It was also stressed, however, that it is necessary to distinguish between NGOs and social movements/organizations emerging from the worlds of small farmers, indigenous peoples, and other disempowered groups. 'Both categories are legitimate, the report concluded, 'but the nature of their legitimacy is different: the latter are empowered to speak *for* those people whose interests they reflect, whereas the former are not'.

While UN liaison offices sought clarity on which to base operational decisions about how to manage the UN–civil society governance interface, the legitimacy-accountability-representativity conundrum began to spark considerable interest among a broad range of actors, including CSOs themselves.[34] A major issue from the outset was the North–South divide. Already in 1995 the Benchmark Survey recorded the perceptions, very widely felt within the civil society world, of dominance by large, Northern, English-language-run NGOs (Benchmark Environmental Consulting 1995:28; Krut 1997:20–21). Rather more pernicious interest in CSO legitimacy has been fuelled by some developments over the past few years, which have impacted strongly on UN governance terrain although they have not been generated within it. One of these is concern for security – for which 11 September 2001 is the focal date – and the attention it has generated for what has been termed 'the dark side' of civil society. Another is the attack on NGOs launched by conservative forces, dominantly but not exclusively in the United States. These campaigns oppose fundamentalist readings of values like 'the family' to NGO defence of rights. They base much of their argumentation on presumed NGO non-accountability in relation not only to their role in global governance but also to their use of the considerable amounts of national and multilateral aid budgets that are channelled through them. As a result of these developments, disproportionate attention has tended to be directed to two components of the civil society basket – religious and nationalist groups, on the one hand, and NGOs, on the other – leaving social movements and people's organizations in the shade.[35]

The cross-system survey provides us with valuable information on how these difficult issues are being dealt with in practice. Respondents were invited to discuss how they are handling the question of global interface with civil society and decisions about who should speak for whom in the intergovernmental forums for which their entities are responsible. This query gave rise to a variety of reflections which appear to be influenced to some degree by the kinds of issues discussed in a particular forum and the nature of the civil society community with which individual UN entities deal: predominantly Northern NGOs or a broader mix. One respondent voices the concern that 'some Member governments tend to take the view that they are elected representatives of the people and do not necessarily have to answer to self-elected CSOs and note that, for their part, many CSOs are not transparent with regard to their financing and membership'. But another respondent suggests that his/her organization

> understands that CSOs are not elected and don't pretend to replace elected governments, and their representation and legitimacy comes from other factors such as representing the interests of disenfranchised populations, track record in promoting grassroots development, and speaking for non-constituency values such as the environment or human rights. We view the 'participatory' democracy provided by civil society as complementary to and not conflicting with the 'representational' democracy represented by governments.

Box 3.3 How the UN Family Interfaces with Civil Society

UN secretariat entities

- *UNDESA-CSD (Commission for Sustainable Development)*: Adopts the classification of civil society into nine Major Groups as defined in Agenda 21. The interface was initially with a CSD NGO Steering Committee, and is now with Major Group Organizing Partners, self-selected Major Group organizations that have agreed to collaborate with the Bureau through the secretariat to facilitate input from Major Groups worldwide into the work of the CSD.
- *UNDESA-DAW (Division for the Advancement of Women)*: The interface mechanism is a self-organized NGO Committee on the Status of Women.
- *UNDESA-FFD (Financing for Development)*: Following the Monterrey Conference, various CSOs have established an International Facilitating Group on Financing for Development. The business sector and parliamentarians have also developed their own independent interface mechanisms.

- *UNDESA NGO Section*: Adopts the classification of NGOs into three categories of Consultative Status. The overall interface mechanism is the Conference of NGOs in Consultative Relationship with the United Nations (CONGO).
- *DPI (Department of Public Information)*: The 1,500 accredited NGOs have elected an 18-member Executive Board which partners with the secretariat.
- *UN-Habitat*: Has an Advisory Committee to the Executive Director with one civil society member.
- *UNCTAD (United Nations Conference on Trade and Development)*: Cooperation is with international organizations and self-organized networks. Has no global interface mechanism.
- *UNDP (United Nations Development Programme)*: Has established a CSO Advisory Committee to the Administrator with 15 members appointed in their individual capacity to advise and guide UNDP in its substantive policy areas.
- *UNEP (United Nations Environment Programme)*: A proposal for establishment of a UNEP Major Group Facilitating Committee with one representative of each Major Group and two from each UNEP region was adopted at 9th Global Civil Society Forum in February 2008.
- *UNHCR (Office of the United Nations High Commissioner for Refugees)*: Formal interface is conducted through annual NGO consultations and through NGO umbrella groups and their forums. Partnerships with beneficiary populations themselves are considered to be an area of great potential but least developed.
- *WFP (World Food Programme)*: Annual consultation conducted with major NGO partners and networks.

Specialized agencies
- *FAO (Food and Agriculture Organization of the United Nations)*: Two self-organized global interface mechanisms. The International CSO Planning Committee for Food Sovereignty (IPC) emerged from the parallel forums to the World Food Summit and its +5 review. It groups some 50 constituency, regional and thematic focal points concerned with food and agriculture, with emphasis on facilitating involvement of social movements in the South (peasant farmers, fisherfolk, indigenous peoples, pastoralists, agricultural workers). The Ad Hoc Group of representatives of INGOs in formal status with the FAO is a forum of Rome-based representatives of these INGOs.
- *ILO (International Labour Organization)*: In a special category because of its tripartite structure which fully involves workers' and employers'

organizations in governance. Maintains a Special List of other categories of NGOs.

* *UNIDO (United Nations Industrial Development Organization)*: No formal interface mechanism. Consultations with CSOs are conducted through seminars, workshops and conferences.
* *WHO (World Health Organization)*: Has no single global mechanism. Relations are maintained with various categories of NGOs: academic, scientific, professional, development, special interest (youth, women, patients, consumers, trade unions, local authorities, parliamentarians).

International financial institutions

* *ADB (Asian Development Bank)*: Has no global advisory committee. Works through existing CSO networks such as the NGO Forum on ADB. Consultations are held on specific topics and in connection with Board of Governors meetings. Some country-level Resident Missions hold regular meetings.
* *AfDB (African Development Bank)*: AfDB–CSO Committee.
* *IDB (Inter-American Development Bank)*: Has no global interface mechanism. Holds annual consultations with CSOs of the region. Civil Society Advisory Councils exist in about half of the 26 country offices.
* *IFAD (International Fund for Agricultural Development)*: In the past an IFAD/NGO Consultation Steering Committee facilitated preparation of biennial IFAD/NGO Consultations. More recently, a forum of representatives of small-scale farmers, fisherfolk, pastoralists and indigenous peoples' organizations, the Farmers' Forum, has been established which interacts with the Governing Council and oversees an effort to replicate such dialogue at country level and mainstream participation throughout IFAD operations.
* *IFC (International Finance Corporation)*: No formal interface mechanism. It is felt difficult to establish one since NGOs are not representative of global civil society. Sector or issue-specific groups are being considered.
* *IMF (International Monetary Fund)*: Has no formal interface.
* *World Bank*: Uses a wide range of constituency and thematic mechanisms for consultation at all levels, using also new technologies like video conferencing. Interface is conducted with CSOs on global policy reviews (for example, indigenous peoples, environmental safeguards). World Bank–Civil Society Joint Facilitating Committee, an outgrowth of the former World Bank NGO Working Group, was established to explore transparent and effective mechanisms for dialogue and engagement between civil society and the World Bank at the global level.

Other
- *OECD (Organisation for Economic Co-operation and Development)*: Formal Business and Industry and Trade Union Advisory Committees were created at the same time as the OECD. No formal mechanism for other CSOs.
- *WTO (World Trade Organization)*: Works with informal business and NGO advisory bodies.

Overall, the consensus that seems to be emerging among responding UN entities points in the direction of holding the CSOs attending intergovernmental meetings themselves responsible for ensuring their representativity, legitimacy and accountability according to agreed criteria and modalities, with the secretariat playing a facilitating but not a coercive role. In several cases, CSO participants are encouraged to group together and present joint statements, which are given priority in the list of speakers. One respondent notes that 'regional positions are encouraged to be brought to international debate'. Another reports that a combination of appointing focal points for constituencies combined with an issue-based approach 'has, over the years, improved the quality of inputs and outputs ... It has become more difficult for "one man show" type NGOs wanting to give a statement – or even large NGOs but not on topic – to monopolize the microphones.' In the words of another respondent, 'The secretariat encourages inclusiveness and transparent and democratic decision-making structures on the NGO side. However, final responsibility of their organization is left to the civil society community.'

When UN secretariats cede overall control of the process, the quality of the way in which the civil society interface mechanism functions emerges as the key success factor. One respondent emphasizes that issues of representativity, legitimacy and accountability can only be addressed if there are verifiable, autonomous and inclusive civil society processes of ongoing consultation in place. Only such mechanisms can give the few people who are able to attend any particular intergovernmental forum a mandate to express the concerns of many and can guarantee that feedback will be widely diffused. Helping such processes to emerge and to engage effectively with the secretariat, member governments and intergovernmental negotiation is, in the view of this respondent, the most delicate and important task of UN civil society offices.

In other words, a good way to address the UN–civil society governance issue is through interface mechanisms whereby each side is held accountable for the legitimacy and transparency of its own consultation and decision-making processes, and together they establish the rules for, and manage the operations of, their interaction. Feedback from the cross-system survey provides an indication of the degree to which the reality of UN family procedures mirrors this awareness. The various approaches currently adopted by respondents are described in Box 3.3.

Respondents report encountering a number of difficulties with regard to interface mechanisms (Boxes 3.4 and 3.5).

Box 3.4 Interface Mechanisms: Difficulties

- Conflicts within the NGO world.

- Difficult to ensure inclusiveness with a limited number of civil society focal points.

- Need to be vigilant and select stakeholders that are representative and well diversified.

- Differences in level and experience of members of civil society interface mechanism.

- Hard to obtain resources to facilitate interface, particularly for participation of developing-country CSOs.

- Frequent changes in people/priorities on the side both of the agency and, more frequently, the NGOs.

- Uneven quality of consultation conducted by different units in the secretariat. Often poorly organized in terms of preparation, logistics, methodology, feedback, leading to 'consultation fatigue' which is reinforced by insufficient perceived civil society impact on policies.

- Consultative interface mechanisms sometimes not embraced by governments, which believe that their efforts to channel civil society demands may be undercut by third-party arrangements that 'impose' a form of dialogue on them.

Box 3.5 Interface Mechanisms: Good Practices

- Transparent consultation with CSO mechanisms and their members.

- Recognize the autonomy of CSOs and their right to self-organization.

- Maintain close consultative relations with the interface mechanism and provide regular support and guidance.

- Monthly conference calls with dissemination of detailed notes on discussions.

- Inclusiveness, legitimacy and effectiveness of NGO engagement can be enhanced when various complementary groups work together in close coordination.

- Empowerment of the interface capacity of the agency's regional offices through continual dialogue.

- Start off from the agenda of civil society interlocutors rather than imposing a UN agenda.

- Adopt appropriate methodologies that allow for a wide spectrum of views to be heard and considered by management.

- Enhance interface capacity throughout the organization through such steps as staff training, preparing a stakeholder consultation sourcebook and establishing a reference centre.

- Mix of 'rotation' and preservation of 'institutional memory' among participating CSOs.

- Relationships with umbrella organizations offer the advantage of having fewer contact points for exchanging information and put the onus on the organizations themselves to decide who should come to the meetings.

As can be seen from the boxes, the range of approaches adopted by respondents to governing interaction with civil society actors is so great as to defy classification. Four major variables can, however, be identified: the form of the interface mechanism, who holds responsibility for establishing it, which actors interface, and the functions or mandates of the mechanism.

Regarding the first variable, situations range from ones where there is no global interface mechanism, either formal or informal, to ones where interface is conducted essentially through a periodic civil society conference whose preparation may be guided by a joint steering committee, to others where a formal ongoing interface mechanism exists. The formal-versus-informal dilemma is inherent in the relationship between civil society and the intergovernmental world. Turning precedents into recognized procedures and obtaining formal recognition of interface structures can win important ground with regard to mainstreaming and guaranteeing access for civil society voices. The existence of a recognized collective interface mechanism underlines the fact that there is an issue of governance involved, not simply one of seeking appropriate contributions to discussions on particular themes as the original provisions for INGO input to UN deliberations implied. Collective mechanisms strengthen the negotiating power of CSOs. But formalization presents dangers as well. As the 2003 meeting of the NGO/CSO focal point network put it:

> Attempts to convert informal practices into more formal mechanisms are likely to become the subject of formal negotiations [among member governments] with the risk of resulting in more restrictive arrangements. In addition ... permanent mechanisms for participation may risk creating 'fiefdoms' of insider civil society groups, as well as forcing respective civil society constituencies to speak with one voice that may mask important differences within each group (UN-NGLS 2003a:11).

On their side, although CSOs set great stock by formal recognition of their rights, they fear that, in the encounter between the UN and civil society, the bureaucratic make-up of the former is likely to prevail. 'The hierarchical nature of the UN system is reflected/mirrored in the hierarchy it creates in multiple ways through which it interacts with CSOs' (UNDESA 2003:9).[36]

The issue of formalizing interaction with CSOs is not only one of empowering CSOs. It is also important in terms of strengthening the hand of the CSO focal points within UN agencies to work for mainstreaming civil society cooperation and developing a corporate appreciation of, and adherence to, a multi-actor approach. A significant aspect of follow-up to world conferences across the system has been the adoption of policy frameworks for civil society cooperation underwritten by top management and/or governing bodies. Getting the right mix of formal procedures and informal networking and sensitization is a delicate task. Jonsson and Soderholm's case study on NGOs active over the human

immunodeficiency virus/acquired immune deficiency syndrome (HIV/
AIDS) provides some interesting insights into the advantages and disadvantages of formal and informal mechanisms. The former raise
problems of representation, limit access, and introduce elements of
hierarchy, while the latter are based on personal relations and are more
vulnerable to turnover of personnel. The two, the authors conclude, are
complementary. Jonsson and Soderholm also cite the example of a
WHO director who successfully provided vital leadership for the
development of a broad informal transnational network but at the cost
of jeopardizing his position within his agency due to his 'readiness to
depart from narrow organizational roles and to base initiatives on a
conception of collective goals, however controversial' (Jonsson and
Soderholm 1996:134–5). The deep links of informal networking and
alliances among women in CSOs, governments and intergovernmental
organizations have undoubtedly contributed decisively to civil society
impact in mainstreaming gender issues across a range of thematic areas
and summit processes.[37] In a broad sense, all UN–civil society focal
points find they need to broker understanding and trust among as wide
a range as possible of agency staff and civil society actors, and much of
this is done through informal contacts and communication.

If the relative desirability of formal or informal interfaces resists an
either-or response, the same is not the case with regard to who should
have the authority to establish the mechanism. Indeed, the two
questions are linked: it could be argued that upholding civil society's
right to self-organize the way it interacts with the UN is the best
guarantee against the worst defects of formalized interface arrangements.
Experience regarding this variable ranges from situations where the UN
entity takes the initiative and selects the members to ones where the
initiative is shared, and others where it is squarely in the civil society
camp. There would appear to be unanimity regarding the need to
respect civil society's rights to self-organization in the pronouncements
of both CSOs and UN–civil society focal points. The review of its CSO
relations commissioned by UNDESA in 2003 recommended that 'the
categories/groupings by which CSOs are organized and chosen should
be made by the CSOs themselves' (UNDESA 2003:38). The report of
the 2003 meeting of NGO/CSO focal points from the UN system and
intergovernmental organizations concurred. 'Experiences shared around
the table suggest that it is important to avoid predetermining what the
interface between civil society and an inter-governmental process
should look like' (UN-NGLS 2003a:10). And yet, as the tabulated

information on interfaces given above indicates, reality does not fully reflect this awareness. In only seven cases, it would appear, does the intergovernmental entity interact with a collective, self-organized civil society mechanism.[38] Even in this short list there are important distinctions to be made, since in most cases the 'universe' of CSOs that organize themselves is pre-delimitated by a selection or categorization process controlled by the UN entity. Only in two or three cases do the CSOs themselves fully determine both the coverage and the membership of their mechanism.

The Major Group (MG) system introduced by Agenda 21 at the very outset of the decade of the summits is an interesting one to analyse from this point of view. The fact that the official UNCED outcome document went into such detail about non-state actors was a reflection of the importance attached to them, and it undoubtedly strengthened the resolve of the CSD secretariat to involve them in the subsequent monitoring and review process. But the document introduced a negative precedent of predefining the categories according to which non-state-actor involvement should take place. The inclusion of business and industry within the same interface mechanism as non-profit CSOs has created a host of problems. The definition of the MGs, as it appears in Agenda 21, is worthy of the Chinese categorization of the animal kingdom imagined by Borges (1975) which humorously listed 'animals included in this classification' as a subgroup of the classification itself. An authoritative review of the civil society–UN experience toward the end of the 1990s put the case in strong terms:

> The list of major groups is arbitrary. It includes women but not men, the young but not the elderly, farmers but not fishing communities, trade unions but not professional associations ... It is illogical because it includes NGOs as a separate category when the other eight major groups are all represented at the UN under the heading of NGOs ... It is repugnant to allocate people to pre-specified groups rather than accepting whatever manner people choose to organize on a voluntary basis (Foster and Anand 1999:258).

A good deal of the positive press from which the MG approach has benefited has been due to a confusion between a system of classification and interface – the MGs – and a particularly successful participation practice – the Multistakeholder Dialogues (MSDs), which happened to have been mainstreamed by the CSD[39] but is in no way exclusively linked to the MG approach. The CSD secretariat has made commendable efforts to promote inclusive and effective civil society participation. The process, however, has been handicapped by several factors: the predetermination of the categories; the fact that the international networks acting as facilitators for the categories were originally selected by the secretariat, as are the limited number of MGs which participate in any particular thematic dialogue (UNDESA 2003:22);[40] and the top-down nature of the interaction, strongly conditioned by the agenda and time constraints of centralized UN consultation.

As the CSD process wended its way toward the 2002 World Summit for Sustainable Development, the defects became increasingly evident. A document produced by NGOs involved in the preparations contended that 'there is a questionable assumption that civil society, compartmentalized into major groups and stakeholders, can sit at round tables to reach consensus. Often the interests of industry and communities (and their organizations) are diametrically opposed' (United Nations 2002a:6). We have recorded above the terms of the collision of the MG approach with the self-defined civil society mechanism that was interfacing with the FAO in the preparation of the World Food Summit:*five years later* (see pp. 56–57 and p. 81). As one participant in the heated exchanges of 2002 put it:

> FAO has developed, over the years, a practice of recognizing and respecting the autonomy and separate identity of specific stakeholders who represent the interests of identifiable social sectors and shoulder the responsibility for doing so ... Stakeholders of this kind do not exist at global level, both because there are no global organizations which represent entire social categories in any meaningful way and because the interests of sectors of the same category are often differentiated in different regions ... FAO does not expect or encourage stakeholders with different interests to reach agreement on complex issues in general terms.[41]

Changes in procedures for MG interaction with the Commission on Sustainable Development in the post-WSSD period may be moving in the direction of eliminating the consensus requirement.

Another interface model that merits a closer look is the CSO Advisory Committee to the Administrator of the UNDP established in 2000. Composed of 15 people named by the UNDP to serve in their personal capacity, the committee 'sets the context for policy partnerships with civil society'.[42] In particular, it 'provides strategic, policy, and substantive guidance to the Administrator and senior management of UNDP; supports and monitors information and advocacy efforts; and pilots joint UNDP/CSO initiatives'. The committee is not said to be representative of civil society globally, but the principles governing membership include that of 'representation in different types of institutions with which UNDP engages' and 'local, national, regional and global perspectives on UNDP thematic areas'. Given the fact that the UNDP does not engage systematically with any self-organized interface mechanism and that the UNDP Governing Council resists direct engagement with civil society actors, the CSO Advisory Committee effectively occupies the available policy dialogue space and could be said to shield the UNDP from interaction with a more accountable and potentially unruly mechanism.[43] The UNDP precedent is of particular importance because of the central role of the UNDP Resident Coordinator's office in the UN system's presence at country level.

The variable of who has the authority to establish the interface mechanism is closely related to that of which actors are actually involved in interfacing. In some cases the interaction is essentially between CSOs and the secretariat, while in others member governments are also involved. In some cases people's organizations are part of the process; in others they are not.[44] As a participant in the 2005 meeting of UN and intergovernmental civil society focal points put it, 'What CSOs are we working with? Is it always the same 1,000? How to enlarge the constituencies?' We have seen above[45] that only three of the 24 entities that responded to the survey questionnaire, the ILO, the FAO and IFAD, reported strong success in reaching out beyond 'traditional' NGOs to social movements and people's organizations. In the case of the ILO, this success is inherent in the fact that the governance of the agency includes trade unions as full partners, an arrangement which would merit further study in terms of its potential to be adapted to other UN entities. In the case of the FAO, the strong interaction with organizations of peasant farmers, artisanal fishworkers, pastoralists and indigenous peoples can be attributed to respect for the autonomy of a civil society networking mechanism that has placed inclusion of people's organizations at the heart of its mission.[46] As we have seen, the IPC has reserved majority membership and leadership for social movements of the South and has asked the FAO to accept both the agenda these organizations have expressed and the consultation methods and rhythms that are appropriate to them. The results have not always been supportive of the 'FAO line' – as the incident of the publication on biotechnology discussed in Chapter 2 demonstrates – if this is what is desired from civil society outreach. But there is inestimable value in the fact that the FAO is in direct and ongoing contact with people's organizations that represent those sectors of the world's population that are the 'ultimate beneficiaries' of its work.

The third UN system agency covered in the survey that has moved decisively in this direction is IFAD. Following an exploratory meeting in 2005 (IFAD 2005), at a workshop held in Rome on 14–15 February 2006, some 34 representatives of farmers', pastoralists' and fisherfolk organizations from all regions came to an agreement with IFAD management and governing bodies to establish a Farmers' Forum as a permanent feature of the IFAD Governing Council. The forum was defined as 'an ongoing, bottom-up process – not a periodic event – spanning IFAD-supported operations on the ground and policy dialogue' which functions as 'a tripartite process involving farmers' organisations, governments and IFAD' (IFAD 2006:iii). At the forum's second global meeting in February 2008, the IFAD secretariat reported to the rural people's organizations on the degree to which it had fulfilled the commitments it had made two years earlier, an innovative extension of the concept of agency accountability beyond member governments to other important stakeholders (IFAD 2008). The establishment of the Farmers' Forum was the culmination of two years of careful preparation aimed at building both a basis of trust with the more radical farmers' movements and crafting a consensus among all components that the forum was a space that worked to everyone's advantage.

Other UN family entities, in contrast, are judged by some CSOs 'to divide civil society organizations into two groupings, based on whether they consider them "constructive" or "destructive". The "destructive" groups are the ones who in any way challenge the orthodoxy of the major IFIs, and those groups aren't even allowed into the room.' Discussions at the 2005 meeting of international organizations' civil society focal points witnessed an interesting discussion around these issues. All participants noted the tendency for a split to develop within the world of civil society between organizations that were taking what some termed more 'pragmatic' views to poverty reduction, and hence were amenable to engagement with the international system on topics like trade, and other organizations which took more radical stances. Some participants felt the international organizations should get on with the job with the former category. Others felt that the latter category could not be ignored and that it was necessary to respond to their assessment of the lack of any fundamental change in the macroeconomic policy of the IFIs and to their criticisms of the Poverty Reduction Strategy Papers process. Indeed, as Schechter points out, 'resistance movements' are extremely important actors in the global governance process. 'They are key to providing alternative perspectives and new ideas … They are key to one of the reasons why NGOs have been turned to by the UN in the first place, offering a legitimate claim to inclusiveness' (Schechter 2001:157).

Finally, the *functions* or *mandates* of the interface mechanisms also vary. Some are advisory mechanisms. Others are considered – rightly or wrongly – to represent the views of civil society actors. In the case of others, the CSOs explicitly reject the role of representation and consider the mechanism above all as a tool for giving visibility to the experiences and proposals of social actors who are on the front line of battles concerning the issues on which the UN deliberates and acts. The overwhelming majority of interface mechanisms, however, are advisory in nature and in most cases the primary direct relationship is with the secretariat. Access to governing bodies and input to decision-making processes is a product of this primary relationship. Often it takes place through civil society consultations held in conjunction with conferences of the governing bodies.[47] In some cases it does not happen at all.[48] This situation of depoliticization has been critiqued not only by CSOs but within UN circles as well. A participant at the 2004 meeting of NGO/CSO focal points had this to say:

> These ideas of mixed commissions, joint facilitation committees, advisory commissions, advisory bodies, liaison committees and so forth are being put forth today as good practice. I have to say I have had my doubts about these things but I am actually less convinced now than before I walked into this meeting. Is it maybe a diversionary tactic? … I think CSOs are interested in dealing with us on policy issues … They do not want to do it through some kind of second committee or something, They want to actually be there, real time, and contribute to the process (UN-NGLS 2004:4).

We will come back to this issue in the concluding chapter. For now let us note that the question of interface mechanisms between the UN and civil society is clearly one of the most fertile areas of challenge for the future exploration of global governance issues and practices. The very richness of the experimentation with various forms of interface taking place throughout the system testifies to the importance attached to it. Interface mechanisms are the practical terrain on which the fundamental issues of civil society representativity, legitimacy and accountability are played out. They are key to evolving shared responsibility for effective and transparent management of the relations between the UN and civil society, and, eventually, for transforming bureaucratic review procedures into dynamic two-way processes, as IFAD is trying to do. They are playing an indispensable role in ensuring the far too infrequent relays that now exist between global and local processes, and will be called upon to intensify such action greatly in the future. Under these circumstances, while recognizing that no one model of interfacing can suit all situations, it would seem important for some basic principles to be adopted throughout the UN system. The engagement to respect civil society's autonomy and its right to self-organization would be a good one with which to start.

UN Reform Proposals, the Millennium Development Goals and Civil Society: Are We on the Right Track?[49]

The international summits of the 1990s were an expression of the inability of the UN system as structured and operating at that time to deal with a host of emerging global issues in a rapidly changing political and economic context. In turn, these conferences gave expression to a UN reform agenda built around the need to achieve greater coherence and effectiveness in implementing summit outcomes. Consolidating the progress in civil society participation achieved through the agency of the world conferences has been one strand of the reform process. The challenge has been to integrate into the UN system's normal way of conducting business the civil society outreach that was facilitated in the exceptional context of the summits without provoking a self-protective 'backlash' on the part of member governments.

The first step in this direction was the ECOSOC 'review of current arrangements for consultation with NGOs', initiated in 1993 in the aftermath of UNCED, to which we have already referred.[50] The review came to a close in 1996 with a resolution that extended eligibility for accreditation to national and regional NGOs but failed to broaden the locus of consultation beyond ECOSOC itself and processes reporting to it, in particular the General Assembly and the Security Council. A compromise decision (United Nations 1996b) requested the General Assembly to examine the highly political question of the participation of NGOs in 'all areas of work of the UN'. At the outset, the United States and other Northern countries opposed NGO access to the Security Council, while the Group of 77 (G-77) and the Non-Aligned Movement held that 'all areas' included not only the Security Council but the Bretton Woods institutions as well.[51] In typical institutional fashion, for want of agreement on any more decisive action the

Secretary-General was asked to prepare a report on current arrangements for interacting with NGOs throughout the system in order to keep the issue on the table.[52]

At the same time, Secretary-General Kofi Annan included 'reaching out to civil society' as one of the thrusts of the reform plans for the United Nations he presented to the General Assembly in 1997:

> In recent years, the United Nations has found that much of its work, particularly at the country level, involves intimately the diverse and dedicated contributions of non-governmental organizations and groups – be it in economic and social development, humanitarian affairs, public health or the promotion of human rights. Similarly, the pronounced growth in the flow of private international economic transactions over the past decade has established the private sector as the major driving force of international economic change, Yet despite those growing manifestations of an ever more robust global civil society, the United Nations is at present inadequately equipped to engage civil society and make it a true partner in its work.
>
> Accordingly, the Secretary-General is making arrangements for all United Nations entities to be open to and work closely with civil society organizations that are active in their respective sectors and to facilitate increased consultation and cooperation between the United Nations and such organizations (United Nations 1997:22, para. 59).

The terms of this text evoked two issues that were making CSOs, and many UN civil society offices, increasingly nervous. On the one hand, it coupled civil society and the business world in a single statement.[53] On the other it laid emphasis on operational country-level cooperation, foreshadowing an attempt by some UN member governments to sidestep the outspoken 'advocacy' CSOs that had been prominent at the summits and to privilege the reputedly more docile 'operational' NGOs who could be expected to knuckle down and get on with the job of implementation without raising such a political fuss. The United Nations Millennium Declaration adopted by the General Assembly in September 2000 used language that was equally ambiguous in failing to distinguish between the identities and roles of CSOs and the private sector, and tepid if not instrumental in its vision of the relationship between civil society and the UN: 'We resolve … to give greater opportunities to the private sector, non-governmental organizations and civil society, in general, to contribute to the realization of the Organization's goals and programmes' (United Nations 2000: para. 30).

The Millennium Declaration had been drafted in an ECOSOC committee to which civil society had no access. How were non-state actors to be enrolled in the implementation of a declaration in whose crafting they had not been involved? The UN designed a three-tiered strategy to help countries achieve the eight Millennium Development Goals to which they committed themselves in adopting the declaration. The strategy involved country reporting (the most politically significant component, since it could conceivably offer an opportunity for calling governments to account), research (a project, aimed at developing a strategy for reaching the goals, undertaken by a high-powered team of academics and UN experts), and campaigning. Civil society involvement has been minimal in the country reporting conducted thus far and was practically nonexistent in the research project (United Nations Millennium Project 2005).[54] In these circumstances, the major civil society outreach mechanism in the Millennium Goals package is the skilfully directed and well-resourced Millennium Campaign launched by the UN in October 2002. On the civil society side, the campaign is led by a core coalition – the Global Call to Action Against Poverty – promoted by INGOs and networks including Oxfam, Action Aid, MWENGO, Social Watch and others. Although the coalition is global, the campaign organizers state that the action should be primarily local, since 'real change is only possible at the country level'. Kofi Annan is cited as stressing that:

> political will shifts only if there is national and local mobilization by the public, and only when leaders are held accountable. Appeals by international organizations are one thing. But what would really make a difference is if, at the local level, the Goals achieve a critical mass of support and even become 'vote-getters'.[55]

Given the style and pace of the campaign, however, it has been more successful thus far in reaching NGOs, celebrities, community groups and individuals[56] than in obtaining the involvement of people's organizations that mobilize the bulk of the citizens of the countries of the South where change is most needed.

In September 2002, the UN Secretary-General put before the General Assembly a comprehensive document, *Strengthening of the United Nations: An Agenda for Further Change* (United Nations 2002b), which dedicated 13 paragraphs to promoting partnerships with civil society and with the private sector. The document noted the 'exponential growth' of civil society actors and transnational networks and the intensification of their interaction with the UN system not only at country level, where partnership with NGOs in humanitarian and development work 'has been the rule for decades', but more recently, as a result of the decade of world conferences, in global intergovernmental processes as well. As a result of the 'explosive growth in participation', the document proceeded, 'the system that has evolved over several years for facilitating the interaction between the United Nations and civil society actors is showing signs of strain'. Problematic areas included pressure on physical facilities, a confusing variety of accreditation procedures, wariness on the part of 'many Member States' to make more room for NGO participation in their deliberations, the imbalance in participation among industrialized and developing country NGOs, the fact that some actors nominally placed in the civil society basket – parliamentarians and private sector in particular – did not consider themselves NGOs and that the modalities for their participation in the activities of the United Nations were unclear. As a first step toward finding solutions to these problems the Secretary-General determined to 'assemble a group of eminent persons representing a variety of perspectives and experiences to review past and current practices and recommend improvements for the future in order to make the interaction between civil society and the United Nations more meaningful'. The fact that the review was presented more in terms of problem-solving than of opportunity-seizing was not appreciated by many CSOs or civil society fans within the UN.

The panel, headed by the former president of Brazil, Fernando Henrique Cardoso, started its work in February 2003.[57] Over the 12-month period allocated for its task it consulted widely with a range of CSOs, governments and UN officials. A background paper prepared by its support team gave a frank summary of some of the concerns that had been expressed in high-level UN coordinating mechanisms:[58]

> Management discussions appreciated the mounting sense of civil society frustration, due to governments' lack of response to their concerns and abnegation of international obligations and also to the UN system seemingly moving towards a pro-globalization stance and closer to the private sector. The UN's response, it was considered, should be to recognize CSOs' contributions and concerns, but at the same time to look carefully into the legitimacy and sources of CSO funding, particularly regarding those most aggressive in the major international events … Management has become concerned about the competing agendas of governments and civil society, about mounting member state questions concerning the legitimacy, representativity and sources of funding of some of the CSOs, and about the impression (again held by some member states) that CSOs may infringe the prerogative of member states in intergovernmental decision-making processes (United Nations 2003:16–17).

The tendency of UN secretariats at the top management level to view relations with civil society primarily in terms of the problems they occasioned was even more evident in this more internal rendition than it had been in the Secretary-General's official presentation of the review.

The panel submitted its report to the Secretary-General on 7 June 2004 (United Nations 2004a). Just a few days before, the head of its support team summarized the four main planks of the panel's analysis and recommendations at a meeting of UN system NGO/CSO focal points:

1. Reinterpret multilateralism to mean *multi-constituencies*
The way multilateral agendas are shaped has changed – with civil society bringing new issues to the global agenda and governments taking effective actions not by consensus but through multi-constituency coalitions of governments, civil society and others (global policy networks). *Recommendations: UN should explicitly adopt this important mode of multilateralism, and use its convening power to create multi-constituency fora, open formal UN fora to all actors necessary to solve critical issues, and regularize the use of a range of participatory modes such as public hearings.*

2. Realize the full power of *partnerships*
Multi-stakeholder partnerships have emerged as powerful ways of getting things done and closing the implementation gap by pooling the complementary capacities of diverse actors. *Recommendations: Achieving the MDGs and other global targets demands a UN that is proactive and strategic in this area.*

3. Link the *local with the global*
A closer connection between the deliberative and operational spheres of the UN is imperative so that local operational work truly helps realize the global goals *and* that global deliberations are informed by local reality. *Recommendations: The UN needs to give top priority to enhancing its relationship with civil society at the country level.*

4. Help tackle democracy deficits and strengthen *global governance*
The substance of politics is globalized (trade, economics, terrorism, culture, pandemics etc.) but its process remains firmly rooted at national/local levels. Representative democracy is being broadened by participatory democracy, with the help of ICT [information and communication technology] and civil society networks. How citizens aggregate politically has changed from communities of locality *to* communities of interest – which, thanks to ICT, can be global as readily as local. *Recommendations: These three factors challenge the familiar outlines of global governance and demand changes in the UN by engaging civil society in policy-making at all levels* (UN-NGLS 2004:10).[59]

A number of the specific measures recommended by the panel were judged to be potentially controversial for a variety of political, turf protection and financial reasons. These included: shifting from a 'fixed-slate' approach involving all accredited NGOs in all forums to engaging with those actors most relevant to the issue in hand; establishing a new Under-Secretary-General function to encourage and coordinate engagement with civil society and other actors; opening the General Assembly and its committees and special sessions to civil society; bringing all accreditation processes together into a single process, located in the General Assembly; reviving multi-constituency forums such as public hearings to review progress on meeting globally agreed goals. In order to put muscle in the country-level approach, the panel recommended appointing civil society and partnership specialists at country level in the resident coordinators' teams, setting up advisory civil society committees, and establishing a fund to enhance UN and Southern civil society capacity for engagement.

Published comments from the civil society world on the panel's report were generally supportive of its overall intentions but critical of the formulation of a number of its proposals. In particular, CSOs voiced concerns about the strong focus on promoting partnerships among what were felt to be imprecisely defined 'constituencies', including private sector actors. The objection was not to the principle of giving the private sector a seat at the table. Many CSOs felt, however, that the report's discourse on partnerships was far too vague and that there was not enough emphasis on the need for the UN, when it acts as convenor, to ensure that common goods and the interests of the less powerful actors are defended (see Hill 2004). Pumping public–private partnerships is also seen as a way of letting governments off the hook regarding their commitments to the summit goals by shifting the terrain of implementation from one of political decision making to one of corporate choice of how to invest private funds. CSOs were also sceptical, with good reason as it turned out, regarding the degree to which the panel's recommendations were likely to be actuated. The report's proposals for how to 'bridge the North–South divide' came in for criticism from Third World Network which felt they 'merely pass the hat around for donations so that NGOs from the South can better engage with UN processes … A very significant reason for the establishment of the Panel has found little thinking space devoted to this issue' (Third World Network 2004:7).[60] In the words of Richard Falk, 'What is missing from the Cardoso report are bold proposals that would give global civil society and its representatives an assured and distinct role in future UN activities' (Falk 2005:177).

In September 2004 the UN Secretary-General placed before the General Assembly his own generally timid recommendations for implementing the panel's report (United Nations 2004d). His proposals concerning NGO[61] participation in the General Assembly, the Security Council and ECOSOC focused on extending and standardizing existing practices, most often parallel to, rather than sited in, the meetings of these organs. Under the heading of improving accreditation, the Secretary-General expressed the view that there was 'considerable merit' in the panel's package of proposals. He was generically sympathetic to the idea of an expanded Partnerships Office. But the component of the panel's vision that received his most wholehearted support was the focus on the country level and on linking the global with the local.[62] Annan concurred with the panel's suggestion for the creation of a single trust fund to provide financial support for NGO representatives from developing countries to attend intergovernmental meetings. NGO participation at country level required enhancement, and the MDGs and the PRSPs were 'key opportunities … to ensure that the rhetoric is put into practice'. The UN Resident Coordinator system needed to enhance its capacity to engage with civil society, and the Secretary-General fully endorsed the panel's recommendations in this regard.[63] He indicated that he had already asked all Resident Coordinators to identify a staff member to serve as a civil society focal point, with an additional dedicated staff member to be appointed 'as soon as resources allow'. He announced his intention to establish a trust fund to cover the costs of capacity enhancement both of NGOs and of the UN system. Finally, he concurred with one of the panel's most pernicious proposals, that of creating NGO advisory groups at country level to guide implementation of UN strategies, replicating the global advisory committee of UNDP and a pilot country-level committee established in Botswana in 2003 'as a forum for policy advice and participation' (United Nations 2004d: para. 46).

The two documents were taken up in the General Assembly in early October 2004. The discussion was reported in an article posted on the UN-NGLS website in tightrope-walking language, which is painfully familiar to those who frequent intergovernmental forums.

> Several Member States recognized the contribution made over the years by civil society organizations and expressed their interest in enhancing civil society participation in the UN's work. However, several speakers

recommended that a cautious approach be taken in reforming current UN practices so that the Organization retains its intergovernmental nature (UN-NGLS, no date, p. 1).

The political issue of access to the General Assembly and the financial issue of support for developing country NGOs to attend global forums polarized the attention of delegates.[64] Wrapping up the two days of discussion, the General Assembly President noted the lack of substantial consensus and 'proposed that further consultations with Member States should be undertaken on the matter' (UN-NGLS, no date, p. 4).

In a certain sense the very diffidence of senior UN management and General Assembly delegates regarding further engagement with civil society could be regarded as proof of the impact of a decade of relatively intense interaction. The cross-system survey, carried out some months later, gives us an opportunity to verify this hypothesis from the viewpoint of the UN staff directly responsible for civil society relations. The final section of the survey questionnaire asked respondents to judge the impact that civil society engagement had had on their entities over the past few years according to seven parameters: (1) the general 'culture' of the organization; (2) its overall understanding of civil society work; (3) the discourse employed and the issues addressed; (4) the sources and kinds of knowledge on which the entity draws; (5) civil society participation in governance of the institution; (6) informal accountability to civil society; and (7) allocation of resources. Respondents' reactions document their view that whatever the limitations, the backlashes, the challenges ahead, the UN family had been profoundly transformed by its interaction with civil society over the previous decade. Impact was judged to be 'strong' on all parameters except that of allocation of resources.[65] Other feedback from within the system coincides with this judgement. The FAO study presented above is a case in point. The 2003 internal review of interaction between UNDESA and civil society testifies to 'the exceptionally rich range of interaction' and 'the important role that civil society plays in the work of the UN' (UNDESA 2003:2). The complementary UNDESA-sponsored review of the relationship as viewed by CSOs and governments concludes that 'overall CSOs are thought to play an important role in making UN processes more democratic and creating an enabling environment for dialogue through their efforts to expand participation in a variety of ways' (UNDESA 2003:32).

At the same time, some CSO focal points report negative reactions on the part of some developing-country governments, attributed to their concern that 'large Northern NGOs have disproportionate place in the policy debates, in a manner that risks further weakening of the power of Southern governments' and that 'increased NGO participation in such exercises simply raises the number of conditionalities on the social/governance questions but without heeding NGO demands for macroeconomic alternatives' (UN–NGLS 2003a:7). In fact, there is no doubt that civil society has been far less successful in impacting on 'hard' economic issues and the intergovernmental institutions that deal with them than on 'soft' rights issues. Some participants at the 2005 meeting of CSO focal points asked themselves whether the UN was moving backward regarding openness to civil society as compared with the decade of the summits and noted the tension that often exists between the facile rhetoric of senior management and the capacity of the system to respond. The fate of the UN reform process was seen to be evidence of this ambiguous trend.

The Millennium Assembly+5 scheduled for 14–16 September 2005 was the first occasion following discussion of the Cardoso report on which the UN could have implemented an albeit cautiously more open approach to civil society actors in General Assembly deliberations. The UN–NGLS circulated widely the Secretary-General's report to the General Assembly, *In Larger Freedom: Towards Development, Security and Human Rights for All* (United Nations 2005)[66] and put together a compilation of the 128 reactions it received from CSOs (UN–NGLS 2005b).[67] Not surprisingly, a large number of the comments centred on the role of civil society, which received little attention in the Secretary-General's report, and on the need to distinguish clearly between civil society and the private sector.[68] There were hopes that space might be made at the General Assembly for civil society actors to express their views, but the decision in the end was to allow access and speaking time to just one civil society representative and one from the private sector. In partial compensation, informal interactive hearings of the General Assembly with representatives of NGOs, CSOs and the private sector were held in New York on 23–24 June 2005, comfortably distant from the intergovernmental forum.[69]

The outcome of the Millennium Assembly+5 itself was disastrously below expectations. The event was dragged under by a persistent deficit of political will – of which the most flamboyant representation was the performance of the newly named US ambassador who introduced dozens of difficult-to-negotiate proposed changes in the outcome document at the twelfth hour – and complicated by the scandals surrounding Kofi Annan's management of the UN secretariat. Where civil society and partnerships were concerned the governing bodies failed to make available the modest amounts of additional funding that would have been necessary to implement them. Governments' priorities were clearly elsewhere.

In the follow-up to the General Assembly's recommendations Annan named yet another high-level panel, this time to deliberate on 'United Nations System-wide Coherence in the areas of development, humanitarian assistance and the environment'. Its report, *Delivering as One*, was submitted to Kofi Annan in November 2006 but was transmitted to the General Assembly by the new UN Secretary-General, Ban Ki-moon, on 3 April 2007. The panel's report argues that the UN 'needs to overcome its current fragmentation and to deliver as one' both globally and at country level. The central recommendations regarding country-level action design a 'one UN' system with one, multisector, 'country-owned' programme managed by one leader, the Resident Coordinator, with one budgetary framework and one office. This approach is currently being tested in eight pilot countries,[70] with the endorsement of Secretary-General Ban Ki-moon.

'Engaging civil society organizations and the private sector' is the object of a five-paragraph section of the report. CSOs are seen as 'indispensable partners in delivering services to the poor, and they can catalyse action within countries, mobilize broad-based movements and hold leaders accountable for their commitments'. Their inputs into the preparation of the One Country Programme are stated to be important 'to ensure full national ownership and relevance'. The section ends with the recommendation that 'the capacity of the Resident Coordinator's office to advocate, promote and broker partnerships between government and relevant civil society organizations and the private sector should be enhanced' (United Nations 2005: paras. 72–76).

Indeed enhancement measures had already been launched in response to the Cardoso report. By July 2007, 42 Resident Co-ordinators had taken the positive first step of naming an officer to serve as a civil society focal point with responsibility for coordinating civil society engagement by UN agencies in the country. In 15 countries civil society advisory committees had been established or were in the process of being so. In only one of these, Bolivia, were people's organizations – as distinct from NGOs – strongly involved: the indigenous peoples' organizations, which are politically unavoidable in the Bolivian context.[71] In Mozambique the members of the committee selected by the UN Resident Coordinator themselves questioned the absence of the 'productive sector', farmers' organizations in particular. In the Philippines, following a crab-walk itinerary, the United Nations Country Team named a national Civil Society Advisory Committee composed of people serving in their individual capacity which subsequently 'established an accountability mechanism for itself by creating a Civil Society Assembly composed of 40 participating CSOs to which the committee members will report'. At its inaugural meeting the assembly then elected the ten CSO representatives who 'constitute the core membership of the committee' (UNDP 2007). Here, too, the membership was drawn exclusively from NGOs. Although membership is organizational, 'members are expected to represent larger constituencies and not their organizations alone'. In terms of agenda and organization, most of the advisory committees adapt themselves to the 'thematic groups' that had already been established – with no significant civil society participation – when the UNDAF exercises were launched in the mid-1990s. Only in the case of Bolivia, not surprisingly, has a new interagency thematic focus been dictated by civil society, that of intercultural issues.

The preoccupied prophecy expressed by a UN civil society liaison officer in 2004 seems to risk coming true:[72] in the post-summit era the UN could be tending to 'clomp in like elephants onto the national level and bring the UN agenda and the UN criteria for selecting civil society partners, and UN coordination mechanisms ...' Nonetheless, it could well be argued that proactive UN initiatives, however fallible, are better than inaction since they set dynamics in motion. To what degree these initiatives can be 'subverted' in favour of ones that enhance meaningful political engagement will depend in good part on the reactions of civil society, people's organizations and social movements in particular. Their reactions, in turn, will depend on the strategic importance they assign to UN-promoted processes at national level and the force with which they are able to advocate more legitimate interface mechanisms, as has happened in Bolivia.

The UN system's efforts to forge a coherent implementation strategy for the global policy deliberations of the summits and to link them with national action are situated in a complex and evolving multilateral context. The build-up of tensions around Iraq, brought to a head by the 11 September attack on the Twin Towers just a year after the Millennium Conference, drew attention away from development toward security as the dominant motivation for pursuing multilateralism. The US determination to unilaterally wage 'war on terrorism' if the UN declined to do its bidding chipped away still further at the civil-society-championed principles of solidarity, equity and sustainability in which the MDGs are embedded. The greater the difficulties encountered by the WTO Doha agenda, the more powerful governmental actors and corporate interests have dug in their heels to defend the neoliberal agenda contested by most CSOs. For its part, the donor community has banded together under the Organisation for Economic Co-operation and Development (OECD) banner to devise what some CSOs see as ever more sophisticated conditionalities in the name of 'enhancing aid effectiveness', conditionalities masked under the veil of a doctrine of 'local ownership' which makes scant provision for participation by non-state actors.[73] Burgeoning public–private partnerships, encouraged by the UN system itself through the Global Compact and the follow-up to the World Summit on Sustainable Development, have joined with the emergence of unthinkably well-endowed private foundations[74] to create a situation in which the bulk of external resources available to support the attainment of development goals are in no way accountable to the UN system, let alone to civil society.

Already in 1997, Riva Krut had ended her discussion paper on NGO influence in international decision making by noting that 'it is ironic that the late twentieth century has seen the unprecedented growth and influence of civil society and unprecedented decline of those national and intergovernmental organizations most open to participation. Having spent five decades lobbying at the gates of the United Nations, non-governmental groups have finally been granted access only to see that real power now lies behind other doors' (Krut 1997:29). Well into the first decade of the twenty-first century the latter part of her conclusion had been confirmed, while the first was at a delicate point of reassessment. Yet never has the UN system been more in need of allies if it is to regain a significant role in global governance and refurbish its legitimacy and accountability. To what degree is the UN convinced of the strategic importance of investing in building alliances with civil society? What would it take to do so? This is what we will turn to in the concluding chapter.

4
Conclusions and Ways Forward

Major Challenges for the UN in Its Relations with Civil Society

Constitute a meaningful political space for global governance

The global summits of the 1990s and their aftermath have testified to the UN's capacity to recognize the key challenges the world is facing. At the same time they have documented the difficulties it encounters in seeking to resolve them. Persistent lack of political will to meet even the modest targets set by the summits; dominance of the powerful few in furtherance of narrow interpretations of national interests over defence of global common goods; inability to address economic issues and structural reform and to police the corporate world; failure to incorporate the innovative stakeholder outreach of the summits into normal practice in order to work towards more legitimate forms of global governance: pack these deficiencies together and they spell something resembling failure in the eyes of civil society organizations (CSOs), but not only in their eyes. The UN system is both a reflection of the present state of political balance, and the only existing international institution that offers a possibility of moving it forward. There is general consensus that civil society participation is indispensable to make this happen. Whether or not this catalytic role can be played, however, depends on the evolution of a delicate dialectical relationship between the UN and civil society actors. The greatest danger, quite simply, is that the most deeply rooted and legitimate sectors of the civil society universe may simply lose interest in the UN as a forum in which to invest their precious energy.

What are these organizations seeking in the UN? An arena in which to effectively present, defend and – if possible – win acceptance for alternatives to the dominant neoliberalization agenda championed by

169

the international financial institutions (IFIs), the corporate world and some powerful UN members. The UN is not offering this kind of platform now, for several reasons which need to be addressed in order to avoid a verdict of irrelevance. On the one hand, the capacity of the UN system and the development establishment to incorporate the language of contesters while maintaining the status quo is almost equal to the centuries-long practice of the Catholic Church. One of the most lucid political analyses of the process of incorporation has this to say about how the post-Washington consensus (PWC) apparently opens the door to alternative agendas but in fact closes it to anything resembling the political process necessary to advance these agendas:

> The PWC ... is an understanding of governance based on (a) a managerialist ideology of effectiveness and efficiency of governmental institutions and (b) an understanding of civil society based on the mobilization and management of social capital rather than one of representation and accountability....The debate on global governance within the international institutions (the United Nations, World Bank, IMF [International Monetary Fund] and WTO [World Trade Organization]) remains firmly within a dominant liberal institutionalist tradition; discussions about democracy beyond the borders of the territorial state are still largely technocratic ones about how to enhance transparency and, in some instances, accountability. They fail, or in some instances still refuse, to address the asymmetries of power of decision-making that characterize the activities of these organizations ... Governance, in its effectiveness and efficiency guise, is 'post-political'. Agendas are set and implementation becomes the name of the game ... Real governance is about political contestation over issues such as distribution and justice; it is concerned with the empowerment of communities from the bottom up rather than just the top down in the promotion of the public good. Both of these issues, in other than rhetorical fashion, still fall into the 'too hard box' for the international policy community (Higgott 2001:134–5).

There was a magic moment, around the Cancun session of the WTO Ministerial, when powerful social movements concerned with food and agriculture issues saw the UN system – the Food and Agriculture Organization of the United Nations (FAO) and the United Nations Conference on Trade and Development (UNCTAD), in particular – as a possible alternative terrain on which to champion a vision of international trade governed not by the unmitigated laws of the market, but by the right of peoples and countries to achieve food security and exercise food sovereignty. The combination of the stall in the WTO negotiations and the eruption of a global food crisis in 2008 has created a further opportunity to question dominant paradigms. But the UN is not fulfilling this expectation. On the contrary, the scenario of UN reform and the proclamation of the Millennium Development Goals (MDGs) have been accompanied by strengthened links between an ever more synergetic World Bank–IMF–WTO trio, on the one hand, and the UN family, on the other, with the apparent effect of cementing over the contradictions between the two spheres that have provided civil society with space to advocate their concerns. The UN has not been able to impact in any meaningful way on the power of a few wealthy governments and corporations to impose a neoliberal agenda on the many poor of this world. It has not even been able to enforce a serious assessment of the impact of market liberalization on food insecurity and poverty or of the World Bank–IMF-promoted Poverty Reduction Strategy Papers on development in the countries in which they have been applied.

Nor has it proved capable of disciplining the unbridled power of the corporate world to pursue its interests and to orchestrate globalization to the tune of profit making, most recently and outrageously in the context of the current food crisis. So far as private sector participation in UN policy forums is concerned, few absurdities in the way the UN works are more flagrant than the zeal that is invested in vetting and policing CSOs that aspire to cross the threshold of a UN meeting hall, as compared with the relative indifference to the antics of representatives of transnational corporations (TNCs) and private companies. In the FAO in recent years the radical farmer leader José Bové would have been excluded from the World Food Summit:*five years later* if the French government had not gone to bat for him. A young, naive member of the delegation of a highly esteemed North American non-governmental organization (NGO) was carried off to be interrogated by the Italian police for passing around notes inviting delegations to refrain from electing the United States to the FAO Council following the invasion of Iraq. At the same time, the transnational sugar lobby conducted itself outrageously in a FAO technical committee, attempting to purchase developing country votes and intervening in a heavy-handed way in the discussions. Yet no disciplinary action was taken by the institution despite the complaints of the technical secretariat itself. While many UN agencies subject individual corporations to vetting processes before entering into financial or other forms of relations, UN regulations allow international business associations to be accredited to global policy forums as 'NGOs' on the grounds that the associations themselves are non-profit, despite the obvious fact that they represent the for-profit interests of their members.[1] When the World Health Organization

(WHO) tried to apply to business associations the same vetting process it uses for individual companies one Northern government objected on the grounds that, after all, all NGOs pursue their own interests and there was no reason to be particularly severe with the private sector. Private companies, like NGOs, can also be incorporated into the national delegations of member governments. Of the 23 members of the US delegation to the July 2008 meeting of the Commission of the joint FAO–WHO Codex Alimentarius, which sets the standards applied by the WTO for international trade in food products, 10 represented food corporations or private firms that consult for them while none represented consumer organizations or other CSOs concerned with the food chain. It is easy for UN secretariats to pass the buck on questions like these by appealing to procedures and the sovereign rights of member governments, but it is a losing and a pusillanimous stance if the issue is to keep the UN alive as an authoritative global policy forum.

The UN's attempts to engage the private sector as a category are also subject to stringent criticism. The lack of a serious monitoring process incorporated into the UN's Global Compact with the business world or in the public–private partnerships launched around the World Conference on Sustainable Development is a cause for concern. As we have seen, the Kofi Annan reform proposals perpetuated vague discourse about partnerships. Since the UN Centre on Transnational Corporations was abolished in 1992, passing its mission on to UNCTAD, the UN has had insufficient focused capacity to track what transnationals are up to, let alone to discipline their action. This is an unpardonable gap in any effort to conceive of an effective mechanism of global governance. Again, UN secretariats can justifiably lament the lack of political will on the part of powerful member governments, but this is no solution. Civil society is strengthening its capacity to address issues of corporate responsibility and monitor corporate behaviour and financial speculation. The challenge for the UN is to have the courage and the capacity to build virtuous alliances with these efforts[2] and to evolve systemic proposals for tracking and disciplining private sector impact on common goods and human rights.

The UN is caught between a tradition of international governance by sovereign states and the emerging need for global governance involving other actors on an equitable basis. Thus far it has not been able to ring in the new. Organizations that are aiming not just to tinker with the system but to work toward paradigmatic changes that can render basic human rights operative are seeking, as Keck and Sikkink (1998:35) put it, 'to amplify the generative power of norms, broaden the scope of practices those norms engender, and sometimes even renegotiate or transform the norms themselves'. The question is whether the UN system, once the dust of the summits has settled, can provide a platform for this to happen. A lot will depend on how effectively it addresses the issues reviewed above, and on how astutely it proves able to govern its relationship with civil society.

Treat the interface with civil society as a political process

There is an exasperating tendency on the part of UN secretariats to get so bogged down in the detail of procedures that they lose sight of what the real issues are. This is not to minimize the value of the painstaking efforts of civil society liaison staff throughout the system to open up doors and push practices forward. The FAO case study and the cross-system survey document how much has been accomplished in this regard over the past decade and a half. However, even the most outward-looking and motivated UN secretariat staff tend to feel that the centre of gravity is located within the UN and the processes it promotes. And civil society liaison staff are rarely if ever decision makers in their institutions. The FAO study testifies to how infrequent it is, and what a difference it makes, when the senior management responsible for overseeing civil society outreach is armed with political acumen and a broad sense of where the institution's long-term interests lie. Too often the directives that percolate down from the top have to do with not antagonizing member governments, sticking to the rules, making the event a success, attracting publicity-drawing personages, keeping costs down ... There is a cultural and cognitive problem involved here as well as an issue of bureaucracy. UN secretariats generally operate on an extremely notional understanding of political process and social change: the niceties of the distinction between getting rock stars on the bandwagon and interacting seriously with people's organizations are not always grasped. The choice before the UN system is between engaging in political process involving the mobilization of social actors on the one hand or, on the other, opting for a diabolic duo of disembodied 'global public opinion', one of the newest buzz words, and global policy networks or epistemic communities of the MDG project variety with a few super-NGOs thrown in to add a civil society flavour.[3] The UN feels far more comfortable with the latter, but its salvation lies with the former however 'messier' and more threatening it may seem. Some UN leaders know this is so. We have quoted above Kofi Annan's statement that political will shifts only if there is broad-based national and local mobilization, an insight shared by the FAO's Director-General Jacques Diouf. But neither has acted unequivocally on this understanding.

The following discussion of major issues in the governance of the UN interface with civil society is deliberately limited to a few essential points and principles in order to avoid getting lost in detail. It does not revisit the terrain of what the UN system already knows how to do with the civil society interlocutors to which it is accustomed. Much of this good practice has been documented above. It focuses instead on what the UN does not know how to do with actors it is not reaching. The thesis here, supported by the evidence emerging from the preceding chapters, is that nothing short of daring to venture into unexplored territory will suffice to pull UN governance into the twenty-first century. Many of the NGOs and the individual thinkers whose voices reach the UN are advocating laudable and sometimes visionary ideas. What are missing are the voices of those most affected by the inequities of current global governance and the political clout their organizations can mobilize.[4] The UN needs above all to create space for engagement with the sectors of civil society that legitimately articulate alternatives to the dominant agenda of liberalization and the social injustice, conflict and depredation of common goods which accompany it. Such alternatives emerge in the first instance from the resistance of those who suffer their consequences directly. There is some experience on which to draw. The FAO's interface with civil society following the World Food Summit: *five years later* is documented in detail in Chapter 2. The International Fund for Agricultural Development (IFAD) has had the courage to set its sedate NGO Committee on a back burner and engage with vociferous small farmer and artisanal fisherfolk organizations in an effort to evolve an autonomous Farmers' Forum which can address its governing council with incommensurately greater authority. UN-Habitat is interfacing with a global network of slum dwellers. Years of frequentation of the Commission on Human Rights by indigenous peoples has led to the establishment of a UN Permanent Forum on Indigenous Issues. These experiences are very diverse and, indeed, it is neither possible nor desirable to suggest universally applicable recipes. The new will come not through global unilateral dictate but from a networked cumulative dynamic of opening new political spaces and devising new ways of occupying them. It will not come if multiple engagements at all levels do not take place. There are no blueprints then, but what can be done is to indicate principles and basic practices that need to be respected for engagement to take place.

The first principle is one we have encountered in the case of the FAO and its relations with the International CSO Planning Committee for Food Sovereignty (IPC). It is to respect the autonomy of civil society and its right to self-organization. Some kind of a Pavlovian electric shock mechanism should be installed within the UN system to induce it to refrain from preselecting categories into which to sort the chaotic world of civil society and from naming focal CSOs to co-ordinate them. The sleight of hand of advisory committees composed of UN-nominated individuals should be banned as an instrument for ongoing dialogue on policies and programmes. This does not mean that the UN should not engage with CSOs in dialogue about desirable characteristics of the interface mechanisms they autonomously estab-lish, such as inclusion and empowerment of people's organizations rooted in the regions of the South. It is proper and desirable that civil society networks be required to indicate how they go about their business and to report on how successful they are in attaining their self-defined objectives. Meeting their responsibility to demonstrate trans-parently the validity of their claims to legitimacy is an area in which CSOs have been deficient, and UN interlocutors can play a useful role by calling them to account.

If the UN system wants to benefit from the reinvigoration that engagement with people's organizations and social movements can bring, it needs to avoid the kind of heavy-handed interference with the internal dynamics of the civil society world that has occurred too often in past years. Ways in which civil society engagement with UN summits has tended to privilege some kinds of CSOs over others have been well documented. To a certain degree this was understandable in the early phases of opening up to an unknown universe, but there is no excuse for perpetuating this kind of behaviour 17 years after UNCED. Yet we have noted a certain tendency on the part of international inter-governmental organizations today to divide the world of civil society into 'good engagers' and 'radical protesters' and to opt for getting on with the job with the former on the grounds that the latter have chosen freely not to be a part of it. This is not useful. If some of your invitees persistently refuse to enter your home, you ought to question the house's design and the modalities of the invitation before you denigrate the invitees' motivations. We have seen how a major global social organization like Via Campesina found the Major Group system untenable but felt at ease in the IPC. During negotiations about the architecture of the Farmers' Forum-in-formation, a Via Campesina leader told IFAD staff, 'If I give away on what you see as a detail I am lost'. Respect for intransigence whose motivations may not always be evident from a UN perspective is a precondition for engagement with social movements.

So is respect for the requirements for conducting dialogue and consultation with far-flung, multilingual, locally rooted interlocutors, quite different from those of the kind of English-speaking, capital-city-based, electronically connected networks with which the UN understandably finds it easier to deal. Here it is useful to recall Higgott's exhortation to avoid saddling civil society engagement to an 'efficiency and effectiveness' nag. The main aim of social organizations is not to have X impact on Y UN outcome. Rather, it is to use the space of global governance that the UN potentially affords to help locally based movements build upward and outward links that can amplify their voices and collectively project alternative proposals to the liberalization agenda. If these movements are obliged to choose, it is less important for them to have a text ready for such and such a date drafted in a form and language that will easily slot into UN negotiations than it is to respect the time and process required for meaningful consultation with their base. And, after all, if we take a deep and long-term view of UN interests, this is just what the UN should want them to do. It is on this kind of practice that their legitimacy is founded. People's organizations follow their own agendas and strategies, of which engagement with the UN is only a part. How important a part will depend on how fertile a terrain the UN offers. The UN system should not expect civil society networks and social movements to focus specifically and uniquely on interaction with what is going on in their institutions. The FAO experience is a good illustration of how, even in the best of circumstances, CSOs need to be strategically selective in determining what processes they engage in, and how. The UN system has to be willing to respect the autonomous arenas of people's organizations and not insist on engaging with them only on UN ground. It has to be sensitive to the need for social movements to conduct a good part of their mobilization and their elaboration of alternatives in their own independent space and in forms that are alien to intergovernmental process. The UN should be open to contamination by the results that emerge. The evolution of the paradigm of food sovereignty described in the FAO chapter is a case in point. Links between global and local levels, in forms more reminiscent of civil society 'praxis' of the 1970s[5] than of the language of 'scaling up' used in UN circles, are clearly fundamental.

Is the best solution to expanded global governance to be found in the realization of the world people's assembly proposed by the Commission on Global Governance and championed by some NGO networks concerned with defence of the UN? The idea is a powerful one and it has the advantage on its side of high visibility.[6] But it has significant disadvantages as well. Establishing an organ of this kind would inevitably involve applying principles of representative democracy to the civil society world, which operates on a different logic: one of participation, demonstration and mobilization.[7] It would risk exacerbating conflicts between different categories of CSOs – NGOs and people's organizations in the first instance – both globally and at national level. It would tend to privilege the NGOs, who normally have more time and resources to invest in presence at the UN. Despite well-meaning intentions of building from the bottom up, it would tend to gain its energies and direction from what goes on globally rather than what is happening locally. Experience points in the direction of starting off, instead, by transforming the terms of engagement at country and regional levels, and letting global forms of interaction emerge from this process. We will return to this strategy below.

A trend of the past few years which illustrates the problems involved in opening space for engagement in global governance by people's organizations as well as NGOs has been the invention of advocacy as the new name for image building and resource mobilization. Big international NGOs (INGOs) with extensive research and public relations capacities have come to occupy the front stage of the advocacy scene. Adding this additional clout to civil society lobbying might be seen as advantageous. In practice, however, the positions that these NGOs advocate, 'on behalf of' the poor, are most often developed without systematic political engagement with concerned people's organizations and may not even reflect the positions for which these organizations themselves are lobbying, OXFAM's stance on cotton being a case in point.[8] Almost without exception, the reports and information materials the NGOs develop cite the plight of individuals in the South but do not highlight the collective resistance struggles that Southern people's organizations are conducting, reserving visibility for the NGO. Fortunately other NGOs, both in the North and in the South, have dedicated years of effort to supporting the emergence of articulate popular organizations representing the disenfranchised and have built up a practice of meaningful partnership. But the inter-governmental system often does not recognize and reward them. It falls instead into the trap of privileging the 'brand name' of the most highly visible INGOs. Seeking to strengthen global civil society networking on food security in 2003, the European Union passed over the IPC mechanism which puts Southern people's organizations in the driver's seat and was legitimized by a global food sovereignty forum process involving hundreds of CSOs around the world. The EU grant was awarded, instead, to a coalition dominated by an already well-resourced INGO which is using the funding to build up its own network in the South on the basis of an agenda of food sovereignty 'borrowed' from Via Campesina and the IPC without citing the source. Decisions like these have political implications, and it is misleading to treat them as though it were simply a technical question of vetting project proposals.[9]

Resources, indeed, are an important and delicate issue where relations with civil society are concerned. The cross-system survey confirms the fact that the rhetoric of participation has not been followed up by a commensurate reattribution of resources, both to enhance UN capacity to engage with civil society and to cover costs on the civil society side. Indeed, reallocation of resources figures last on the list of parameters of change in the UN institutions resulting from interaction with civil society that participants in the cross-system survey were asked to rank.[10] While apparent recognition of the importance of partnering with civil society has increased enormously within the FAO over the past 10 years, in the same period the number of dedicated staff responsible for these relations has declined from five to one. Kofi Annan's relatively modest proposals for the implementation of the recommendations of the Panel of Eminent Persons were scuttled due to lack of resources. It is true that the UN in general is terribly and perpetually underresourced. But it is also true that some sectors are maintained or even increased, while others drop off the budget charts. It is equally true that efforts to raise extrabudgetary funds for various activities are carried out with greater or lesser intensity according to the priority attached to the activity in question by top management. These too are political choices, and UN family secretariats have a substantial share in the responsibility for making them.

This section, in fact, has been directed in the first instance to what UN secretariats can do to set the stage for meaningful engagement, because it is they – indeed – who do set the stage. But, of course, the main actors with which civil society actors need to enhance their political interaction are the governments. This is an area to which social movements and civil society actors advocating paradigmatic changes have not dedicated sufficient attention on an ongoing strategic basis, outside the highly orchestrated events of international conferences. The conclusions of an authoritative analysis of the results of the Hong Kong WTO ministerial conference point in this direction:

> Alliances among developing countries are vital and have been successful in changing the power dynamic in the negotiations, but these alliances may not be sufficient to change the nature of the current agreement or the existing trade model. Visionary leadership is needed to build a more just and sustainable trading system. Alternative approaches exist and are widely promoted by civil society groups and constituencies around the world. Convincing governments to adopt these approaches will require a more concerted effort at the national and regional level to build support for these alternatives and for a new international trading system (TIP/IATP 2006).

Government lobbying is an established practice in Europe and North America, although there is room for refinement. It is in the developing regions that most effort is required, and we will now turn to global–local links with this in mind.

Build the political process from the local to the global level

We have seen in Chapter 3 that one of the few points on which all parties agree is the imperative of strengthening engagement with civil society at the country level and linking upwards from there to global governance. But other arenas in the South, which tend to receive less attention in the UN world, are equally important. At the subregional level, economic organizations and markets are being established, regional policies are being adopted and bilateral trade agreements negotiated. At the continental level states adopt concerted political positions which could, in the best of circumstances, constitute a bulwark against the impact of liberalization and a platform for alternatives. It could well be argued – and many social movements do – that strategies for working toward democratic and equitable global governance should privilege advocacy and mobilization by Southern civil society to induce their governments to better defend the bulk of their citizens' interests in international negotiations. The example of the West African farmers' movement and its impact on regional policies and negotiations is indicative.

In the world of social movements, alternative practices of building horizontal links among local spaces and struggles are relatively well developed, as the regional and world social forums illustrate. Researchers in disciplines ranging from anthropology to geography and ecology have documented and analysed such geographies of resistance.[11] As we have seen in the concluding section of Chapter 2, there is also a rich literature on the topic of transnational civil society networks and their vertical interactions with international institutions.[12] The experience of bringing networked local resistance and alternatives to bear decisively on global forums in which 'hard' policies are decided, however, is far from conclusive. As one of the most attentive observers of these dynamics put it several years ago:

> Presently there is a political gap from the local to the global which is only partially being filled in by the stretch from local networks to planetary social movements, international NGOs or global civil society. This is not merely an institutional hiatus but as much a programmatic hiatus and a *hiatus of political imagination* (Pieterse 2000:199).[13]

The itineraries of the IPC, reviewed in Chapter 2, of Shack/Slum Dwellers International and its interface with UN-Habitat, or of the widely dispersed indigenous peoples coming together around the UN Permanent Forum on Indigenous Issues are significant examples of work-in-progress to span this hiatus.

If social movements can be faulted with a certain deficit of political imagination, what can we say about how the UN views the 'why' and the 'how' of the imperative to strengthen civil society outreach at the country level and to bridge the 'local–global gap'? The problem is partly one of developmental culture. Some areas of the UN system have not yet acknowledged the progressive demise of the North–South divide and the rearticulation of confrontation around models of development and visions of society that are not geographically circumscribed. There is a lag between recognition of the global nature of the problems the world faces, promoted by the thematic summits of the 1990s, and operational UN activities. The latter often continue to be conditioned by an ageing development paradigm based on North–South technology transfer which is increasingly being discredited as a winning recipe for addressing the gap between the 'haves' and the 'have-nots', but has the support of powerful economic interests. There is little space in such a paradigm for the knowledge and protagonism of local people and their organizations. The problem is political as well as cultural. As Higgott (2001:134–5) has pointed out, large parts of the UN system operate on the premise that civil society engagement ought to be directed at propagating good governance on an 'efficiency and effectiveness' track which avoids addressing the structural issues that generate poverty and injustice. For social movements and people's organizations, on the contrary, the aim of engagement with the UN is to open up political space to address precisely these issues. The neoliberal paradigm which conditions a good deal of development discourse also makes it difficult for the UN system to comprehend an important objective that is shared by the governments and the civil societies of many Southern countries and to take advantage of it as one basis for facilitating dialogue between the two actors. This common ground is the ambition to reconquer and defend the sovereignty that has been compromised by the colonial history of most of these countries and further drastically reduced by structural adjustment and globalization. UN–civil society engagement at national level is inevitably conditioned by these divergent visions of what is at stake.

What can the UN do to improve its performance in country-level engagement with civil society without undergoing an improbable major cultural revolution? A great deal. To start with, it can resolutely limit its role to the highly significant one of helping to set the stage for meaningful political process and refrain from meddling with the process itself. It is worthwhile recalling here the injunction of the UN civil society liaison staff cited above to 'be really careful that we do not clomp in like elephants onto the national level'. Both the FAO study and the cross-system survey document how little the UN knows about civil society and people's organizations at national level. Acting in ignorance is the first mistake to avoid. Another is that of perpetuating the situation documented in the system-wide survey cited above whereby UN cooperation with CSOs tends to imprison them in traditional operational roles. Finally, the UN system needs to meditate on the fact that its dominant partners at country level today are national NGOs (as information purveyors and service providers), community-based organizations (politically toothless generators of local social capital), and national NGO platforms (as an experienced UN informant put it, 'we go for the harmless umbrella organizations to appear participatory'[14]). Bottom of the basket in both the FAO study and the cross-system survey are structured people's organizations representing the disenfranchised at levels above that of the community. Yet, as we have noted, it is precisely these organizations whose engagement in national and regional political processes and development programmes should be facilitated.

The UN system interacts with CSOs at national and regional levels in three major ways. Involving CSOs in programme implementation is the most common form of partnership, and a frequent injunction to the UN from civil society is to go beyond it. This is not to suggest that there is not room for improvement in this area, much to the contrary. It is noteworthy, to cite just one example, that in post-Tsunami programmes even UN system staff who had been directly involved in the Cardoso Panel exercise did not think to look beyond the usual humanitarian INGOs and make contact with the well-publicized and successful efforts by artisanal fisherfolk and peasant farmer organizations themselves to channel support to local communities for self-determined relief and rehabilitation.[15]

Support for capacity building of Southern CSOs, a second form of collaboration, is a constant refrain at UN–civil society forums, yet it can be a poisoned apple. As a United Nations Research Institute for Social Development (UNRISD) study on rural social movements comments,

> Over the past decade, the development agenda has been fundamentally recast in terms of structural adjustment, liberalization, privatization, institutional development, decentralization, good governance and now poverty reduction with an accent on civil society actors. In this context, there is a general consensus within the development community regarding the necessity of building well-structured rural producer organizations ... Nudging this process along has become an object of great interest to development partners. Views of what form a structured farmers' movement should take and what functions it should perform, however, vary from donor to donor, and the development programmes they fund tend to become instruments whereby each donor promotes the implementation of its vision. At the same time, the political implications of a strong organization representing the interests of the rural population are not lost on governments. Donor conditionality intervenes to complicate positioning between the governments and farmers' movements (McKeon et al. 2004:51).

Strong movements are able to resist manipulation and enforce their own agendas; weak ones, who most need the reinforcing, are not. One corrective approach that some UN system programmes are applying is that of adopting a subregional perspective to capacity building, promoting horizontal exchanges between stronger and weaker people's organizations and supporting their own collective reflection on priority needs and how to meet them. IFAD and the FAO deserve credit for applying this approach on some occasions, giving the people's organizations the determining voice in deciding the content and the methodology of the training. It can be done.

Facilitating civil society participation in policy dialogue is the most important area of country-level collaboration and the one in which the

UN system has the greatest comparative advantage. It is also, however, the one in which it most needs to improve its performance. We have seen in Chapter 3 how, on the admission of UN staff themselves, the actual practice of stakeholder consultation is a ghostlike reflection of the rhetoric of participation. What needs to be done is known and much of it is by no means politically impossible. What is needed has to do with taking the trouble to understand the dynamics of civil society and social movements in a given country or subregion, identifying those organizations that objectively mobilize some portion of the disenfranchised, taking the time and budgeting the necessary resources to enable them to carry out their own processes of consultation with their bases to be fed into multistakeholder forums. Top on the list of what to avoid is pre-empting the political space that rightly belongs to national social organizations and filling it with surrogates such as advisory committees made up of individual civil society figures selected by the UN system. Vying for pole position on the list of 'worst practices' is the burgeoning promotion of public–private partnerships without due regard for their impact on access to resources and services by the poor and without facilitating their organizations' involvement in the negotiations.

Nevertheless, facilitation of civil society participation is not an unattainable utopia. To cite just two examples, in Africa IFAD and the FAO, joined at a later stage by the United Nations Economic Commission for Africa (ECA), have teamed up to support the four regional farmers' networks develop their input to the agriculture component of NEPAD (New Partnership for Africa's Development) and to undertake their own autonomous assessment of the impact of the European Union–Africa Caribbean Pacific (EU–ACP) Economic Partnership Agreements (EPAs) on small farmers. The resulting networking and capacity building enabled the four regional organizations to come together in Addis Ababa in May 2008 and form an autonomous Pan African Farmers' Platform, which will interface with the African Union in defence of rural people's interests. In South America, IFAD has backed the creation of a platform of family farm organizations of the Common Market of the South (Mercosur) region to advocate both public policies favourable to family agriculture and agrarian reform and has helped the platform obtain official recognition as an interlocutor by the Mercosur Common Market Group.

In short, the UN system should be applying at national and regional levels the same principles we have evoked regarding global interface with civil society: respect the organizations and the processes of people's movements; support their own capacity-building initiatives; system-atically facilitate space for them in national and regional policy dialogues and negotiations, and ensure that they have timely access to strategic documentation; refrain from influencing how they use the space, leaving it up to people's organizations and governments to engage directly; require people's organizations to report on their progress in fulfilling their own self-defined objectives of inclusiveness and transparency. It will not be possible to shift gear simultaneously around the globe, but that is no reason not to start where it is possible. It can be done and it is being done.

Issues for Further Investigation

The pages above have sparked as many questions as they may have answered, or at least illuminated. The most important of these can be grouped into three interlinked areas meriting further investigation. There is no pretence here of identifying totally new research topics; rather our aim is to help map out territory that has already been delimitated by other writers and activists.

The first of these areas has to do with how the UN system can best articulate its interface with civil society in order to encourage the emergence of forms of global governance that extend political process beyond nation-states and strengthen the system's capacity to defend the values on which it is founded. The hypothesis advanced here is that a blueprint for such expansion cannot be designed abstractly and simplistically. Certainly not in the form of a world people's assembly which could risk violating the very logic of how civil society operates and undermining the legitimacy on which its contribution to global governance is based. It is suggested here that appropriate forms for expanded global governance can best emerge from multiple experiences of engagement, starting at the national level and building upwards, which respect a certain number of principles and meaningfully include social actors with which the UN now has far too little commerce. This position is advanced on the strength of extensive direct experience and some cross-system comparison, documented in this study. Further investigation is warranted, since this is a key issue for the future prospects of locally rooted governance of UN-civil society relations.[16] It is also a matter of urgency since the plans for UN reform currently under discussion point toward a stronger role for the UN Resident Coordinator system which, generally speaking, has not distinguished itself by the political sensitivity of the approaches to civil society outreach it has adopted. UN civil society offices are seeking to improve such outreach and assign it greater priority, and their efforts merit high-level support.

Undertaking research of this kind will require more extensive comparative analysis of existing experience. Virtuous and less virtuous instances of interface at all levels need to be collected and compared. More work is also required on how, and with what success, people's organizations and global networks in which they play a leading role – like the IPC or Shack/Slum Dwellers International – actually conduct the essential task of extended consultation with local groups and the figuring upwards of their experiences and proposals. What kinds of alliances with NGOs playing what kinds of roles are most effective in this regard? Our theoretical understanding of the dynamics involved in the encounter between social activism in the North and the South also needs to be improved by carrying out the kind of further comparative research 'going beyond the traditional Northern constituency of social movement that is familiar to Northern movement scholars', for which Donatella della Porta called in an UNRISD study (della Porta 2005:28).[17] The relatively recent body of studies making a link between social movement themes and analysis of Southern rural people's organizations and change processes are an important resource in this connection.[18]

The second research area is situated on the terrain of institutional change and focuses on the differential impact of civil society engagement on UN system entities over the past 15 years. This area is very closely related to the first, since the thesis advanced in this study is that civil society interface that makes space for political process is a powerful instrument for institutional change in the UN system. Some insights on the question of UN institutional change and civil society engagement exist in the literature, but there is nothing that even remotely approaches a systematic and systemic assessment. Over a decade ago, Gordenker and Weiss speculated about how the quality and characteristics of particular UN institutions can help or hinder the development of effective partnerships and noted that 'too few resources have been devoted to analysing the composition and behaviour of international secretariats' (Weiss and Gordenker 1996:220). In the same volume – the earliest authoritative survey of NGOs, the UN and global governance – Ken Conca (1996:115) noted the temptation of environmental NGOs to shift their attention to the new, more permeable and multidisciplinary Commission on Sustainable Development, and pointed to the danger that this could draw resources away from the specialized agencies, arguably more able to constitute an alternative forum to the WTO. More recently, Keck and Sikkink (1998:202) have noted that 'institutional openness to leverage varies significantly across issue areas within a single institution', a phenomenon to which the FAO case study also attests. Pianta (2005:28) hypothesizes that 'opportunity could come forward in fields where an institutional architecture at the global level is still emerging – as in the cases of the environment or the International Criminal Court – and where intergovernmental organizations and CSOs have long cooperated'. O'Brien et al. (2000: 214), in their excellent comparative study of the multilateral economic institutions (MEIs), advance the concept of 'complex multilateralism' to describe the movement of these organizations from an exclusively state-based structure, and identify four transformation variables: subject-area culture, structure, role of executive head, and vulnerability to social movement action. The *Whose World Is It Anyway?* review of civil society, the UN and the multilateral future (Foster and Anand 1999) and, above all, the rich and varied offerings of the UN-NGLS provide a wealth of material on institutional change within the UN system that has not been sufficiently exploited.

This study has contributed some additional elements. The evidence we have assembled underscores the variegated nature of different parts of the UN system and points to some of the important variables, including institutional differences of mission, governance and structure. The longitudinal FAO case study sheds further light on the issue by tracing changes over time in a single agency relative to a certain number of significant factors. These include the political and the paradigmatic context in which a particular UN organization operates at a given moment; the political awareness and commitment of senior management and the astuteness of the staff directly responsible for civil society relations; the strength and the quality of civil society networking on themes with which the organization deals; the strategic importance of the agency for hegemonic political and economic interests. The cross-system survey and the discussion of UN reform in Chapter 3 reiterate the need to extend this investigation and to undertake a serious systemic analysis of institutional change within the UN family.

While social movement scholars have made efforts to categorize civil society campaigns and networks according to differences in how they approach international organizations (Pianta 2005; Sikkink 2003), most often using political opportunity concepts, very little systematic attention has been devoted to understanding what variables explain the differences in how these approaches are received. Much of the discussion about closed and open structures at the international level tends to make the mega-distinction between the UN and the IFIs and to stop there.[19] Plucking examples from individual agencies to compose a nosegay of 'best practices' may be heartening, but it is insufficient. The fact that the Joint UN Programme on HIV/AIDS (UNAIDS) has found it possible to include representatives of the 'direct beneficiaries' in its governing board is unlikely to have an impact on how the World Bank runs its shop. Winning greater access to the UN itself is close to irrelevant if the doors remain closed at the WTO and if the UN's capacity to address hard economic issues remains marginal. As we have seen in this study, there are significant differences among UN family components in the ways in which they react to demands on the part of CSOs to engage in political process, as is illustrated by the history of Via Campesina's differentiated interactions with the World Food Summit:*five years later* and the World Summit on Sustainable Development. A systemic assessment of institutional change should home in on these differences. In doing so, it should shed more light on the secretariats' margins for manoeuvre in their relations with member governments and devote some attention to the hitherto little-studied civil society liaison officers and offices,[20] and to the phenomenon of networking among them.

The third area, also closely related to the others, is a standard one in the literature on social movements and change which takes on a special dimension at global level. It is the question, posed at the outset of this study, of the impact of civil society–UN engagement in terms of evolutions in development discourse.[21] What we are interested in here is not only how successful civil society has been in getting new topics on the agenda, a well-documented phenomenon (see, for example, Keck and Sikkink 1998; Joachim 2007), but what impact they have had on the paradigms that underlie global agendas and condition their implementation. The world of civil society is generally recognized as a major locus of production of concepts and visions tending toward the advancement of the values on which the UN rests. A better understanding of the dynamics at play is hence of general interest in the context of improving the quality of global governance.

The respondents in the cross-system survey presented in Chapter 3 gave relatively high marks to CSO impact on development discourse but did not cite specific examples. The FAO case study provides more in-depth analyses of three conceptual or paradigmatic efforts: the right to food, an agro-ecological model of agriculture, and food sovereignty.

It examines some of the complex interaction that takes place among the multiple levels involved in paradigmatic change. These include inter-relations between civil society analytical elaboration and social process and practice, between local and global arenas, between technical and political dimensions of paradigm development, and between social movements' capacity to undertake autonomous formulation of alternatives in their own spaces and their success in bringing the results to bear on international institutions and dominant discourse.

More work is needed on what is required to reach the point where 'what was once unthinkable becomes obvious' (Keck and Sikkink 1998:211).[22] As Kathryn Sikkink states the case,

> we do not know exactly what makes particular norms attractive at particular historical moments. But such methodological and theoretical difficulties should not dissuade scholars from examining these issues, for without attention to global norm structures and power structures, we will not understand the contours of the current global order or the possibilities for systems change (Khagram et al. 2002:306).

The questions are legion and intriguing. What factors have intervened in those cases in which CSOs have had the greatest success?[23] What relations could potentially be built between campaigns like those on land mines, debt and the Multilateral Agreement on Investment (MAI), which seem to work best when they focus on specific targets, and the broader and deeper structural and conceptual transformations that are required to dethrone the neoliberal paradigm? What makes the difference between paradigmatic change which alters the way reality is conceived and institutions operate, on the one hand, and the kind of co-optation described by Higgott in the case of the post-Washington consensus, on the other? Is it conceivable that the easier-to-influence 'soft' issues, such as human rights, can be used as entry points for 'hard' economic and structural paradigmatic change, for example, by gradually working toward the recognition and subsequent judicialization of the right to food and to food sovereignty?[24] Is there something in our very understanding of human nature that deflects into self-replicating spirals our efforts to change society and institutions? How are we to ensure that the production of alternative concepts and visions does not, itself, become entrapped in the logic of competition and efficiency it purports to oppose? The risk that outside actors may more or less unwittingly alter the balance of power among different sectors of civil society and in their relations with governments is a real one which has been flagged on several occasions in this study. How are we to ensure that international and bilateral support for policy engagement actually empowers the organizations of the poor?[25] Autonomous civil society experiments, such as the IPC and Shack/Slum Dwellers International, in which NGOs share their technical and analytical capacity with people's organizations while the latter make the political decisions about what to advocate, take on all their significance in this context.

Investigation in the three interrelated areas outlined above will require methodological innovation in order to find ways of involving social activists in the design and conducting of research along with academics from various disciplines, concerned UN practitioners and government officials. What is at stake is not only cognitive correctness – the example of the misreading of the United Nations Convention to Combat Desertification (UNCCD) experience cited above is illustrative. Even more important is the participation of social actors in the negotiation of meanings, a practice that cannot be dissociated from the effort to build more equitable and inclusive global governance, which is the object of this study.[26]

Notes

1 Setting the Stage

1   Undertaken in the context of a United Nations Research Institute for Social Development (UNRISD) research programme on 'UN World Summits and Civil Society Engagement', this study complements an overall analysis from the viewpoint of civil society (Pianta 2005) and six national case studies with a focus on civil society dynamics carried out in countries in which UN summits and preparatory committee meetings were held.

2   Moreover, the author's first-hand experience of managing this FAO–civil society interface provides an authoritative basis for filling this gap in the literature.

3   And by the two schools reflecting together, as in Khagram et al. (2002).

4   An enduring classic is Keck and Sikkink (1998). For a recent consideration of networks in global social movements, see Marchetti and Pianta (2007).

5   The literature on NGOs and civil society, their interactions with states and their role on the global scene is dauntingly vast. Uncensored testimony on how this universe is perceived from within the UN – outside of official papers and reports – is less rich. See Donini (1996), McKeon (1989, 2004), UN-NGLS (1996, 2003a), Hill (2004).

6   *Charter of the United Nations, Preamble* (see www.un.org/aboutun/charter).

7   On the history of the UN, see Goodrich et al. (1969), Meiler (1995) and Kennedy (2006).

8   The work of the Commission on Global Governance was funded by the UNDP, nine governments and several foundations.

9   See also Childers, with Urquhart (1994:1) for the results of a painstaking reflection undertaken by people familiar with the workings of the existing system and calling for reforms that would not require extensive constitutional change.

10   The commission came down strongly in favour of a continued and strengthened leadership role for the UN, and advanced proposals for a major restructuring of the UN to help bring this about, including a new Economic Security Council with authority over the Bretton Woods institutions and the WTO, restructuring of the existing Security Council and elimination of veto power, establishment of international taxation, an International Court of Justice, a Trusteeship Council to protect the environment and an 'Assembly of the People' to represent civil society. Although some of the commission's proposals have been implemented and others continue to be discussed, its overall vision did not gain approval.

11 International governance has been defined as '… the output of a non–hierarchical network of interlocking international (mostly, but not exclusively governmental) institutions which regulate the behavior of states and other international actors in difference issue areas of world politics' (Rittberger 2001:2).

12 Studies reflecting on global governance with particular attention to the role of civil society include Smith et al. (1997), Archibugi et al. (1998), Holden (2000), Edwards and Gaventa (2001), Scholte (2002; and forthcoming), Clark (2003), Van Rooy (2004), Held and Koenig-Archibugi (2005), Mayo (2005), Falk (2005), Karagiannis and Wagner (2007), and Archibugi (2008).

13 This was the campaign against the Multilateral Agreement on Investment (MAI), which industrialized countries attempted to negotiate in the Organisation for Economic Co-operation and Development (OECD). See Keck and Sikkink (1998).

14 See the reports of two interesting workshops organized by the UN–NGLS in 2003, one grouping the liaison offices of the UN system and international organizations and the other spokespersons from a number of international civil society networks that interact with the UN (UN-NGLS 2003a, 2003b).

15 The literature on the evolution of relations between the UN and civil society organizations (CSOs) is extensive. See Charnovitz (1997), Krut (1997), Foster and Anand (1999), Kaldor (2003), Hill (2004), Friedman et al. (2005), MIF (2005), Falk (2005) and Smith (2008).

16 In Article 71 of the United Nations Charter, the result of determined lobbying by a group of US and international NGOs. The former UN Under-Secretary-General for Economic and Social Affairs, Nitin Desai, holds that the designation of ECOSOC as the only UN organ that allowed for consultation with NGOs was 'simply a spill over from the experience of the pre-Second World War League of Nations with social and humanitarian work in which NGOs had played an important role' (Falk 2005:156).

17 This relation was termed 'praxis' in the language of the time, and popularized in the 'conscientization' work of the school of Paolo Freire.

18 See Foster and Anand (1999) for a detailed, careful and well-documented account of the interaction toward the end of the summit cycle, and Pianta (2005).

19 Pat Mooney (Executive Director of ETC Group at the time of writing), a long-time participant in UN–civil society interaction, has termed this phenomenon of co-optation the 'Stockholm syndrome' referring to a case in 1972, at the time of the Stockholm Conference on the Human Environment, in which hostages grabbed by a gang of bank robbers bonded to their captors to the point where two of the victims were eventually betrothed to their bandit heroes.

20 A vivid memory of mine, dating some 20 years back, is of returning to the capital of Sierra Leone following a stay in the countryside that had been rhythmed after dusk by the drums of secret society initiations, to find the hotel dining room off limits to guests since it was reserved for the confabulations of the tuxedo-clad, power-exuding members of the Freetown chapter of an international service organization.

21 See p. 152 for a discussion of this categorization.

22 See Higgott (2001). Kaldor (2003) presents a clear and succinct discussion of the development of the term 'civil society' and the breakdown of its composition.

23 See, for example, Walzer (1995); Kaldor (2003); Keane (2003); Wild (2006). See also the yearbook *Global Civil Society*, published annually by the Centre

for the Study of Global Governance and Centre for Civil Society of the London School of Economics and Political Science (Anheier et al. 2001).

24 It is a misapprehension that a UN–NGLS publication on decision-making processes in the United Nations helps to unmask. See UN-NGLS, with Gretchen Sidhu (2003) and also Smith (2006).

25 Many of the most important summits had secretariats housed in the UN Department of Economic and Social Affairs, which is not responsible for operational follow-up on summit results.

2 The FAO, Civil Society and the Global Governance of Food and Agriculture

1 Not only in the colonies but also in the rich countries themselves.

2 Speech by Stanley Bruce to the General Assembly of the League of Nations, 11 September 1935 (cited in Cépède 1984:283).

3 And of rich consumer states like Britain, who depended on low-cost food imports from the United States. See Weiss and Jordan (1976), cited in Fouilleux (2008).

4 It is worth noting that the founding members of the FAO also rejected a proposal for a tripartite structure, along the lines of the International Labour Organization (ILO), involving producers and consumers in the decision-making process along with governments. See Marchisio and Di Blasé (1991:12).

5 The functions of the World Food Board were to stabilize world agricultural prices, manage an international cereal reserve, direct surpluses to needy countries on concessionary terms, and cooperate with the organizations responsible for agricultural development loans and international trade policy. 'Food is more than a commodity', Boyd Orr declared, anticipating contemporary civil society advocacy by half a century, observing that 'a world food policy based on human needs' was therefore required.

6 Following his resignation, Boyd Orr dedicated himself to building a movement of public opinion and lobbying on food issues.

7 Close to half of the participants at both congresses came from developing countries. The Second World Food Conference (WFC) was enlivened by a Youth Conference held just prior to the official meeting and a parallel New Earth Village where the younger participants camped.

8 The First WFC was preceded by the drafting of a Proclamation on the Right to be Free from Hunger signed by some 50 eminent persons, including 18 Nobel Prize laureates. President Kennedy made the inaugural speech at the congress.

9 The Union of Soviet Socialist Republics (USSR) had opted not to become a member of the FAO, and this absence impacted on the form and content of the debate in its governing bodies.

10 Proponents of protective isolation included the past Director-General of the FAO, B.R. Sen, and the incumbent at that time, A. Boerma. The Independent Chairman of the FAO Council at the time, Gonzalo Bula Hoyos of Colombia, like others, was more concerned by 'the danger that FAO may find itself isolated, reduced to impotence, immured in its ivory tower like a cold technical relic' (FAO 1975).

11 The Canadian NGO delegation was particularly successful in breaking out of this isolation, for reasons analysed in Van Rooy (1997).

12 The WFC gave birth to an institution that is still a strong player in the food and agriculture world today, the International Fund for Agricultural Development (IFAD). Another offspring, the more policy-oriented World Food Council, hosted by the FAO but reporting to the UN General Assembly, was abolished in 1993.

13 The United Nations Development Programme (UNDP) came to learn from the Freedom from Hunger Campaign/Action for Development (FFHC/AD) in the late 1980s when it decided to open up an NGO/CSO programme.

14 This networking led on several occasions to the creation of autonomous regional networks, such as the Asociación Latinoamericana de Organizaciones de Promoción (ALOP/Latin American Association of Development Organizations) and the Asian Cultural Forum for Development (ACFOD).

15 Such as funding to carry out action-oriented research on emerging issues, training for activists, exchange of experience.

16 The FAO, through the FFHC, and UNICEF were the founding members of the United Nations Non-Governmental Liaison Service (UN-NGLS) in 1975, as the only two UN bodies seriously concerned with development education, as distinct from public information work, at that time.

17 The dialogue included, for example, an in-depth analysis by European and African NGOs of the image of Africa projected by media – and many NGOs – during the drought of the mid-1980s and the negative impact of emergency assistance on emerging rural people's associations and strategies. See McKeon (1988).

18 Such as agro-ecological approaches to production in Latin America, participatory models of support to peasant associations in drought-prone areas of Africa, community-based retrieval and multiplication of local varieties of food crops in South Asia.

19 NGOs were the most enthusiastic consumers of the 'Peasants' Charter' adopted by the conference. International NGOs (INGOs) in formal status with the FAO were so disturbed by the lack of opportunity given to them to intervene in a forum that was of such interest to them that, at the suggestion of the International Federation of Agricultural Producers (IFAP), they took the initiative of forming an 'Ad Hoc Group of INGO Representatives to FAO Residing in Rome' in order to build more constant and effective interaction with the secretariat.

20 *Ecologist*, Vol. 21 (2).

21 In Saoma's case the commitment was to the World Food Day celebrations instituted by the FAO Conference at his initiative.

22 Saoma distanced himself from this distaste years later when, addressing the 2004 World Food Day ceremony at FAO headquarters, he denounced political and economic interests pursued without moral values and suggested that civil society is the basis of the legitimacy of international organizations.

23 That management accepted it in the end had a good deal to do with the fact that NGO donors were willing to channel some $5 million through the FFHC programme, including $1 million from Bob Geldof's highly publicized Band Aid initiative.

24 Particularly the International Agricultural Trade Research Consortium (IATRC) established in 1980. See Coleman (2001).

25 The World Bank organized an international meeting on the issue of hunger in Washington in late 1993, while IFAD had teamed up with the Liaison Committee of Development NGOs to the European Union to plan a conference on hunger and poverty in Brussels in November 1995 with strong civil society participation.

26   Input was sought from the Coordinator of UN-NGLS, which was playing an important role in facilitating the NGO outreach efforts of the other UN conferences.

27   In the longer run, however, this procedure turned out to have its advantages, since the precedents established in the World Food Summit process weighed directly on mainstream governance practice.

28   Statutes, membership and members of executive committee, and so on.

29   The Italian development NGO federations involved were Coordinamento delle Organizzazioni non Governative per la Cooperazione Internazionale allo Sviluppo (COCIS/Network of NGOs for International Development Cooperation), Coordinamento di Iniziative Popolari di Solidarietà Internazionale (CIPSI/Network of Popular Initiatives for International Solidarity) and Federazione Organismi Cristiani Servizio Internazionale Volontario (FOCSIV/Federation of Christian Organisms of International Voluntary Service). A key figure in this process was Antonio Onorati, president of the NGO Centro Internazionale Crocevia, which had long-standing partnership relations with peasant and indigenous people's organizations as well as NGOs in the South, and a strong record of interaction with the FAO in the field of biodiversity.

30   CLONG's food security working group, coordinated by Clive Robinson of Christian Aid, had developed close interaction with the FAO as the concept of food security took shape in the first half of the 1990s.

31   The Italian component was broadened into a committee grouping not only development NGOs but also trade unions, farmers' organizations, and environmental and social associations.

32   They were Daniel Van Der Steen for the Liaison Committee of Development NGOs to the European Union, Antonio Onorati for the Italian Committee for the NGO Forum on Food Security, Filipo Cortesi for the Ad Hoc Group of INGOs in formal status with the FAO, Joanna Koch for the Geneva Working Group on Nutrition (a network of INGOs in formal UN status that had been involved in organizing the International Conference on Nutrition), and Gary Sealy for the Global Network on Food Security.

33   Eko-Liburnia from Croatia; International Collective in Support of Fishworkers, Indigenous People's International Centre for Policy Research and Education; Fédération des ONG du Sénégal (FONGS – a national peasant farmer federation from Senegal); Assessoria e Serviços a Projetos em Agricultura Alternativa (AS-PTA/Advisory Services for Alternative Agricultural Projects – a Brazilian NGO); Innovations et Réseaux pour le Développement (IRED/Development Innovations and Networks – an NGO network in Eastern/Southern Africa); Asian NGO Coalition (ANGOC); Land Research Committee (Palestine); and Via Campesina.

34   The steering committee members were Antonio Onorati, Victoria Corpus of the Indigenous People's International Centre for Policy Research and Education, Jan Marc Von der Weid of the Brazilian NGO AS-PTA, Ranko Tadic of Croatian NGO Eko-Liburnia, and Daniel Van Der Steen. Rafael Alegria, coordinator of Via Campesina, was also nominated to the group but was unable to attend the International Support Committee (ISC) meeting at which the composition was ratified. The term 'political body' is quoted from the final report of the Forum (Italian Committee for the NGO Forum on Food Security 1997:30).

35   This tension was one that affected the entire UN system. It came to a climax during the ECOSOC review of procedures for granting accreditation to NGOs carried out between 1993 and 1996, when some INGOs in formal

status actually opposed the extension of accreditation to national NGOs.

36   Private sector associations did, of course, participate as observers in the official summit.

37   For reasons which are made clear below.

38   The civil society dynamics around the WFS process add some dimensions to those discussed in Friedman et al.'s (2005) survey of state–society relations at UN world conferences, which records North–South differences and NGO autonomy from states as the only issues on which civil society frames were 'unaligned'.

39   On the grounds of violation of the territorial rights of the indigenous peoples who inhabited the tropical forests and of damage to the environment and the global climate.

40   Major FAO-promoted forums in which such interaction had taken place included the negotiations on plant genetic resources leading to the establishment of the International Commission for Plant Genetic Resources in 1983 and the adoption of the Global Plan of Action for the Conservation and Utilization of Plant Genetic Resources in 1996 (the Rural Advancement Foundation International/RAFI – now the Action Group on Erosion, Technology and Concentration/ETC Group – and GRAIN were the major international networks operating in this area); the formulation of the Code of Conduct for Responsible Fisheries adopted by the FAO Conference in 1995 (the Madras-based International Collective in Support of Fishworkers was a major player, along with trade unions and environmental NGOs such as Greenpeace and the World Wide Fund For Nature/WWF); the work of the Codex Alimentarius (Pesticides Action Network and Consumers International – International Consumers Union at that time – were active participants); the FAO-sponsored meetings leading up to the UN Conference on Environment and Development (UNCED) in which the concept of Sustainable Agriculture and Rural Development (SARD), later enshrined in Chapter 14 of Agenda 21, had been developed; and the controversial discussions surrounding the Tropical Forestry Action Plan in FAO's Committee on Forestry (NGOs such as Third World First and the Rainforest Network).

41   These are the Committee on Agriculture, the Committee on World Food Security, the Committee on Fisheries, the Committee on Forestry, and the Committee on Commodity Problems. The Commission on Plant Genetic Resources and Codex Alimentarius, which have secretariats housed in the FAO but are independent bodies, are two other important global food and agriculture policy forums.

42   In 1992, at the instigation of the ex-FFHC unit then housed in the Office of External Affairs, the FAO broke new ground by providing technical assistance to a national farmers' federation in Senegal to understand the language and the implications of agricultural structural adjustment and build its own lobbying capacity.

43   With a grant of 500 million lire, approximately $329,000 at the time. In-kind support to the NGO Forum was provided by the municipality and the Province of Rome and the region of Lazio, and through the voluntary services of many NGOs and individuals.

44   The main items of expense were rental of premises, the secretariat and travel of participants from developing countries.

45   A total of some $800,000 was contributed by the governments of Canada, Denmark, the Netherlands, Norway and Sweden, the European Commission (EC), the World Bank, and the Kellogg and Jennifer Altman Foundations.

The main items of expenditure were the costs of organizing the regional and global NGO consultations and travel of NGO observers from the South to attend the WFS itself. Participants travelling both to the WFS and to the NGO Forum benefited from price reductions on air tickets negotiated by the FAO.

46   The FAO field offices were asked to suggest NGOs to be invited and to receive travel support, as were the NGO Forum organizers.

47   The meetings were from 20 to 21 May, 6 to 7 June and 29 July to 2 August.

48   Collected in three volumes and published by the FAO (1996a), the papers covered topics such as 'Lessons from the green revolution: Towards a new green revolution', 'Socio-political and economic environment for food security', 'Investment in agriculture: Evolution and prospects', 'Food and international trade', 'Assessment of feasible progress in food security', and represented a major investment of secretariat time and effort.

49   The Asian and Pacific consultation was co-organized by the Asian NGO Coalition for Agrarian Reform and Rural Development (ANGOC). A host of networks involved in Forum preparations participated in the Latin American and Caribbean meeting. For the African meeting the WFS Secretariat called for assistance on the FAO's NGO unit, which was able to involve the major NGO networks of the region and the nascent Platform of Peasant Organizations of the Sahel. The Near East consultation suffered from the generally low level of development of the NGO sector in the region, with only eight countries represented.

50   One hundred and thirty-five of these representatives were from developing countries.

51   A paper consolidating the proposed changes and additions to the draft summit documents produced by the working groups was also made available informally to the government delegates in English only, but it was definitely a secondary product.

52   *The [Bread] Bracket* was an independent newsletter of CSOs at the World Food Summit 1996.

53   These initiatives included the First Latin American and Caribbean Conference on Food Security in Managua, Nicaragua (October 1995), a Southeast Asian NGO Conference on Trade and Food Security in the Philippines (February 1996), the Conference on Food Security and Sustainable Agriculture organized by the Association of Protestant Development Organizations in Europe (APRODEV) in Denmark (March 1996), and a North American Workshop on Global Food Security (March 1996).

54   These 'constituencies' were defined as cooperatives, family farmers, consumers, indigenous peoples, trade unions, women, religious organizations, sustainable agriculture, academia and science, food assistance, and the Ad Hoc Group of INGO representatives residing in Rome.

55   The choice of these delegates had been made by the ISC. Despite the efforts made by the organizers, the representation of indigenous people's organizations was not as numerous as had been hoped.

56   The forum secretariat in Rome, directed by Antonio Onorati, put together the first ever comprehensive mailing list of CSOs that dealt with some aspect of the food and agriculture agenda, a total of 8,200 in all. Of these, some 2,500 demonstrated interest in attending the forum and were invited. The delegates whose travel costs and living expenses were covered were selected on the basis of balance by region and type of organization.

57   Coordinated by Clive Robinson of Christian Aid (UK), the drafting committee included ANGOC (Asia), FONGS (Africa), EKO-Liburnia (East

and Central Europe), the World Sustainable Agriculture Association (WSAA – North America), the Comité de Liaison des ONG/CLONG (Western Europe), and AS-PTA (Latin America). It took as its base the declaration of the September 1996 NGO consultation and worked under the steering committee's instruction to 'imagine a world with values, criteria and priorities other than those dictated by the market and its rules', foreshadowing the World Social Forum slogan 'Another World is Possible'.

58   The report also contains the text of the final statement.

59   The Forum had originally designated an African peasant organization to present its statement but it was unable to do so. The selection of the Latin American woman had the interesting effect of obliging the WFS secretariat to instantly accredit Via Campesina in order to allow her to enter FAO headquarters, despite the fact that the organization did not fulfil the requirements since it did not have statutes and a 'legal personality'. This precedent has since been used to extend FAO invitations to global forums to other informal networks.

60   Particularly *Vivre Autrement Rome 96*, produced in French by Environmental Development Action (ENDA).

61   Exceptions included members of the delegations of Argentina, Canada, Cuba, France, Great Britain, India, Italy, Japan, the Netherlands, Palestine, Senegal, Tunisia and the United States.

62   One was a jointly organized workshop presenting the experience of an innovative programme of FAO technical assistance to the peasant farmers' movement in Senegal to build their analytical capacity regarding agricultural policy and international trade. Another was a workshop on the Food for All Campaign foreseen in Commitment Seven of the WFS Plan of Action, organized by the Global Network on Food Security and other NGOs with the participation of the FAO unit responsible for promoting the campaign. The third was the input of the FAO division responsible for commodity and trade issues, which responded to an invitation from the forum organizers by sending a strong delegation of technical staff headed by the division director himself to take part in the day-long series of workshops on trade on 15 November.

63   The units involved were the NGO cooperation unit and the technical unit responsible for rural institutions.

64   They were organized by groups ranging from advocacy NGOs, including the Institute for Agriculture and Trade Policy (IATP) and Collectif Stratégies Alimentaires (CSA), and development NGOs such as Danchurchaid, to farmers' organizations, such as Coordination Paysanne Européenne, teaming up with the Kenyan National Farmers' Union.

65   On the relationship between officially recognized international norms and collective beliefs held by transnational movements, see Khagram et al. (2002).

66   The Brazilian Institute of Social and Economic Analyses (IBASE – Brazil) and Asociación Nacional de Empresas Comercializadoras de Productores del Campo (ANEC/National Association of Rural Producers – Mexico) from Latin America; International Agriculture, Peasant and Modernization Network (APM – Cameroon) from Africa; EWB (Germany), Crocevia (Italy), Réseau d'ONG Européennes sur l'Agro-alimentaire, le Commerce, l'Environnement et le Développement (RONGEAD/European Network on Agriculture, Food and Development – France) and Fondation Charles Leopold Mayer pour le Progrès de l'Homme (FPH/Foundation Charles Leopold Mayer for the Progress of Humankind – France) from Western Europe; IATP from the United States; and the Network for Safe and Secure

Food and the Environment (NESSFE – Japan) from Asia. The only people's organization involved in the original drafting group was ANEC.

67   The World Food Summit adopted a Rome Declaration on World Food Security and a Plan of Action articulated into seven commitments covering: (1) the political, social and economic environment; (2) policies aimed at eradicating poverty and improving access to food; (3) food, agriculture, fisheries, forestry and rural development policies and practices; (4) food, agricultural trade and overall trade policies; (5) natural disasters and man-made emergencies; (6) public and private investments; and (7) monitoring and follow-up. See FAO (1996b).

68   The US team was the only delegation that held that the human right to food 'is a goal or aspiration to be realized progressively but does not give rise to any international obligations', as reported in PANUPS (1996).

69   Now the ETC Group (Action Group on Erosion, Technology and Concentration).

70   *What to Do after the Tents Come Down. A Way Forward!*, 9 November 1996 (unpublished three-page document circulated among participants at the NGO Forum). A similar proposal was advanced in civil society circles in the context of the 2008 global food crisis.

71   *Towards a Global Forum on Food Security* (unpublished eight-page document circulated among participants at the NGO Forum).

72   Antonio Onorati for Crocevia, NGO Forum Report (see Italian Committee for the NGO Forum on Food Security 1997:69).

73   See FAO 1996b, Objective 7.1 (c).

74   The Committee on World Food Security was entrusted with responsibility for monitoring follow-up of the Plan of Action.

75   It was specified that this arrangement did not create a precedent for any other meeting of the CFS or other FAO governing bodies.

76   The NGO/CSO unit had had to protest vigorously against an early version of the secretariat paper which foresaw government involvement in the selection of civil society spokespersons as one option to be considered by the committee. This incident illustrates the power of UN secretariats to influence the ways in which debate is framed and decisions are taken.

77   Commitments One, Two, Five and parts of Seven.

78   Commitments Three, Four, Six and the relevant parts of Seven. The logic behind this separate clustering was precisely what CSOs were opposing when they championed 'people-centred development'.

79   The entire operation was undertaken by three 'Freedom from Hunger Campaign (FFHC) survivors', relatively powerless in a hierarchical sense, who received very little backing from their superiors and were armed only with their extensive relations with the civil society world, their capacity to manoeuvre within the institution, and their dedication to the cause.

80   These exercises documented and drew lessons from positive and negative past experience, described benefits of, and hindrances to, closer relations, identified key areas in which improved cooperation would make the most difference and the kinds of civil society partners with which the FAO should be working, and pointed to policy issues that needed to be addressed at a corporative level.

81   The convenor of the food security working group of the Liaison Committee of Development NGOs to the European Union, Clive Robinson of Christian Aid (see Robinson 1996).

82   Italics in original.

83   The rest of this chapter will focus on a specific self-organized civil society interface mechanism that emerged from the networking that took place

initially at the WFS and subsequently at the WFS:*five years later*: the International CSO Planning Committee for Food Sovereignty (IPC). This focus is due to two innovative characteristics of the IPC. First, it is a rare case of a global civil society network in which people's organizations from the South play the dominant role in the functioning and decision-making processes. Second, it has created a platform for broadening the analysis and magnifying the impact of organizations with a range of technical expertise related to food and agriculture systems which had previously been interacting with the FAO in a sectoral fashion. This special focus is in no way intended to diminish the value of other dimensions of NGO–FAO interaction during the period that have not been directly related to the IPC dynamic.

84   This cobbling-together was undertaken in a committee of the UN General Assembly from which CSOs were excluded. See p. 158.

85   The observers 'would be encouraged to form caucuses and to designate ten representatives to sit as observers at the plenary meetings ... Each ... would be allowed to make an oral statement of no more than 4 minutes duration to the plenary meeting.' To be fair, it should be noted that even heads of state of government were allocated only seven minutes, due to the cramped schedule of a summit inserted into the agenda of a normal biennial FAO Conference.

86   The roundtable discussions proposal was inspired by experience at the UN Millennium Summit, where civil society organizations had played no role, given the restrictive rules governing NGO participation in UN General Assembly sessions.

87   In the end, as the atmosphere cooled down, the Italian government agreed to the summit taking place in Rome, but the postponement was maintained.

88   The person in question was Henri Carsalade, director of the French Agricultural Research Centre for International Development (CIRAD/ Centre de Coopération Internationale en Recherche Agronomique pour le Développement) before coming to the FAO in 1995 at the invitation of the Director-General, initially to head the newly established Sustainable Development Department.

89   The Network of Farmers' and Agricultural Producers' Organizations of West Africa (ROPPA) groups national peasant platforms in 12 West African countries and is now reaching out to the other three, English-speaking members of the Economic Community of West African States (ECOWAS).

90   The weakest component of the food- and agriculture-related social movements, in addition to indigenous peoples, continued to be the pastoralists.

91   In particular, on the global scene, the International Union of Food, Agricultural, Hotel, Restaurant, Catering, Tobacco and Allied Workers' Associations (IUF).

92   Depending on their capacity and the degree of internal democracy.

93   The rationale for coupling the two processes had emerged from the 8th session of the UNCED follow-up mechanism, the Commission on Sustainable Development (CSD), held in April 2000, which had focused on SARD. The session had featured a 'multistakeholder dialogue' involving five of the nine 'Major Groups' into which Agenda 21, the action plan adopted at Rio, had divided up the universe of non-state actors. The report of the CSD session had underlined the desirability of continuing this kind of civil society input in major events in the run-up to the World Summit on Sustainable Development scheduled for 2002, which was the +10 of the Rio Conference. These major events included the March 2001 session of the FAO's Committee on Agriculture, one of the FAO's leading policy-making technical committees. The FAO was a player in both the WFS:*fyl* and the

World Summit on Sustainable Development (WSSD), and some of the civil society organizations most closely involved in the CSD session had also been active at the 1996 NGO Forum. It therefore seemed opportune to try to build links between the two processes despite the foreseeable difficulties involved, of which the most obvious was the inclusion of business and industry in the Major Groups mechanism.

94   Concrete projects and programmes translating the principles of the WFS Plan of Action into practice were foreseen as one expected product of collaboration with civil society in the run-up to the summit, including a possible civil society 'food watch' activity.

95   See Franck Amalric (2001) for an interpretation of the strategic choice the IPC faced and a series of interviews with participants at the May 2001 meeting.

96   As of October 2001 reports on national preparation for the WFS:*fyl* had been received from 109 countries out of a total of 112 covered by FAO representatives. Of these, 61 reported the involvement of stakeholders.

97   Travel and meeting costs were met by the FAO.

98   The Regional Conferences were also the occasion for initiating a practice that subsequently became a tradition within the FAO, that of adding a civil society slot to the programme of meetings with ministers of agriculture that the FAO's Director-General normally undertakes during his attendance at the Regional Conferences.

99   The African consultations laid emphasis on protection of local markets against dumping; it also added human immunodeficiency virus/acquired immune deficiency syndrome (HIV/AIDS), gender and the financing of agriculture to the list of priority themes. African governments were lobbied to obtain participation by farmers' organizations and other civil society sectors in the formulation of the agricultural component of the New Partnership for Africa's Development (NEPAD), which was being discussed in a region-wide forum for the first time at the FAO Conference in Cairo in February 2002. This initial lobbying effort was carried forward at the WFS:*fyl* and eventually led to an IFAD-funded initiative which allowed small farmer organizations in all the subregions of Africa to reflect and exchange on their visions of the future of African agriculture. Whatever the impact on NEPAD may have been, the contribution to building an Africa-wide network of small farmers' organizations was important. The Asian consultation came down in favour of taking agriculture out of the World Trade Organization, establishing a moratorium on genetically modified organisms, and seeking governments' commitment to an international convention on food sovereignty and a code of conduct on the right to food to be coordinated by the FAO. Piggy-backing with the consultation, held in the capital of a civil-war-torn Nepal, the nascent South Asian Peasants' Coalition organized its second conference, with the FAO Representative in attendance. The European consultation, with relatively good representation from the eastern and central parts of the region, launched a platform for reform of the Common Agricultural Policy (CAP) 'with food sovereignty at the centre', to the benefit both of Europe and of other countries affected by European agricultural and trade policies. Protection of biodiversity, recognition of the multifunctional role of agriculture and defence of the rights of agricultural workers got special mention, along with an appeal for an immediate moratorium on GMOs. The Latin American meeting echoed several of the same themes as the Asian one and added a denunciation of the privatization of natural resources and the power of transnationals. It also launched a plea for defence of the state and of

the FAO's role in food and agricultural policy, seen to be under attack from the WTO and the World Bank. The Near East consultations began finally to assemble an articulate group of civil society spokespersons, although people's organizations were perennially absent. Themes that attracted particular attention included the impact of war and occupation on food security, gender discrimination, and the need to ensure sustainable management of bio-diversity and water resources, and to increase political space for CSOs.

100 The four Major Groups and focal points that had been identified by the CSD secretariat to take part in the review of Chapter 14 of Agenda 21 were NGOs (NGO Caucus on Sustainable Agriculture and Food Systems), workers and trade unions (the International Confederation of Free Trade Unions/ICFTU through the Trade Union Advisory Committee of the Organization for Economic Co-operation and Development/OECD and IUF), farmers (originally only IFAP, but Via Campesina was added as a second focal point on the grounds that IFAP did not sufficiently represent the interests of peasant farmers/smallholders), and business and industry (International Agri-Food Network). The stakeholder delegations were expected to include representatives of indigenous people, youth and scientists and to reflect gender balance.

101 They clashed, for example, in their assessments of the market-assisted approaches to land reform championed by the World Bank.

102 There were 20 on the opening day, 150 on the second day, and 250 on the two successive days.

103 A shocking example of intervention by the Italian security forces was the refusal of entry to FAO headquarters to an authoritative member of the IPC, an international expert in human rights, on grounds that 'he was a dangerous extremist', an allegation that at first the secret services refused to substantiate. Only pressure from top management of the FAO led to the revelation that the person in question had been 'docketed' in the secret service files because the young man with whom he shared a hotel room during the 1996 summit had borrowed his pass without permission in order to get into FAO headquarters and had been caught by the guards. In the end the security forces had to admit that this was hardly grounds for refusing the human rights expert entrance and the order was rescinded.

104 The result of a decision to confer their drafting to one of the wisest and most eloquent staff members of the FAO, Andrew MacMillan, rather than the usual interdepartmental committee or outside consultant.

105 The adjectives 'voluntary', 'progressive' and 'national' had all been added by the US delegation to guard against any suggestion that the right to food might give rise to any international obligations. Despite the watered-down wording of the paragraph, the United States still expressed a reservation to it.

106 The format proposed for the Multistakeholder Diaologue's organization was an interesting one. The topic was the same as that of the three high-level roundtables from which civil society was excluded, 'the WFS Plan of Action – results achieved, obstacles and means of overcoming them'. The intention was to provide civil society representatives with an opportunity to have their views on this central issue expressed and reflected in the WFS:*fyl* process. It was suggested by the FAO secretariat that representatives of the regional groups of FAO member governments and the IPC should shape up the event together, a joint planning process which would have represented a step forward in civil society dialogue with the permanent representatives of member countries to the FAO. Unfortunately the permanent representatives were in such a dither about the official roundtables in which their heads of delegation were to participate that they did not feel able to take on an

additional task, an expression also of the feeling of apathy of many members regarding the WFS:*fyl* as a whole and the relatively low priority attached to civil society dialogue. In the end, the event was thrown together at the last minute by two very able co-chairs, Sarojeni Regnam of the Pesticides Action Network – Asia, and Hilde Frafjord, the Development Cooperation Minister of Norway. The CSOs made presentations on a regional basis but the governments did not. Although a number of government delegates were present in the room (54 out of a total of 280 participants), relatively few took the floor and they did so as individual country representatives. The report was presented to the plenary, but its impact was nowhere near what it would have been had a real process of dialogue taken place.

107   This assessment was undertaken shortly after the event, with input from involved FAO staff and members of IPC.

108   Some regions, such as Asia, were stricter about applying this last criterion than others.

109   The Italian embassies/consulates were generally unhelpful in this regard. One exemplary case involved a delegation of Thai artisanal fisherfolk who were refused visas because they did not have credit cards.

110   It amounted to €453,000. The Municipality of Rome also provided considerable in-kind support. The European Commission and the Canadian and Irish governments contributed funds for civil society participation in the WFS:*fyl* more generally to an FAO-held fund.

111   These included, for example, Food First, Pesticides Action Network–Asia and the Pacific, IBON Foundation, and Crocevia.

112   It should be noted that a certain amount of confusion reigned during the forum in so far as communication regarding the timing and venues of meetings was concerned, and this unfortunately exacerbated the perception of disenfranchisement of some participants.

113   The European and North American plenary delegates included, in addition to IPC members, representatives of three European federations of development NGOs and one national one (EuronAid, CLONG, Coopération Internationale pour le Développement et la Solidarité [CIDSE/International Cooperation for Development and Solidarity] and Associazione ONG Italiane), one international NGO (Action Aid), the relatively marginal Belgian member of the OXFAM International family, and seven national NGOs (Canadian Food Banks, Comité catholique contre la faim et pour le développement, Comité français pour la solidarité internationale, Bread for the World Germany, Both Ends, Terra Nuova and SOS Faim). To these should be added 14 nonvoting accredited organizations (in addition to the obviously numerous Italian NGOs for whom participation was no-cost): Norwegian Development Foundation, Coordination Sud, Church of Sweden Aid, British Overseas NGOs for Development (BOND), OXFAM America, Catholic Relief Services (CRS), OXFAM Canada, Caritas Internationalis, Counterpart International, Christian Aid, World Vision, SOS Sahel, Hilfswerk der Evangelischen Kirchen Schweiz (HEKS) and Vredeseilanden-COPIBO (the latter five were represented by nationals from field offices).

114   The African farmers' organizations valued NEPAD as a proposal that at least had been born in Africa, and they used it as an opportunity to network and to gain official recognition as interlocutors in policy discussions.

115   The author's personal notes on the meeting.

116   The draft position paper whose adoption had been scheduled for the opening plenary session of the forum was rejected by the dominant social movement voices as being too soft.

117   The four substantive pillars of the Action Agenda are: a rights-based approach to food security and food sovereignty, local people's access to, and management of, resources; mainstreaming family-based farming and agro-ecological approaches; and trade and food sovereignty. A fifth section deals with access to international institutions.

118   This section draws on the assessment of the FAO–NGO/CSO interface during the WFS:*fyl* referred to above (FAO 2002c).

119   Key members of the team were the five NGO/CSO focal points from the FAO regional offices, whose supervisors had agreed to fund their participation in the summit and the forum, despite the fact that travel by regional office staff to the events in Rome was not encouraged. This was a testimony to the strengthened relations that had been built in the regions over the preceding months.

120   The three senior FAO staff at the final plenary were the Assistant Directors-General of the Technical Cooperation and the Agricultural Departments and the Legal Counsel.

121   For each of these themes the document recalled the NGO/CSO Forum's position and related it to relevant objectives in the FAO's Strategic Framework and the WFS commitments. It then listed and described the FAO policy forums in which discussion and negotiation relevant to the theme take place and major normative and operational activities that could offer a terrain for concrete cooperation. Each section wound up with a presentation of a few illustrative examples of how the FAO and CSOs were already working together.

122   For its part, the IPC appreciated the content of the document and interpreted the time and effort that had clearly gone into its preparation as a confirmation of the FAO's commitment.

123   See IPC (2002c), available at www.foodsovereignty.org, where the history and the current structure and activities of the IPC can also be found. By 2008 the IPC had grown to include some 50 organizations and networks of small farmers, pastoralists, fisherfolk, indigenous peoples, agricultural workers, rural youth, rural women and NGOs, reaching thousands of national, regional and global groups concerned with food and agriculture.

124   The draft letter was sent for clearance to all FAO department and regional office heads in order to ensure that it would be recognized as a corporate engagement.

125   This section and the following one do not review all of the fronts on which the IPC has interacted with the FAO since the November 2002 meeting but rather highlight some of the most significant areas from which some lessons can begin to be drawn.

126   Access to land is discussed on p. 98 in the context of the International Conference on Agrarian Reform and Rural Development.

127   This is an excellent example of the strong, although not determinant, influence that UN secretariats exercise on intergovernmental decision making.

128   The wording adopted was: 'At meetings of the IGWG [Intergovernmental Working Group], or of any subsidiary bodies that it may create ... stakeholders will participate fully in the discussions. However, only Members will have the right to make decisions. Stakeholders may participate as observers when decisions are being made.' A footnote specified that 'fully' was meant as 'without having to wait until all members have spoken'.

129   With Brazil and South Africa as strong front runners.

130   The third session was preceded by an open-ended intersessional meeting on 2–5 February 2004.

131   The Foodfirst Information and Action Network (FIAN) was able to access resources to cover the costs of a certain number of Southern CSOs; others were taken in charge from a trust fund established within the FAO to support the IGWG process.

132   See IPC (2004b) for the final NGO/CSO evaluation of the voluntary guidelines.

133   The potential down side of adopting a human rights approach has been discussed by Keck and Sikkink (1998:198) with regard to women's movements. 'What the human rights discourse implied was that if women's organizations were going to use international and regional human rights bodies and machinery, they would have to enhance their knowledge of international law. This requires privileging lawyers and legal expertise in a way that the movement had not previously done nor desired to do.'

134   This was Jean Marc Von der Weid of the Brazilian NGO AS-PTA, who had been interacting with the FAO for years and was highly respected by FAO technical staff, as well as being a leading figure in the organization of the 1996 NGO Forum.

135   The FAO Background Paper for the 1 November 2002 meeting had identified some 23 different normative and operational activities related to agro-ecological principles and objectives.

136   The agroecology working group, as finally constituted, was coordinated by Jean Marc Von der Weid assisted by Patrick Mulvany, one of the IPC expert focal points for biodiversity, and included two people who were not IPC members, Cristina Grandi (Argentina) of the International Federation of Organic Agriculture Movements (IFOAM) and Ibrahima Seck, a technical advisor of the West African farmers' movement. Efforts were made to add an Asian expert, but without success. The IPC dedicated a portion of its scarce resources to covering the costs of the working group, including a consultant from the civil society world to prepare documents and write up reports.

137   The Technical Cooperation Programme was the FAO's only regular programme-funded technical assistance activity. One institutional objective of the joint effort was to open up this in-house resource to agro-ecological approaches and to civil society cooperation.

138   'Priority Areas for Integrated Action' (PAIAs) were introduced by FAO management in the process of planning the 2004–2009 Medium Term Plan to promote interdisciplinary work around key issues like biodiversity, sustainable livelihoods, biotechnology and others. They were seen as a potentially privileged terrain for FAO/civil society normative cooperation. The person in question was Peter Kenmore, one of the most creative thinkers and politically astute actors in the FAO secretariat.

139   Brazil, Kenya, Mali, Niger, Senegal, Lebanon, Bangladesh and Kazakhstan.

140   Undertaken by Jean Marc Von der Weid, in collaboration with ROPPA and the national farmer platforms of the two countries, on an individual basis since the IPC itself had frozen collaboration with the FAO as a result of the biotechnology crisis.

141   Although formal follow-up to the specific proposals generated by the agro-ecology initiative did not materialize, in practice there has been a reorientation of the FAO flagship Special Programme for Food Security (SPFS) in the direction of the agroecology farm development approach, thanks in good part to a period of enlightened management of the FAO's operational division and to the influence of staff coming from the Integrated Pest Management (IPM) experience. While there is no formal exclusion of purchased inputs in

the SPFS guidelines, there is a recognition that, in most cases, they are not necessary for improving farm performance in ways that benefit family food security and – in any event – most of the poorest rural families have no access to purchased input supplies.

142   Patrick Mulvany of Practical Action (formerly Intermediate Technology Development Group/ITDG).

143   As documented in Windfuhr and Jonsén (2005). See, in particular, 'Appendix: Food Sovereignty: Historical Overview of the Development of the Concept', pp. 45–52. For further information on food sovereignty see, in a rapidly burgeoning body of literature, Pimbert (2008), McMichael (2007) and the websites www.foodsovereignty.org, www.nyeleni2007.org and http://viacampesina.org.

144   See, in this regard, campaigns against genetically modified organisms and, in the context of the Brazilian government–FAO international conference on agrarian reform (Porto Alegre, March 2006), renewed attention to issues of access to land and other accompanying measures.

145   Although Windfuhr and Jonsén (2005:1, 35) also cite debate in the European Parliament and incorporation into the Greens/European Free Alliance political platform.

146   ROPPA, the IPC focal point for West Africa, groups the national small farmers' platforms of 12 West African countries (see www.roppa.info). See also McKeon, Watts and Wolford (2004).

147   Civil society organizations in Cameroon have also mobilized successfully in the name of food sovereignty to push the government to establish barriers against the importation of cheap frozen chicken parts from Europe, a low-cost expedient for European industrial producers to get rid of products that do not have a market in Europe, which impacts negatively on local African producers and creates nutritional threats for consumers in countries in which the cold chain cannot be guaranteed.

148   Invitation letter addressed by ROPPA to potential participants, 29 September 2006.

149   ROPPA's successful advocacy and mobilization regarding the Economic Partnership Agreements (EPAs) was conducted in collaboration with the other African subregional farmers' networks and in partnership with two UN family organizations – the FAO and IFAD – and some European NGOs (Terra Nuova, Collectif Stratégies Alimentaires and Crocevia). See McKeon (2008) and www.europafrica.info.

150   This position was created, with considerable pushing by FIAN and other CSOs, in 2000 and was occupied until 2008 by Jean Ziegler, who included sections on 'food sovereignty' in his February 2004 report to ECOSOC (United Nations 2004b) and in his Interim Report submitted to the General Assembly in September 2008 (United Nations 2004c). He was succeeded by Olivier De Schutter, who took an active and positive part in the IPC-organized consultation on the global food crisis held in Rome in June 2008, discussed later in this chapter.

151   As an associate of the IPC, Peter Rosset (2003:1) noted in the fall Food First *Backgrounder*, 'Food sovereignty goes beyond the concept of *food security*, which has been stripped of real meaning. Food security means that every child, woman, and man must have the certainty of having enough to eat each day; but the concept says nothing about where that food comes from or how it is produced.'

152   The FAO teamed up with the government of the Netherlands to organize an International Conference on the Multifunctional Character of Agriculture

and Land in September 1999. The initiative and its results were strongly denounced by members of the Cairn Group (the United States and Australia, in particular) in the FAO's governing bodies.

153   On key themes such as justifications for the protection of small-scale family-based agriculture and the impact of the WTO on the autonomy of national agricultural policies.

154   Available at www.foodsovereignty.org.

155   Publication of the paper by Windfuhr and Jonsén in 2005 to some extent filled the information gap, but without the added advantage of serving as a tool for ongoing dialogue between the FAO and civil society.

156   Most recently during the November 2006 session of the FAO Council which received the report of the Committee on World Food Security in which a WFS+10 Special Forum, discussed later in this chapter, had been held.

157   See www.nyeleni2007.org for information on, and documents of, the forum.

158   Via Campesina, World Forum of Fish Harvesters and Fish Workers, World Forum of Fisherpeople, Friends of the Earth International, World March of Women, Réseau des Organisations Paysannes et de Producteurs Agricoles de l'Afrique de l'Ouest, Coordination Nationale des Organisations Paysannes-Mali, IPC, Food and Water Watch, Development Fund-Norway. One motivation behind the organization of the Nyéléni forum was the realization by Via Campesina that it needed to devote more attention to building strategic alliances among people's movements, a process that required soft-pedalling Via Campesina visibility.

159   The forum adopted the practice that had been pioneered by the IPC of applying quotas for different constituencies and regions.

160   A solution that cost little more than holding the meeting in a city, with the added advantage of siting it in a setting consonant with the themes under discussion.

161   *Misticas*, staged presentations of themes important to rural people, are a traditional component of Via Campesina meetings.

162   An orientation opposed by the developing countries, who set great stock by the FAO's field activities both as an additional source of funds – however miserly compared with funders like the World Bank – and, more politically significant, as an independent and potentially more supportive source of policy advice.

163   The secretariat of the CGIAR is housed by the World Bank.

164   The Food Insecurity and Vulnerability Information and Mapping Systems (FIVIMS).

165   FAO's normative activities in the field of organic agriculture, for example, have been developed in very close collaboration with IFOAM and other specialized NGOs.

166   When the World Resources Institute (WRI) contested findings in an issue of the FAO's *State of the World's Forestry Resources*, the Forestry Department adopted a positive and proactive stance and concluded a technical cooperation agreement with the WRI, including input into future issues of the publication.

167   Despite the fact that many FAO staff did not support the positions taken in the document.

168   UN secretariats often complain if CSOs seek to have their expenses covered when they are provided with an occasion to contribute to normative activities. This objection ignores the resource situation of all but the big, well-heeled NGOs. Providing adequate resources to people's organizations to participate in normative exercises can be a win–win proposition that helps the

people's organizations to systematize their experience and positions and provides UN institutions with invaluable input to which they would not otherwise have access.

169   Available at www.foodsovereignty.org.

170   In fact, the 2006 and 2008 rounds of consultations were curtailed due to lack of funds, with civil society events of some kind taking place only in Africa, Europe and Latin America. Only in Latin America did the FAO office team up with the regional IPC focal points to put together the necessary resources for a full-fledged meeting to take place in 2008, a reflection of the political atmosphere in that region. The IPC holds that it is the FAO's responsibility to mobilize the necessary resources when it seeks civil society participation in an official FAO event, while it is up to the IPC to fundraise for its own autonomous activities.

171   In practice this amounted to transforming the CFS into a multistakeholder forum for the space of debate on this agenda item, and then turning it back into a purely intergovernmental forum to take decisions on the basis of the discussions, an adaptation of the methodology developed for the Inter-governmental Working Group on the right to food.

172   The author of this study, who had been directly responsible for civil society outreach for many years, had left the organization two years earlier and had been admirably replaced by her successor. This was an important passage in terms of institutionalizing the FAO's commitment to partnerships rather than identifying it with the efforts of a few committed individuals.

173   The long-time secretary of the CFS, a woman skilled in handling relations with governments and not adverse to civil society participation, had gone into retirement and her replacement was either unwilling or unable to play a similar mediating role. This is another demonstration of the weight of strategically placed individuals in brokering institutional change.

174   The report, however, was a summary prepared by the chair. The report of the 32nd CFS (FAO 2006a:3) specifies that the chairperson's summary 'was neither negotiated nor agreed upon by the participants in the Special Forum. It is therefore not binding to the Committee, its Members or to the Civil Society or other Organizations which participated in the Special Forum.'

175   Parviz Koofkhan was the head of the secretariat.

176   Two other actors did join the Steering Committee – Action Aid International and the IFAD-based International Land Coalition, a hybrid body which counts the World Bank and the FAO among its members along with CSO networks. The IPC let it be known, however, that it would strongly contest the conference if civil society actors other than the people's organizations, which are the primary direct protagonists of agrarian reform, were allowed to 'represent' civil society in the Steering Committee. Instead, a transparent practice of holding meetings between the FAO secretariat, the IPC and other interested CSOs prior to each meeting of the Steering Committee was established, and the minutes were posted on the International Conference on Agrarian Reform and Rural Development (ICARRD) website.

177   On agrarian reform, Via Campesina and ICARRD, see Borras (2008).

178   The African Union is currently developing continental guiding principles for land reform with technical and financial support from the FAO, including for consultation with the African regional farmers' networks.

179   While noting the significant exceptions to this rule and the progress that had been made in some important areas like the Special Programme for Food Security and Integrated Pest Management programmes and in capacity-

building programmes with rural people's organizations. In some regions, Latin America in particular, joint programming had been initiated with the backing of the Regional Office.

180   Input was sought from FAO country representatives and regional offices, headquarters departments, and global civil society networks with which the FAO collaborates.

181   Not all respondents replied to all questions, so the total is not necessarily 42.

182   For information on the International Alliance against Hunger (IAAH), see www.iaahp.net.

183   Even the most radical members of the IPC established warm and respectful relations with her as a person.

184   Australia, Germany, the United Kingdom, Canada, Japan and the United States made their intention known in a letter to the Director-General, dated 4 April 2006.

185   www.donorplatform.org.

186   'Members of WTO reaffirm their commitment to the rapid and successful conclusion of the WTO Doha Development Agenda and reiterate their willingness to reach comprehensive and ambitious results that would be conducive to improving food security in developing countries' (FAO 2008:49).

187   Among the many lucid documents on the food crisis emanating from CSOs are GRAIN (2008), Guzman (2008), Polaski (2008), Bello (2008).

188   See text at www.foodsovereignty.org.

189   GRAIN (2008) does a particularly effective job of documenting the huge profits that global agribusiness firms, traders and speculators are making from the world food crisis.

190   These considerations are based on notes taken during the IPC annual meetings and a collective interview conducted in June 2008.

191   Limitations in NGO effectiveness in impacting on the UN has been attributed in part to the tendency to take sectoral, non-systemic approaches to the UN. See Juan Somoza in UNRISD (1997:4).

192   ROPPA's 12 national peasant farmer platforms represent some 45 million farmers, the majority of the population of these West African countries.

193   Artisanal small-scale fisheries was introduced as an agenda item on the agenda of the FAO Committee on Fisheries in 2005 and 2007 thanks to civil society lobbying and alliances with the secretariat and 'like-minded governments'. This mounting momentum led to a Global Conference on Smallscale Fisheries in October 2008 with the two international federations of artisanal fisherfolk represented in the planning committee. This process has been facilitated by the IPC.

194   The IPC mobilized resources to bring a delegation of pastoralist representatives from 14 countries to the First International Technical Conference on Animal Genetic Resources for Food and Agriculture organized by the FAO in September 2007 and provided them with the support they needed to be able to make their views known.

195   Report of the May 2006 meeting of the FAO Programme Committee (FAO 2006c: para. 48). Behind this verdict was the irritation of the major donors at the fact that their assessed contributions to the FAO's Regular Programme budget could be used to promote lobbying activities aimed at pushing these very members to make more substantial political and financial commitments.

3 UN–Civil Society Relations: A Comparative Look

1   See, for example, Klandermans and Staggenborg (2002), della Porta (2005:28) and Van Rooy (1997).

2   See, for example, Clark et al. (1998), Corell and Betsill (2001), Weiss and Gordenker (1996), Keck and Sikkink (1998), Krut (1997), Pianta (2005), Smith (2008), Van Rooy (1997). Foster and Anand (1999) look at both the civil society and the United Nations (UN) sides of the coin. Friedman et al. (2005) have interesting things to say about the interface between civil society and states, but are less concerned about the UN as an institution.

3   The questionnaire used in the survey is available on the UNRISD website (www.unrisd.org/research/cssm/unsummits) along with the responses presented in tabulated form. Responses were received from 24 of the 29 offices to which the questionnaire was addressed (see the Annex on page 228).

4   See, for example, Klandermans and Staggenborg (2002:26–8).

5   In contrast, reports that tag the views and information cited tend to suffer from self-censorship and institutional face-saving. See United Nations (2001, 2003).

6   See the Annex for a list of the responding entities.

7   Two institutions that are not members of the UN system although sharing many of the same concerns and participating in the UN-NGLS promoted network meetings: the World Trade Organization (WTO) and the Organisation for Economic Co-operation and Development (OECD).

8   The International Fund for Agricultural Development (IFAD), however, provides an interesting contrast with the other international financial institutions (IFIs) from this point of view.

9   Other related problems included the politicization of the ECOSOC accreditation process and the delays caused by the steady increase in applications for accreditation and lengthy processing procedures. Applications are vetted by the secretariat in the United Nations Department of Economic and Social Affairs (UNDESA) but the decision-making process takes place in the intergovernmental ECOSOC NGO Committee. Final decisions are taken by ECOSOC on the basis of a recommendation from its NGO Committee. In the case of a national NGO, the government of the country concerned has the right to comment on an application but not to veto it.

10   Communication during the Third Annual Meeting of NGO CSO Focal Points of International and Regional Organizations, Paris, 16–17 June 2005 (UN-NGLS 2005a).

11   The Department of Public Information (DPI) maintains a separate accreditation system on the grounds that its relations with NGOs are based specifically on information dissemination. Some of the most field-oriented UN programmes and funds, such as the World Food Programme, do not have formal accreditation procedures. They lay particular emphasis, instead, on the effective selection of operational partners.

12   The General Assembly resolution authorizing the Rio conference spoke only of international NGOs (INGOs) in consultative status. It required long and difficult negotiations at the August 1990 Preparatory Committee (PrepCom) in Nairobi to open up to others (see Falk 2005:156). Acting as PrepCom for the World Summit on Sustainable Development (WSSD), the Commission on Sustainable Development (CSD) later accredited 737 NGOs without ECOSOC status to the Johannesburg Summit. The following year ECOSOC deliberated to allow these organizations to

participate in the first post–WSSD CSD implementation cycle and then seek consultative status with ECOSOC if they decided to continue to engage in WSSD follow-up.

13   In the case of the FAO, for example, the vast majority of the concrete field collaboration that takes place involves CSOs with which the organization has no form of formal relations.

14   Report of working group on accreditation at the June 2005 meeting of international organizations' civil society focal points.

15   These activities, presented in the order of the extent to which respondents reported adopting them, were: briefings, seminars or side events, easy access to media/delegates, civil society position papers, clear participation guidelines, supporting existing civil society networking, parallel civil society forums, multistakeholder dialogues, central well-equipped civil society space, roundtables, civil society input into the agenda, civil society input into secretariat papers, direct civil society/bureau contact, publicizing civil society comments on official documents, free civil society intervention on selected agenda items, preparatory country/regional meetings, free civil society interventions by selected caucuses, separating deliberation (with free civil society intervention) from negotiations, exhibitions, preparatory e-conferences and public hearings.

16   See pp. 11–15 for a discussion of the distinctions between NGOs and social movement/people's organizations.

17   One of these, the ILO, is in a category of its own since it has included labour movements within its governance structure from its foundation, which was well before that of the UN itself. Another, the FAO, reports that it has intensified its interaction with rural social movements (peasant farmers, artisanal fisherfolk, pastoralists, agricultural workers and indigenous peoples) thanks to their participation in the autonomous civil society mechanism which grew up around the World Food Summit in 1996 and the WFS:*fyl* in 2002. The third, IFAD, has also made determined efforts to build up its institutional dialogue specifically with rural social movements over the past few years.

18   The Division for the Advancement of Women is credited in this report for the alliance it has fostered between statisticians, activists and those knowledgeable about grassroots conditions promoting awareness about the need to disaggregate data by gender.

19   Krut (1997:39), based on the 1995 Benchmark Survey of INGOs, which found that many respondents were pleased with their success in defining the problem area but only 52 per cent felt they had been successful in altering the final text of the event.

20   UNDESA, responsible for many of the global summits of the 1990s.

21   Interview in 2003.

22   Charles Yongo in Schechter (2001:119). Enhancing governmental and intergovernmental accountability is identified by many authors as a major contribution that civil society can make to global governance. See Scholte (2005).

23   Princen and Finger (1994), cited in Weiss and Gordenker (1996:19).

24   The UN/IFI divide was problematic at the time and the links were far from clear between the Common Country Assessments/United Nations Development Assistance Frameworks (CCA/UNDAFs) and the authoritative World Bank-promoted programming exercises – the traditional Country Assistance Strategies, the innovative but unwieldy Comprehensive Development Frameworks promoted by World Bank president Wolfensohn, and the

Poverty Reduction Strategy Papers (PRSPs) introduced in response to criticism of the social costs of structural adjustment.

25 Three of the 24 respondents did not reply to this section of the questionnaire because they have no responsibility for country-level action.

26 'Generally less civil society involvement in programme formulation than in other phases.' 'Generally more civil society involvement in programme implementation, as service providers or contractors.'

27 Twelve respondents report medium or strong civil society involvement as against nine failing to reply or reporting no or weak involvement. Comments include: 'Varies by sector and country' and 'Participation is too often window-dressing: snap "validation" at capital city-sited workshops'.

28 Twenty respondents report medium or strong involvement with national NGOs as compared with 17 for INGOs.

29 Fifteen report medium or strong involvement of community-based organizations (CBOs) as compared with ten for national people's organizations/social movements. Among the comments: 'It's easier and "safer" to engage with capital-city-based NGOs, but the social organizations hold the key to meaningful participation and good governance.'

30 See p. 170.

31 These were: lack of enabling environment, insufficient capacity of CSOs, lack of dedicated resources for civil society outreach, inappropriate attitudes or insufficient experience of UN staff, lack of motivation on the part of UN staff, inappropriate procedures for programme formulation and implementation, insufficient guidance for staff, insufficient coordination on the part of UN agencies, and restrictive information disclosure practices.

32 These were, in order of ranking by respondents: include civil society cooperation in staff briefings, provide capacity building for CSOs, promote regional CSO networking, make available seed money for civil society cooperation, promote multistakeholder partnership programmes including CSOs, provide staff with guidelines regarding civil society cooperation, promote the establishment of national civil society platforms with which the UN can interact, coordinate implementation of the UN Millennium Development Goals (MDGs), publicize good experiences of civil society cooperation, provide governments with guidance regarding civil society cooperation, foresee a specific budget line for civil society participation in the formulation of policies and programmes, review project procedures to make them more civil-society-friendly, appoint civil society focal points in national and regional offices, include civil society cooperation in staff terms of reference and performance reviews.

33 The exceptions to the application of this rule, as in the case of the Security Council, are obvious.

34 See, for example, Edwards (2003), Kaldor (2003), Van Rooy (2004), Bendell (2006), Jordan and Van Tuijl (2006), Smith (2008).

35 See the useful categorization of social actors in Kaldor (2003).

36 See also the phenomenon of what Tarrow (1998) calls 'taming', or co-optation in CSO language.

37 See, for example, Chen, in Weiss and Gordenker (1996); UNDESA (2003), Krut (1997), Keck and Sikkink (1998).

38 United Nations Department of Economic and Social Affairs – Division for the Advancement of Women (UNDESA-DAW), UNDESA-Financing for Development (FFD), UNDESA-NGO Section, the DPI, the FAO, IFAD, the United Nations Environment Programme (UNEP). The ILO is in a separate category.

39   Although they were pioneered by UN-Habitat.
40   Generally five of the nine Major Groups take place in each CSD review session.
41   Internal communication, 2 August 2002.
42   www/undp.org/partners/cso.
43   At the same time, the Advisory Committee, currently under evaluation, has undoubtedly been effective in bringing civil society concerns to bear on the framing of UNDP policies in areas such as engagement with indigenous peoples and the risks and benefits of partnerships with the private sector.
44   Only two of the current 15 members of the UNDP Civil Society Advisory Committee come from people's organizations as distinct from NGOs: one is from the International Confederation of Free Trade Unions (ICFTU – which is relatively structured and hierarchical as compared to other people's organizations) and one is from the Indigenous Peoples' International Centre for Policy Research and Education (Tebtebba – an NGO very closely related to indigenous peoples).
45   See p. 130.
46   It is no coincidence that the global peasant movement, Via Campesina, has remained a strong actor in the International CSO Planning Committee for the World Food Summit:*five years later* (IPC) and the interface with the FAO, whereas it has deserted the Major Groups.
47   For example UNEP, IFAD.
48   For example most of the IFIs. The United Nations Conference on Trade and Development (UNCTAD), on the contrary, has decided to institutionalize annual meetings of its Trade and Development Board with civil society. The Joint UN Programme on HIV/AIDS (UNAIDS), an exceptional case within the UN system, has five CSO members on its programme coordination board.
49   The documents and analyses contained on the website of the NGLS (www.un-ngls.org) are a rich source of information on this and other aspects of UN–CSO relations.
50   For detailed discussions of the ECOSOC review process, see Foster and Anand (1999:249–52) and United Nations (2003:14–15).
51   The originally North–South nature of the division blurred during the course of the confrontation.
52   The Secretary-General's report on arrangements for interacting with NGOs, issued in 1998 (see United Nations 1998), has been described in the following terms in Foster and Anand (1999:275): 'a poorly drafted, incomplete report making trivial proposals for reform and avoiding all the contentious political questions'. It was followed, in 1999, by an equally inconclusive further document recording the comments of member states, specialized agencies and NGOs.
53   At the World Economic Forum (Davos, Switzerland, January 1999), the UN Secretary-General announced the creation of the much-critiqued Global Compact which would join companies together with UN agencies and civil society to support universal environmental and social principles. Its operations began the following year.
54   Directed by Professor Jeffrey Sachs of Columbia University, the research project submitted its final report to the UN Secretary-General in January 2005.
55   See www.millenniumcampaign.org.
56   Particularly through its 'Stand Up' campaign which reaches down directly to individual citizens.

57   The other members were Baher Asadi (Islamic Republic of Iran), Manuel Castells (Spain), Birgitta Dahl (Sweden), Peggy Dulany (United States), André Erdos (Hungary), Juan Mayr (Colombia), Malini Mehra (India), Kumi Naidoo (South Africa), Mary Racelis (the Philippines), Prakash Ratilal (Mozambique) and Aminata Traoré (Mali).

58   These mechanisms were the UN system-wide High Level Committee on Programmes which reports to the Chief Executive Board that brings together the UN Secretary-General and the heads of UN programmes and agencies and the Senior Management Committee, which is limited to the UN Secretariat and the funds and programmes run directly by the UN.

59   Italics in original.

60   'The Cardoso Report on UN–Civil Society Relations: A Third World Network Analysis', August 2004.

61   The restrictive term 'NGOs' is used throughout the UN Secretary-General's report despite the fact that the panel's terms of reference speak of civil society.

62   Thirteen of a total of 58 paragraphs of his document are devoted to these areas of action.

63   Proposals 10 and 11.

64   Only six of the 50 delegations taking the floor referred to country-level engagement, and two of these (India and Pakistan) cautioned that government was the natural interlocutor of the UN, not civil society.

65   With percentages ranging from 90 to 71.

66   The report drew on the Cardoso Panel as well as the reports of the Millennium Project and of the High-level Panel on Threats, Challenges and Changes.

67   It should be noted that all of the organizations that took the trouble to respond were NGOs; people's organizations and social movements were simply not following the debate and did not invest energy in the Millennium Summit process. See also Table 5.2 in Falk (2005), which groups the range of global civil society positions on UN reform into six categories without listing a single people's organization.

68   In fact, the Secretary-General's report contains only four references to civil society, none of them operational, in contrast with the specific proposal to create a Council of Development Advisors in the follow-up to the Millennium Development Project team (United Nations 2005: para. 201).

69   This initiative did, however, constitute the first time that such an opportunity for interaction with the General Assembly had been provided.

70   Albania, Cape Verde, Mozambique, Pakistan, Rwanda, Tanzania, Uruguay and Viet Nam.

71   The focus on indigenous peoples' organizations was also facilitated by the fact that the UN terminated the celebration of the Second International Decade of the World's Indigenous People with the adoption of an Action Programme and the creation of a Permanent Forum on Indigenous Issues, giving this particular category of social organizations a formal, recognized relation with the UN system.

72   See p. 141.

73   See OECD/DCD-DAC 2005. Civil society organizations hoped to win more of a voice at the High Level Forum on Aid Effectiveness in Accra on 2–4 September 2008.

74   The Bill & Melinda Gates Foundation's Annual Report for 2007 quotes the endowment assets available at 31 December 2007 for the foundation's charitable actions at $38.7 billion.

4 Conclusions and Ways Forward

1   The Financing for Development process has accredited individual private sector companies.

2   Drawing on precedents that date back to the Nestlé baby bottle campaign of the late 1960s and 1970s, conducted by the Berne Declaration with the wholehearted support of the FAO and WHO nutritionists.

3   The MDG Project approach was praised by Annan in his report on UN relations with civil society. See Slaughter (2004) for a commendatory treatment of global governance by interconnected expertise.

4   Needless to say, this gap is not filled when international institutions or NGOs record the testimony of individual poor people rather than engaging with the organizations mandated to represent them politically, as did the World Bank with its highly publicized 'Voices of the Poor' programme (see www.worldbank.org/prem/poverty/voices), or Action Aid with the piteous messages collected from African poor people by a *Matatu* bus that travelled from South Africa to the G-8 meeting in Gleneagles, Scotland, in July 2005. See, in contrast, the forceful and politically charged 'Message to Blair and the G-8' (ROPPA 2005) released at the same time by the Network of Farmers' and Agricultural Producers' Organizations of West Africa.

5   See endnote 17, p. 191.

6   For an articulate defence of this idea, see Falk (2005:180).

7   In her penetrating study of democracy and capitalism, Wood (1991:176) argues that 'We have yet to see an economy whose driving force is neither direct coercion by the state nor the compulsions of profit but democratic self-determination. That kind of advance in democracy would require a system of social relations as different from capitalism as capitalism was from feudalism.'

8   OXFAM's 2004 study, '"White Gold" Turns to Dust' advocated an end to US subsidies to domestic cotton production in order to increase the price of raw cotton on the world market, while West African farmers' organizations themselves were advocating diversification away from export crops and local processing and marketing of West African cotton.

9   Lobbying by European NGOs on the Economic Partnership Agreements between the European Union and the Africa Caribbean Pacific (ACP) regions has made some significant strides in the direction of respect for the agendas of Southern peoples' organizations, thanks largely to the political weight of ROPPA and to the determined efforts of its European NGO partners in the context of a joint EuropAfrica campaign. See www.europafrica.info. Some of the big INGOs have expressed awareness of the issues involved in 'branding'.

10   In the order in which they were ranked, these parameters were: general 'culture' of the organization, overall understanding of civil society work, 'discourse' used and issue addressed; source/kinds of experience/knowledge drawn upon; civil society participation in governance, informal accountability to civil society, allocation of resources to civil society relations.

11   See, for example, Goodman and Watts (1997); Webster and Engberg-Pedersen (2002); Pile and Keith (1997); Gills (2000); Escobar (2001).

12   In addition to the authors cited on pp. 115–17, two particularly stimulating thinkers, coming at the issue of bringing linked local experiences to bear on the global scene from very different perspectives, are Saskia Sassen (2008) with her conceptualization of 'the world's third spaces', and Jan Douwe van der Ploeg (2005) with his theorization of opposition to the re-patterning of the social and natural worlds under globalization (which he terms the 'Empire') by a 'newly emerging peasantry' in Europe characterized in the first instance by its autonomy.

13   Italics in original.

14   Interview in autumn 2004.

15   Interview conducted in June 2005. See also Telford and Cosgrave 2006.

16   And it is not now being given adequate attention, as is demonstrated by the work of the High Level Panel on UN System-Wide Coherence in the Areas of Development, Humanitarian Assistance and the Environment (www. un.org/reform). Of the regional consultations held by the panel, the Asian meeting (Pakistan, 24–25 May 2006) grouped representatives of the UN system, governments and other multilateral and bilateral donors to the exclusion of civil society. The African meeting (Mozambique, 5–6 May 2006) opened up to CSOs from the host country only, despite the fact that how the UN system should relate to civil society at country level was one of the specific questions on the table. This is a good example of how the UN system is capable of neglecting to apply its own recommendations on inclusiveness from one High Level Panel to another.

17   The country case studies carried out in the context of the UNRISD project on UN Summits and Civil Society are a step in this direction.

18   See Edelman (2003); McMichael (2007); Borras (2008); Desmarais (2007).

19   An exception is O'Brien et al. (2000:233), who suggest that the results of their studies could be extended to the rest of the UN system.

20   One of the few mentions of these figures in the literature is the WHO official cited on p. 151.

21   There is, of course, a vast body of literature on development discourse in general, both within the field of cultural studies and from other standpoints. See, for example, Crush (1995), Escobar (1995), Grillo and Stirrat (1997).

22   The school of 'discursive institutionalism' in which Fouilleux (2008) sites her examination of the FAO's failure to exert significant influence on international discourse on agricultural policies also offers some interesting research perspectives, particularly since the third determining factor she identifies is that of difficulties in establishing alliances with social movements and NGOs.

23   Pianta hypothesizes that a winning combination is that of a universalistic frame such as human rights, a relatively unstructured international institutional set-up (such as climate change as compared to trade) and strong public opinion interest (discussion, July 2008).

24   The IPC's goal of a global convention on food sovereignty. See Sikkink (2005a) for considerations regarding linkages between domestic, regional and international judicialization of politics.

25   In this regard it would be interesting to contrast the impact of initiatives such as the UK Department for International Development-funded, Overseas Development Institute-managed Civil Society Partnerships Programme (see www.odi.org.uk/cspp), in which the dominant Southern participants are think tanks and NGOs, with others like those funded by the International Fund for Agricultural Development, in collaboration with some European NGOs, which are deliberately and uncompromisingly managed by Southern small farmers' networks themselves, calling on the technical support of consultants and organizations of their own choosing.

26   See Khagram et al. (2002:viii–ix); 'Grassroots Globalization and the Research Imagination' in Appadurai (2001:1–20); and Watts and Peet (1996). An experimentation with the kind of further investigation suggested in this concluding paragraph is now being undertaken by the author of this study and Carol Kalafatic of Cornell University in the context of a UN-NGLS action/research project funded by the Ford Foundation.

Bibliography

Amalric, Franck (2001) 'Strategically Speaking: The World Food Summit, five years later and Responses to Franck Amalric'. *Development*, 44 (4) December, 6–16.

Anheier H., M. Glasius and M. Kaldor (eds) (2001) *Global Civil Society 2001* (first edn), Oxford University Press, Oxford.

Appadurai, Arjun (ed.) (2001) *Globalization*, Duke University Press, Durham, NC.

Archibugi, Daniele (2008) *The Global Commonwealth of Citizens: Toward Cosmopolitan Democracy*, Princeton University Press, Princeton, NJ.

Archibugi, Daniele, David Held and Martin Kohler (1998) *Re-Imagining Political Community: Studies in Cosmopolitan Democracy*, Polity Press, Cambridge.

Ayres, Jeffrey and Michael Bosia (2008) *Bridging Global Summits and Local Markets: Food Sovereignty and Micro-Resistance to Globalization*, paper presented at the ISA's 49th Annual Convention 'Bridging Multiple Divides', San Francisco, CA, 26 March 2008. www.allacademic.com/meta/p253316_index.html (accessed October 2008).

Bello, Walden (2008) 'Destroying African Agriculture', *Foreign Policy in Focus*, 3 June 2008. www.fpif.org/fpiftxt/5271 (accessed October 2008).

Benchmark Environmental Consulting (1995) *Democratic Global Civil Governance. Report of the 1995 Benchmark Survey of International NGOs*, Royal Ministry of Foreign Affairs, Oslo.

Bendell, Jem (2006) *Debating NGO Accountability*, NGLS Development Dossier, NGLS, Geneva.

Bill and Melinda Gates Foundation (2007) *Annual Report 2007*. www.gatesfoundation.org/nr/public/media/annualreports/annualreport07/index.html (accessed October 2008).

Borges, Jorge Luis (1975) *Other Inquisitions 1937–1952* (translated by Ruth L.C. Simms), Texas Pan American Series, University of Texas Press, Austin, TX.

Borras, Saturnino M. Jr. (2008) 'La Via Campesina and Its Global Campaign for Agrarian Reform', *Journal of Agrarian Change*, 8 (2/3), April and July, 258–89.

The [Bread] Bracket (1996) 2 (2), 30 October.

Les Brèves du CSA (1996) Various issues: August-September, October, December, Collectif Stratégies Alimentaires (CSA).

Brock, Karin and Rosemary McGee (2004) *Mapping Trade Policy: Understanding the Challenges of Civil Society Participation*, IDS Working Paper 225, May.

Bullard, Nicola (2005) 'Why UN Reform Is Not a Priority', *Focus on the Global South*. focusweb.org/content/index.php?option=com_content&task=view&id=637&Itemid=133 (accessed October 2008).

Cépède, Michel (1984) 'The Fight against Hunger. Its History on the International Agenda', *Food Policy* (November) 282–90.

Charnovitz, Steve (1997) 'Two Centuries of Participation: NGOs and International Governance', *Michigan Journal of International Law*, 18 (2) (Winter), 183–286.

Childers, Erskine, with Brian Urquhart (1994) *Renewing the United Nations System*. Development Dialogue 1994:1–2, Dag Hammarskjöld Foundation, Uppsala.

Clark, Ann Marie, Elisabeth J. Friedman and Kathrya Hochstetler (1998) 'The Sovereign Limits of Global Civil Society: A Comparison of NGO Participation in UN World Conferences on the Environment, Human Rights, and Women', *World Politics*, 51 (1) (October), 1–35.

Clark, John (ed.) (2003) *Globalizing Civic Engagement: Civil Society and Transnational Action*, Earthscan, London.

CLONG (Liaison Committee of European Non-Governmental Development Organizations/ NGDOs to the European Union) (1996) *Suggestions for Amendments to the Draft Policy Statement and Plan of Action*, Intersessional Working Group of the Committee on World Food Security (CFS), 29 July – 2 August 1996, Doc. No. ISWG4/Inf 35, FAO, Rome.

Coleman, William D. (2001) 'Policy Networks, Non-State Actors and Internationalized Policy-making: A Case Study of Agricultural Trade', in Daphne Josselin and William Wallace (eds), *Non-State Actors in World Politics*, Palgrave Macmillan, New York.

Commission on Global Governance (1995) *Towards the Global Neighbourhood. The Report of the Commission on Global Governance*, Oxford University Press, Oxford.

Conca, Ken (1996) 'Environmental Organisations and the UN System', in Thomas G. Weiss and Leon Gordenker (eds), *NGOs, the UN and Global Governance*, Lynne Rienner Publications, Boulder, CO.

Corell, Elisabeth and Michele M. Betsill (2001) 'A Comparative Look at NGO Influence in International Environmental Negotiations: Desertification and Climate Change', *Global Environmental Politics*, 1 (4) (November), 86–107.

Crush, Jonathan (ed.) (1995) *The Power of Development*, Routledge, London.

della Porta, Donatella (2005) *The Social Bases of the Global Justice Movement: Some Theoretical Reflections and Empirical Evidence from the First European Social Forum*, Programme on Civil Society and Social Movements, Paper No. 21, UNRISD, Geneva.

Desmarais, Annette Aurélie (2007) *La Vía Campesina: Globalization and the Power of Peasants*, Pluto Press, London.

Donini, Antonio (1996) 'The Bureaucracy and the Free Spirits: Stagnation and Innovation in the Relationship between the UN and NGOs', in Thomas G. Weiss and Leon Gordenker (eds), *NGOs, the UN and Global Governance*, Lynne Rienner Publishers, Boulder, CO.

Douglas, Mary (1986) *How Institutions Think*, Syracuse University Press, Syracuse, NY.

Ecologist, 21 (2) (1991) 'The United Nations Food and Agriculture Organization: Promoting World Hunger', special issue, March–April.

Edelman, Marc (2003) 'Transnational Peasant and Farmer Movements and Networks', in Mary Kaldor, Helmut Anheier and Marlies Glasius (eds), *Global Civil Society 2003*, Oxford University Press, Oxford.

Edwards, M. (2003) 'NGO Legitimacy – Voice or Vote', BOND, February. www.global policy.org/ngos/credib/2003/0202rep.htm.

Edwards, Michael and John Gaventa (eds) (2001) *Global Citizen Action*, Earthscan, London.

ENDA (Environmental Development Action in the Third World) (1996) *Vivre autrement*, 7th series, No. 1, 13 November.

Escobar, Arturo (1995) *Encountering Development: The Making and Unmaking of the Third World*, Princeton University Press, Princeton.

—— (2001) 'Culture Sits in Places: Reflections on Globalism and Subaltern Strategies of Localization', *Political Geography*, 20 (2), 139–74.

ETC Group (2003) *Lessons Learned from 30 years of UN Summits. Stop the 'Stockholm Syndrome'. Tough love for the UN … Change the Rules and the Game*, draft, Dag Hammarskjöld Foundation, Stockholm.

—— (2008) *Food's Failed Estates = Paris's Hot Cuisine. Food Sovereignty – à la Cartel?* ETC Group Communiqué, issue 97, Ottawa, January.

Falk, Richard (2005) 'Reforming the United Nations: Global Civil Society Perspectives and Initiatives', in Marlies Glasius, Mary Kaldor and Helmut Anheier (eds), *Global Civil Society 2005/6*, 150–89, Sage Publications, London.

FAO (Food and Agriculture Organization of the United Nations) (1970) *Report of the Second World Food Congress*, FAO, Rome.

—— (1975) *Report of the Eighteenth Session of the FAO Conference*, Doc. No. C 75/LIM/8, FAO, Rome.

—— (1995a) *Statement on the Occasion of the Twenty-Eighth Conference, Rome, 20 October–2 November 1995*, FAO Office of the Director-General (Dr Jacques Diouf), Rome. www.fao.org/DG/1995/H7F.HTM (accessed October 2008).

—— (1995b) *FAO Conference Resolution 2/95, 'World Food Summit'* (adopted on 31 October 1995), FAO, Rome. www.fao.org/wfs/resource/english/resolute.htm (accessed October 2008).

—— (1995c) *Strategy Framework for NGO Involvement in the World Food Summit – November 1996*, FAO, Rome.

—— (1995d) *Report to the Committee on World Food Security, Twentieth Session, Rome, 25–28 April 1995*, Doc. No. CFS 95/4, FAO, Rome.

—— (1996a) *World Food Summit. Vol. 1: Technical Background Documents 1–5*, Vol. 2: *Technical Background Documents 6–11*, Vol. 3: *Technical Background Documents 12–15*, FAO, Rome.

—— (1996b) *Rome Declaration on World Food Security and World Food Summit Plan of Action*, World Food Summit (Rome, 13–17 November 1996), FAO, Rome. www.fao.org/docrep/003/w3613e/w3613e00. HTM (accessed October 2008).

—— (1998) *Expert Meeting Report on Civil Society Involvement in Follow-up to the World Food Summit* (Rome, 26–27 January), FAO, Rome.

—— (1999a) *FAO Policy and Strategy for Cooperation with Non-Governmental and Civil Society Organizations*, FAO, Rome.

—— (1999b) *Report of the 25th Session of the Committee on World Food Security (Rome, 31 May – 3 June 1999)*, Hundred and Sixteenth Session (Rome 14–19 June 1999), Doc. No. CL 116/10. www.fao.org/docrep/meeting/X2194e.htm (accessed October 2008).

—— (1999c) *The Strategic Framework for FAO: 2000–2015*, Office of the Director-General, FAO, Rome. www.fao.org/docrep/x3550e/x3550e00.htm (accessed October 2008).

—— (2000a) *Follow-up to the World Food Summit: Report on the Progress in the Implementation of Commitments I, II, V, and Relevant Parts of Commitment VII of the Plan of Action*, Committee on World Food Security, Twenty-Sixth Session (Rome, 18–21 September), Doc. No. CFS: 2000/3-Rev.1. ftp://ftp.fao.org/unfao/bodies/cfs/cfs26/X8175e.doc (accessed October 2008).

—— (2000b) *Report of the Council of the FAO, Hundred and Nineteenth Session (Rome, 20–25 November 2000)*, Doc. No. CL 119/REP, FAO, Knowledge and Communication Department, Rome. www.fao.org/docrep/meeting/003/X8984e/X8984e00.htm (accessed October 2008).

—— (2001a) *Proposal: Participation by NGOs and CSOs in the World Food Summit:five years later and in the Preparation of FAO's Task Manager Report on Chapter 14 of Agenda 21 for the World Summit on Sustainable Development*, unpublished internal document, 8 February, FAO, Rome.

—— (2001b) *Arrangements for the World Food Summit: Five Years Later (Rome, 5–9 November 2001)*, FAO document CFS/2001/5, FAO Committee on World Food Security, Twenty-Seventh Session (Rome, 28 May – 1 June 2001). ftp://ftp.fao.org/unfao/bodies/cfs/cfs27/Y0021E.doc (accessed October 2008).

—— (2001c) *Report of the 27th Session of the Committee on World Food Security (Rome, 28 May – 1 June 2001)*, Doc. No. CFS:2001/REPORT. www.fao.org/DOCREP/MEETING/003/Y0818E.HTM (accessed October 2008).

—— (2002a) 'Declaration of the World Food Summit: Five Years Later', in *Report of the World Food Summit: Five Years Later (Rome, 10–13 June 2002), Appendix*, FAO, Knowledge and Communication Department, Rome. www.fao.org/DOCREP/MEETING/005/Y7106e/Y7106 E00.htm (accessed October 2008).

—— (2002b) *Summit News: World Food Summit: Five Years Later Reaffirms Pledge to Reduce Hunger*, Rome, 27 August 2002. www.fao.org/worldfoodsummit/english/newsroom/news/8580-en.html (accessed October 2008).

—— (2002c) *Assessment of the FAO-NGO/CSO Interface during the WFS:fyl*, unpublished internal document, FAO, Rome.

—— (2002d) *Follow-up to the World Food Summit:five years later with NGOs/CSOs*, Background Paper for Discussion with the International NGO/CSO Planning Committee, unpublished document, October.

—— (2002e) *Information on NGO/CSO Participation in the WFS:fyl and Their Involvement in the Follow-up in Pursuit of the WFS Goal*, Doc. No. CL/123/INF/8, Hundred and Twenty-Third Session (Rome, 28 October – 2 November 2002). ftp://ftp.fao.org/unfao/bodies/council/ cl123/Y7827e.doc (accessed October 2008).

—— (2002f) *Establishment of an International Working Group for the Elaboration of a Set of Voluntary Guidelines to Support the Progressive Realization of the Right to Adequate Food in the Context of National Food Security*. Doc. No. CL/123/22. Hundred and Twenty-Third Session (Rome, 28 October – 2 November 2002). www.fao.org/DOCREP/ MEETING/005/ Y7576e.HTM (accessed October 2008).

—— (2005a) *Strengthening FAO's Alliances with Civil Society at Country Level: Report of a Consultative Review*, unpublished document, FAO, Rome.

—— (2005b) *FAO Reform: A Vision for the Twenty-First Century*, Rome, October.

—— (2006a) *Hundred and Thirty-First Session (Rome, 20–25 November 2006). Report of the 32nd Session of the Committee on World Food Security (Rome, 30 October – 4 November 2006)*, Doc. No. CL 131/6. ftp://ftp.fao.org/unfao/bodies/council/cl131/j8689e.doc (accessed October 2008).

—— (2006b) *International Conference on Agrarian Reform and Rural Development (Porto Alegre, 7–10 March 2006), Final Declaration*, Doc. No. ICARRD 2006/3. www.icarrd.org/ en/news_down/C2006_Decl_ en.doc (accessed October 2008).

—— (2006c) *Report of the Ninety-Fifth Session of the Programme Committee (Rome, 8–12 May 2006)*, Doc. No. CL 131/11. ftp://ftp.fao.org/unfao/bodies/council/cl131/j7777e.doc (accessed October 2008).

—— (2007) *FAO: The Challenge of Renewal. Report of the Independent External Evaluation of the Food and Agriculture Organization of the United Nations (FAO)*, Doc. No. C2007/7.A.1 – Rev. 1, FAO, Rome.

—— (2008) *High-Level Conference on World Food Security: The Challenges of Climate Change and Bioenergy (Rome, 3–5 June 2008), Report of the Conference*, Doc. No. HLC/08/REP, June. www.fao.org/fileadmin/user_upload/foodclimate/HLCdocs/HLC08-Rep-E.pdf (accessed October 2008).

FAO and IPC (2003a) Exchange of Letters, dated 16 January 2003 (Reference TCD-DG/03/55). www.foodsovereignty.org/public/documenti/Letter%20of%20Agreement% 20FAO-IPC%2016.01.03.doc (accessed October 2008).

—— (2003b) *Agroecology in FAO: Developing a Common Civil Society/FAO Approach*, unpublished document, FAO, Rome.

—— (2003c) *Agroecology: Developing a Common Civil Society/FAO Approach*, Report of Side Event, 1 December 2003, 32nd FAO Conference, FAO, Rome. www.foodsovereignty. org/public/documenti/AgroecologySideEventReport_b.doc (accessed October 2008).

Foster, John W. and Anita Anand (eds.) (1999) *Whose World Is It Anyway? Civil Society: the United Nations and the Multilateral Future*, United Nations Association in Canada, Ottawa.

Fouilleux, Eve (2008) 'Acteurs et concurrences dans la fabrication des référentiels internationaux. La FAO et les normes de politique agricole', in Y. Scheweil and W-D Eberwein, *Le mystère de l'énonciation: Normes et normalités en relations internationales*, L'Harmattan, Paris.

Friedlander, Eva (2003) 'The UN Department of Economic and Social Affairs and Civil Society: The Relationship as Viewed by Civil Society Organizations and Member States', unpublished document, New York.

Friedman, Elisabeth Jay, Kathryn Hochstetler and AnnMarie Clark (2005) *Sovereignty, Democracy and Global Civil Society: State–Society Relations at UN World Conferences*, State University of New York Press, Albany.

Gills, Barry (ed.) (2000) *Globalization and the Politics of Resistance*, St Martin's Press, New York.

Goodman, David and Michael J. Watts (1997) *Globalising Food: Agrarian Questions and Global Restructuring*, Routledge, London.

Goodrich, Leland M., Edward Hambro and Anne Patricia Simons (1969) *Charter of the United Nations: Commentary and Documents*, Columbia University Press, New York.

GRAIN (2008) *Making a Killing from Hunger: We Need to Overturn Food Policy, Now!* Against the Grain series, April. www.grain.org/2/?id=39 (accessed October 2008).

Grillo, R.D. and R.L. Stirrat (eds) (1997) *Discourses of Development: Anthropological Perspectives*, Berg Publishers, Oxford.

Guzman, Rosario Bella (2008) *The Global Food Crisis: Hype and Reality*, Special Release, a publication of Pesticide Action Network Asian and the Pacific (PAN AP) and Peoples' Coalition on Food Sovereignty (PCFS), Issue No. 7, July. www.foodsov.org/resources/resources_ 000008.pdf (accessed October 2008).

Held, David and Mathias Koenig-Archibugi (eds) (2005) *Global Governance and Public Accountability*, Blackwell Publishing, Oxford.

Higgott, Richard A. (2001) 'Economic Globalization and Global Governance: Towards a post-Washington Consensus', in Volker Rittberger (ed.), *Global Governance and the United Nations System*, United Nations University Press, Tokyo, New York, Paris.

Hill, Tony (2004) *Three Generations of UN–Civil Society Relations: A Quick Sketch*, NGLS, Geneva.

Holden, Barry (ed.) (2000) *Global Democracy: Key Debates*, Routledge, London.

IFAD (International Fund for Agricultural Development) (2005) *Towards a Farmers' Forum at IFAD's Governing Council. Workshop Report – 14–15 February 2005*, IFAD, Rome.

—— (2006) *Report of the Meeting of the Farmers' Forum in Conjunction with the Twenty-Ninth Session of IFAD's Governing Council, February*, IFAD, Rome.

—— (2008) *Partnerships in Progress*. Report to the global meeting of the Farmers' Forum in conjunction with the Thirty-First Session of the Governing Council of IFAD, 11–12 February, IFAD, Rome.

IPC (International CSO Planning Committee for Food Sovereignty) (2001) 'Call for Action and Mobilisation at the World Food Summit: Five Years Later', May, unpublished document.

—— (2002a) *Food Sovereignty: A Right for All. Political Statement of the NGO/CSO Forum for Food Sovereignty, 8–13 June 2002*. www.foodsovereignty.org/public/documenti/political%20statement%20-%20ngo%20forum.doc (accessed October 2008).

—— (2002b) *NGO/CSO Forum for Food Sovereignty: A Right for All. Acts of the Forum Held in Parallel to the World Food Summit: Five Years Later*, Rome, 8–13 June 2002.

—— (2002c) *Developing a New Relationship between the Food and Agriculture Organization and Non-Governmental and Civil Society Organizations: A Summary of Principles and Action Proposals Presented by the International Planning Committee to the Director-General of FAO, Jacques Diouf* (Rome, 1 November 2002). www.foodsovereignty.org/public/documenti/summary2002.doc (accessed October 2008).

—— (2003) *FAO and Agroecology: Strengthening FAO's Capacity to Support Resource-Poor Farming Families' Food Production and Food Security*, unpublished document.

—— (2004a) *FAO Declares War on Farmers Not on Hunger (An Open Letter to Mr Jacques Diouf, Director General of FAO), 16 June*. www.grain.org/front_files/fao-open-letter-june-2004-final-en.pdf (accessed October 2008).

—— (2004b) *No Masterpiece of Political Will. NGO Caucus (IGWG3): Final Evaluation Report*. www.dd-rd.ca/site/what_we_do/index.php?id=1599&subsection=themes&subsubsection=theme_documents (accessed October 2008).

—— (no date) *Civil Society Statement on the World Food Emergency: No More 'Failures-as-Usual'*. http://viacampesina.org/main_en/images/stories/pdf/22-05-2008_csofoodemergency-en.pdf (accessed October 2008).

Italian Committee for the NGO Forum on Food Security (1997) *Profit for Few or Food for All. Final Report of the NGO Forum on Food Security, Rome, 11–17 November 1996*, Rome.

Joachim, Jutta M. (2007) *Agenda Setting, the UN, and NGOs*, Georgetown University Press, Washington, DC.

Jonsson, Christer and Peter Soderholm (1996). 'IGO-NGO Relations and HIV/AIDS: Innovation or Stalemate?' in Thomas G. Weiss and Leon Gordenker (eds). *NGOs, the UN and Global Governance*, pp. 121–8. Lynne Rienner Publishers, Boulder, CO., and London.

Jordan, Lisa and Peter Van Tuijl (2006) *NGO Accountability. Politics, Principles and Innovations*, Earthscan, London.

Kaldor, M. (2003) 'Civil Society Accountability', *Journal of Human Development*, 4 (1) 5–27.

Karagiannis, Nathalie and Peter Wagner (2007) *Varieties of World-Making: Beyond Globalization*, Liverpool University Press, Liverpool.

Keane, John (2003) *Global Civil Society?*, Cambridge University Press, Cambridge.

Keck, Margaret E. and Kathryn Sikkink (1998) *Activists Beyond Borders*, Cornell University Press, Ithaca, NY.

Kennedy, Paul (2006) *The Parliament of Man: The Past, Present and Future of the United Nations*, Vintage Books, New York.

Khagram, Sanjeev, James V. Riker and Kathryn Sikkink (eds) (2002) *Restructuring World Politics. Transnational Social Movements, Networks and Norms*, University of Minnesota Press, Minneapolis.

Klandermans, Bert and Suzanne Staggenborg (eds) (2002) *Methods of Social Movement Research*, University of Minnesota Press, Minneapolis.

Krut, R. (1997) *Globalisation and Civil Society: NGO Influence in International Decision-Making*, Discussion Paper No. 83, UNRISD, Geneva.

McKeon, Nora (1988) *Synthesis of the African National Reports*, Image of Africa Project, Rome.

—— (1989) 'Luci della ribalta per le ONG?', *Volontari e terzo mondo*, Anno XVII, No. 2/3, 93–101.

—— (2004) 'Collaboration between NGOs and Intergovernmental Organisations: The Case of FAO', in Federica Sera (ed.), *Le ONG protagoniste della cooperazione allo sviluppo*, LED, Milan.

—— (2005) 'Poverty Reduction in the Sahel: What Do Farmers Have to Say?', in Nicola Boccella and Andrea Billi (eds), *Distribution du revenue, inégalités et politiques pour la réduction de la pauvreté*, Karthala, Paris.

—— (2008) 'ACP Farmers' Organizations and EPAs: From a Whisper to a Roar in Two Short Years', *Trade Negotiation Insights*, 7 (1) (February).

McKeon, Nora, Michael Watts and Wendy Wolford (2004) *Peasant Associations in Theory and Practice*, Programme on Civil Society and Social Movements, Paper No. 8, UNRISD, Geneva.

McMichael, Philip (2007) *Sustainability and the Agrarian Question of Food*, paper prepared for plenary presentation to the European Congress of Rural Sociology, Wageningen University, 20–24 August.

Marchetti, Raffaele and Mario Pianta (2007) *Understanding Networks in Global Social Movements*, working paper. University of Urbino.

Marchisio, Sergio and Antonietta Di Blasé (1991) *International Organization and the Evolution of World Society. Vol. 1: The Food and Agriculture Organization (FAO)*, Martinus Nijhoff Publishers, Dordrecht, Boston, London.

Mayo, Marjorie (2005) *Global Citizens. Social Movements and the Challenge of Globalization*, Canadian Scholars' Press, Toronto, and Zed Books, London.

Meiler, Stanley (1995) *United Nations: The First Fifty Years*, Atlantic Monthly Press, New York.

MIF (Montreal International Forum) (2002) *World Conference on Civil Society and the Democratization of Global Governance (GO2), Track 7, Transnational Civil Society: Post GO2 Track Report*, MIF, Montreal.

—— (2005) *Global Democracy: Civil Society Visions and Strategies*, May 29–June 1, 2005, conference report, MIF, Montreal.

O'Brien, Robert, A.M. Goetz, J.A. Scholte and M. Williams (2000) *Contesting Global Governance: Multilateral Economic Institutions and Global Social Movements*, Cambridge University Press, Cambridge.

OECD/DCD-DAC (Organisation for Economic Co-operation and Development/Development Co-operation Directorate-Development Assistance Committee) (2005) *The Paris Declaration.* www.oecd.org/document/18/0,2340,en_2649_3236398_35401554_1_1 1,00. html (accessed October 2008).

PANUPS (Pesticide Action Network North America Updates Service) (1996) *World Food*

Summit Concludes without Firm government Commitments, Pesticide Action Network North America (PANNA), San Francisco, CA, 16 December.

Pianta, Mario (2005) *UN World Summits and Civil Society: The State of the Art*, Programme on Civil Society and Social Movements, Paper No. 18, UNRISD, Geneva.

Pieterse, Jan Nederveen (2000) 'Globalization and Emancipation: From Local Empowerment to Global Reform', in Barry Gills (ed.), *Globalization and the Politics of Resistance*, St Martin's Press, New York.

Pile, Steve and Michael Keith (1997) *Geographies of Resistance*, Routledge, London.

Pimbert, Michel (2008) *Towards Food Sovereignty: Reclaiming Autonomous Food Systems*, International Institute for Environment, online book, www.iied.org/pubs/display.php?o=G02268&n=2&l=2&k=towards%20food%20sovereignty (accessed October 2008).

Polaski, Sandra (2008) *Rising Food Prices, Poverty, and the Doha Round*, Carnegie Endowment for International Peace, Policy Outlook No. 41, May 2008.

Princen, Thomas and Matthias Finger (1994) *Environmental NGOs in World Politics: Linking the Local and the Global*, Routledge, New York.

Rittberger, Volker (ed.) (2001) *Global Governance and the United Nations System*, United Nations University Press, Tokyo, New York, Paris.

Robinson, Clive (1996) *FAO's Cooperation with NGOs*, unpublished document, FAO, Rome, November.

ROPPA (Réseau des organisations paysannes et de producteurs de l'Afrique de l'Ouest) (2005) *Message from the West African Network of Smallholder Farmers' Organisations and Agricultural Producers to Prime Minister Tony Blair and Members of G8* (unofficial translation). www.europafrica.info/english/docs/msg_roppa_g8_en.htm (accessed October 2008).

—— (2006) *Niamey Call for West African Food Sovereignty*, 10 November. www.roppa.info/spip.php?article93 (accessed October 2008).

—— (2008) *Appel des paysans et producteurs de l'Afrique de l'Ouest membres du ROPPA aux chefs d'état et aux honorables députés des parlements nationaux et du parlement de la CEDEAO*. www.roppa.info/IMG/pdf/view.pdf (accessed October 2008).

Rosset, Peter (2003) 'Food Sovereignty: Global Rallying Cry of Farmer Movements', *Food First Backgrounder*, Fall, 9 (4), Institute for Food and Development Policy, Oakland, CA.

Sassen, Saskia (2008) *The World's Third Spaces*, Open Democracy, 8 January. www.opendemocracy.net/article/globalisation/world_third_spaces (accessed October 2008).

Schechter, Michael G. (ed.) (2001) *United Nations-Sponsored World Conferences: Focus on Impact and Follow-up*, United Nations University Press, Tokyo, New York, Paris.

Scholte, Jan Aart (2002) 'Civil Society and Democracy in Global Governance', *Global Governance*, 8 (3), 281–304.

—— (2005) 'Civil Society and Democratically Accountable Global Governance', in David Held and Mathias Koenig-Archibugi (eds), *Global Governance and Public Accountability*, Blackwell Publishing, Oxford.

—— (forthcoming) *Civil Society and Global Democracy*, Polity, Cambridge.

Seedling (2005) 'Food Sovereignty: Turning the Global Food System Upside Down', GRAIN, Barcelona, April.

Sen, B.R. (1982) *Towards a Newer World*, Tycooly International Publishing, Dublin.

Sikkink, Kathryn (2003) 'A Typology of Relations between Social Movements and International Institutions', *American Society of International Law, Proceedings 2003*, 301–305.

—— (2005a) 'The Transnational Dimension of the Judicialization of Politics in Latin America', in Rachel Sieder, Line Schjolden and Alan Angell (eds), *The Judicialization of Politics in Latin America*, Palgrave Macmillan, New York.

—— (2005b) 'Patterns of Dynamic Multilevel Governance and the Inside-Outside Coalition', in Donatella della Porta and Sidney Tarrow (eds), *Transnational Protest and Global Activism*, Rowman & Littlefield, Lanham, MD.

Slaughter, Anne-Marie (2004) *A New World Order*, Princeton University Press, Princeton, NJ.

Smith, Courtney B. (2006) *Politics and Process at the United Nations*, Lynne Rienner, Boulder, CO.

Smith, Jackie (2008) *Social Movements for Global Democracy*, Johns Hopkins University Press, Baltimore, MD.

Smith, Jackie, Charles Chatfield and Ron Pagnucco (eds) (1997) *Transnational Social Movements and Global Politics: Solidarity Beyond the State*. Syracuse, NY; Syracuse University Press.

Tarrow, Sydney (1998) *Power in Movements: Social Movements and Contentious Politics*, 2nd edition, Cambridge University Press, Cambridge.

—— (2005) *The New Transnational Activism*, Cambridge University Press, Cambridge.

Telford, John and John Cosgrave (2006) *Joint Evaluation of the International Response to the Indian Ocean Tsunami*, Tsunami Evaluation Coalition, London.

Third World Network (2004) *The Cardoso Report on UN–Civil Society Relations: A Third World Network Analysis*, August. www.un-ngls.org/08twn.pdf (accessed October 2008).

TIP/IATP (Trade Information Project/Institute for Agriculture and Trade Policy) (2006) *Geneva Update, 17 January 2006: Breaking out of the Mould: Reflections on the WTO Ministerial Conference in Hong Kong.* www.ourworldisnotforsale.org/showarticle.asp?search=1238 (accessed October 2008).

United Nations (1996a) *Consultative Relationship between the United Nations and Non-Governmental Organizations*, UN Doc. Resolution 1996/31, 49th Plenary Meeting, United Nations Economic and Social Council (ECOSOC), New York, 25 July. www.un.org/esa/coordination/ngo/Resolution_1996_31/index.htm (accessed October 2008).

—— (1996b) *Decision on Non-Governmental Organizations*, UN Doc. No. E/1996/297, United Nations Economic and Social Council (ECOSOC), New York. www.globalpolicy.org/ngos/ngo-un/ecosoc/1996/e96-297.htm (accessed October 2008).

—— (1997) *Renewing the United Nations: A Programme for Reform. Report of the Secretary-General*, UN Doc. No. A/51/950, United Nations General Assembly, New York, 14 July 1997. http://daccessdds.un.org/doc/UNDOC/GEN/N97/189/79/IMG/N9718979.pdf?OpenElement (accessed October 2008).

—— (1998) *Arrangements and Practices for the Interaction of Non-Governmental Organizations in All Activities of the United Nations System, Report of the Secretary-General*, UN Doc. No. A/53/170, United Nations, New York, 10 July 1998.

—— (2000) *Resolution Adopted by the General Assembly. 55/2 United Nations Millennium Declaration*, UN Doc. No. A/RES/55/2, United Nations General Assembly, New York, 18 September. www.un.org/millennium/declaration/ares552e.pdf (accessed October 2008).

—— (2001) *Reference Document on the Participation of Civil Society in United Nations Conferences and Special Sessions of the General Assembly during the 1990s*, United Nations, New York, August 2001. www.un.org/ga/president/55/speech/civilsociety1.htm (accessed October 2008).

—— (2002a) *Multi-Stakeholder Dialogue Segment*, Commission on Sustainable Development acting as the preparatory committee for the World Summit on Sustainable Development (Bali, Indonesia, 27 May – 7 June 2002), UN Doc. No. A/CONF/199/PC/18/Add.4, United Nations General Assembly, New York, 10 May. http://daccessdds.un.org/doc/UNDOC/GEN/N02/377/82/PDF/N0237782.pdf?OpenElement (accessed October 2008).

—— (2002b) *Strengthening of the United Nations: An Agenda for Further Change, Report of the Secretary-General*, UN Doc. No. A/57/387, United Nations, New York, 9 September 2002. www.unog.ch/80256EDD006B8954/(httpAssets)/4636334EE32718D1C1256F5C005D37C7/$file/A-57-387.pdf (accessed October 2008).

—— (2003) *UN System and Civil Society. An Inventory and Analysis of Practices*, Background Paper for the Secretary-General's Panel of Eminent Persons on United Nations Relations with Civil Society, United Nations, New York, May 2003.

—— (2004a) *We the Peoples: Civil Society, the United Nations and Global Governance: Report of the Panel of Eminent Persons on United Nations–Civil Society Relations*, UN Doc. No. A/58/817, United Nations, New York, 11 June 2004.

—— (2004b) *Economic, Social and Cultural Rights: The Right to Food. Report Submitted by the Special Rapporteur on the Right to Food, Jean Ziegler, in Accordance with Commission on Human Rights Resolution 2003/25*, UN Doc. No. E/CN.4/2004/10, United Nations Economic and Social Council (ECOSOC), New York, 9 February. www.unhchr.ch/huridocda/huridoca.nsf/(Symbol)/E.CN.4.2004.10.En (accessed October 2008).

—— (2004c) *The Right to Food*, UN document No. A/59/385, United Nations General Assembly, New York, 27 September. http://domino.un.org/unispal.nsf/2ee946874755 6b2d85256cf60060d2a6/1b855814a29e512485256f390072ebd2!OpenDocument (accessed October 2008).

—— (2004d) *Report of the Secretary-General in Response to the Report of the Panel of Eminent Persons on United Nations–Civil Society Relations*, UN Doc. No. A/59/354, United Nations General Assembly, New York, 13 September. www.unog.ch/80256EDD006B8954/ (httpAssets)/F77BEFE7DDC2FB88C1256F5C005D9679/$file/A-59-354.pdf (accessed October 2008).

—— (2005) *In Larger Freedom: Towards Development, Security and Human Rights for All. Report of the Secretary-General*, UN Doc. No. A/59/2005, United Nations General Assembly, New York, 21 March 2005. www.gtz.de/de/dokumente/en-report-largerfreedom.pdf (accessed October 2008).

—— (2006) *Delivering as One. Report of the Secretary-General's High-Level Panel on United Nations System-Wide Coherence in the Areas of Development, Humanitarian Assistance and the Environment*, United Nations, New York.

UNDESA (United Nations Department of Economic and Social Affairs) (2003) *Review of Interaction between the United Nations Department of Economic and Social Affairs and Civil Society*, UNDESA, New York.

UNDP (United Nations Development Programme) (2001) *Civil Society Engagement in the CCA and UNDAF Processes: A Desk Review*, Jennie Richmond. www.ngocentre.org.vn/files/ docs/UNDAF-CCAPaper-CS.doc (accessed October 2008).

—— (2007) *More National Civil Society Advisory Committees Launched*, UNDP News Release, 1 October 2007. http://content.undp.org/go/newsroom/2007/march/national-cso-advisorycommittee-20070323.en?categoryID=349425&lang=en (accessed October 2008).

United Nations High Level Task Force (2008) *High Level Task Force on the Global Food Crisis. Comprehensive Framework for Action, July 2008*. www.un.org/issues/food/taskforce/ Documentation/FINAL%20CFA%20July%202008.pdf (accessed October 2008).

United Nations Millennium Project (2005) *Investing in Development: A Practical Plan to Achieve the Millennium Development Goals*, Earthscan, Sterling, VA and London. www.unmillen niumproject.org/reports/fullreport.htm (accessed October 2008).

UN-NGLS (United Nations Non-Governmental Liaison Service) (1995) *Mobilizing NGOs for the World Food Summit: Some Preliminary Thoughts*, unpublished document, NGLS, Geneva.

—— (1996) *The United Nations, NGOs and Global Governance*, NGLS, Geneva.

—— (1997) 'The World Food Summit', *NGLS Roundup*, January. www.un-ngls.org/ pdf/11wfs.pdf (accessed October 2008).

—— (1998) *Inter-Agency Consultation on Operational Collaboration with NGOs (Geneva, 20–21 November 1997), Final Report*, NGLS, Geneva.

—— (2003a) *Summary Report of the Meeting of NGO and Civil Society Focal Points from the UN System and International Organizations (6–7 March 2003)*, NGLS, Geneva.

—— (2003b) *Report of the Consultation with Civil Society on 'The Crisis in Global Governance: Challenges for the United Nations and Global Civil Society'* (4–6 June 2003), NGLS, Geneva.

—— (2004) *Informal Meeting of NGO/CSO Focal Points (1–2 June 2004)*, NGLS, Geneva.

—— (2005a) *Summary Report. International Organizations Civil Society Focal Points Conference (16–17 June 2005)*, NGLS, Geneva.

—— (2005b) *Compilation of NGO Comments on: 'In Larger Freedom: Towards Security, Development and Human Rights for All' (A/59/2005). Report of the Secretary-General of the United Nations*. www.un-ngls.org/UNreform/NGO-Comments-SG-Reports-last%20 version.pdf (accessed October 2008).

—— (no date) *General Assembly Takes up UN–Civil Society Relations*. www.un-ngls.org/ GAarticle.doc (accessed October 2008).

UN-NGLS, with Gretchen Sidhu (2003) *Intergovernmental Negotiations and Decisions Making at the United Nations. A Guide*, United Nations, Geneva.

UNRISD (United Nations Research Institute for Social Development) (1997) *Advancing the*

Social Agenda: Two Years After Copenhagen. Report of the UNRISD International Conference and Public Meeting (Geneva, 9–10 July 1997), UNRISD, Geneva.

Valente, Flavio Luiz Schieck (1999) *Report on Food for All Campaign and Civil Society Participation in the WFS Follow-up at National and International Level*. Global Forum on Sustainable Food and Nutritional Security.

van der Ploeg, Jan Douwe (2005) *Empire and the Peasant Principle*, paper presented to the XXI Congress of the European Society for Rural Sociology, Keszthely, Hungary, 22–26 August. www.jandouwevanderploeg.com/en/empire-peasantry-and-resistance (accessed October 2008).

van Rooy, A. (1997) 'The Frontiers of Influence: NGO Lobbying at the 1974 World Food Conference, the 1992 Earth Summit and Beyond', *World Development*, 25 (1), 93–114.

—— (2004) *The Global Legitimacy Game: Civil Society, Globalization and Protest*, Palgrave Macmillan, Basingstoke.

La Via Campesina (2008) *La Via Campesina and the Global Food Crisis: Adequate Food is Simple Justice*, Friday, 25 July 2008. www.viacampesina.org/main_en/index.php?option=com_content&task=view&id=590&Itemid=38 (accessed October 2008).

Waites, Alan (ed.) (2002) *Masters of Their Own Development? PRSPs and the Prospects for the Poor*, World Vision, Monrovia, CA.

Walzer, Michael (ed.) (1995) *Towards a Global Civil Society*, Berghahn Books, Providence, RI.

Watts, Michael and Richard Peet (1996) 'Towards a Theory of Liberation Ecology', in Richard Peet and Michael Watts (eds), *Liberation Ecologies: Environment, Development, Social Movements*, Routledge, London.

Webster, Neil and Lars Engberg-Pedersen (2002) *In the Name of the Poor: Contesting Political Space for Poverty Reduction*, Zed, London.

Weiss, Thomas G. and Leon Gordenker (eds) (1996) *NGOs, the UN and Global Governance*, Lynne Rienner Publishers, Boulder, CO, and London.

Weiss, Thomas G. and R.S. Jordan (1976) 'Bureaucratic Politics and the World Food Conference: The International Policy Process', *World Politics*, 28 (3), 422–39.

Weitz, Charles (1999) 'Freedom from Hunger Campaign: Involving Civil Society Before It Became Fashionable', in John W. Foster and Anita Anand (eds), *Whose World Is It Anyway? Civil Society, the United Nations and the Multilateral Future*, United Nations Association in Canada, Ottawa.

Wild, Leni (2006) *Strengthening Global Civil Society*, Institute for Public Policy Research, London.

Windfuhr, Michael (1998) 'The Code of Conduct on the Right to Adequate Food: A Tool for Civil Society', in FAO, *The Right to Food in Theory and Practice*, FAO, Rome.

—— (2005) *Up-Date Information for the Guidelines List Serve Regarding Voluntary Guidelines for the Progressive Implementation of the Right to Adequate Food*, 25 October, unpublished document.

Windfuhr, Michael and Jennie Jonsén (2005) *Food Sovereignty: Towards Democracy in Localised Food Systems*, ITDG Publishing, Bourton-on-Dunsmore, Rugby.

Wood, Ellen Meiksins (1991) *The Pristine Culture of Capitalism: A Historical Essay on Old Regimes and Modern States*, Verso, London.

World Bank (2005) *World Bank – Civil Society Global Policy Dialogue Forum (Washington, DC, 20–22 April 2005), Summary Report*, World Bank, Washington, DC.

—— (2008) *Defining Civil Society*. http://go.worldbank.org/4CE7W046K0 (accessed 30 July 2008).

World Social Forum (2002) *World Social Forum Charter of Principles*, www.forumsocial mundial.org.br/main.php?id_menu=4&cd_language=2 (accessed October 2008).

Websites

EuropAfrica – www.europafrica.info
Fian International – www.fian.org
Global Donor Platform for Rural Development – www.donorplatform.org
International Alliance against Hunger – www.iaahp.net
IPC Food Sovereignty – www.foodsovereignty.org
MillenniumCampaign.org – www.millenniumcampaign.org
Nyéléni 2007 – www.nyeleni2007.org
Overseas Development Institute, Civil Society Partnerships Programme – www.odi.org.uk/cspp
Reform at the United Nations – www.un.org/reform
Third World Network – www.twnside.org
La Via Campesina – http://viacampesina.org
UNDP civil society organizations – www.undp.org/partners/cso
UN-NGLS – www.un-ngls.org
World Bank – www.worldbank.org

ANNEX: Cross-System Survey Responding Entities

UN Secretariat Departments and Programmes

1. Department of Public Information (DPI)

Name of civil society unit: NGO Section, Civil Society Service, Outreach Division.

Activities undertaken by the entity in which the unit is located: Global policy dialogue/ negotiation, normative work, field programmes, public information.

Intergovernmental forums for which the unit manages civil society participation: Regular seminars, briefings and commemorations involving CSOs; annual DPI/NGO Conference.

Outreach capacity at country level: Access to over 60 UN Information Centres and Services, most of which have an NGO focal officer. Reliance on UNDP country offices as well.

Activities at country level: Information dissemination.

Civil society interface mechanism: The 1,500 accredited NGOs have elected an 18-member Executive Board which partners with the secretariat.

2. Division for the Advancement of Women (DAW), United Nations Department of Economic and Social Affairs (UNDESA)

Name of civil society unit: Coordination and Outreach Unit.

Activities undertaken by the entity in which the unit is located: Global policy dialogue/ negotiation, normative work, policy advice at national/regional levels, field programmes, public information.

Intergovernmental forums for which the unit manages civil society participation: Commission on the Status of Women, Committee on Elimination of Discrimination against Women, Follow-up to the Fourth World Conference on Women.

Outreach capacity at country level: Not applicable (no separate field offices or staff).

Activities at country level: Policy advice, technical assistance programmes, capacity building.

Civil society interface mechanism: The interface mechanism is a self-organized NGO Committee on the Status of Women.

3. Financing for Development Office (FFD), UNDESA

Name of civil society unit: One NGO focal point working in the Multistakeholder Engagement and Outreach Branch.

Activities undertaken by the entity in which the unit is located: Global policy dialogue/ negotiation, normative work, policy advice at national/regional levels, public information.

Intergovernmental forums for which the unit manages civil society participation: Follow-up to International Conference on Financing for Development including Special High-Level meeting of the United Nations Economic and Social Council (ECOSOC) with the Bretton Woods institutions and the World Trade Organization (WTO), as well as High-Level Dialogue on Financing for Development.

Outreach capacity at country level: None.

Activities at country level: None.

Civil society interface mechanism: Following the Monterrey Conference, various CSOs have established an International Facilitating Group on Financing for Development. The business sector and parliamentarians have also developed their own independent interface mechanisms.

4. Commission for Sustainable Development (CSD), UNDESA

Name of civil society unit: Major Groups Programme, Major Groups and Partnership Branch, Division for Sustainable Development, UNDESA.

Activities undertaken by the entity in which the unit is located: Global policy dialogue/ negotiation, normative work, policy advice at national/regional levels.

Intergovernmental forums for which the unit manages civil society participation: UN Commission on Sustainable Development, International Meeting on Small Island Developing States, World Summit on Sustainable Development (WSSD).

Outreach capacity at country level: No reply.

Activities at country level: No reply.

Civil society interface mechanism: Adopts the classification of civil society into nine Major Groups as defined in Agenda 21. Interface was initially with a CSD NGO Steering Committee. Now with Major Group Organizing Partners, self-selected major group organizations that have agreed to collaborate with the CSD Bureau through the secretariat to facilitate input from Major Groups worldwide into the work of the CSD.

5. NGO Section, UNDESA

Name of civil society unit: NGO Office for ECOSOC Support and Coordination.

Activities undertaken by the entity in which the unit is located: Global policy dialogue/negotiation, normative work, policy advice at national/regional levels, public information.

Intergovernmental forums for which the unit manages civil society participation: ECOSOC and its various segments, international meetings, General Assembly Special Sessions and Special Events, Ministerial roundtables at ECOSOC, various commissions and forums of ECOSOC (for example, Forum on Indigenous Issues).

Outreach capacity at country level: No reply.

Activities at country level: Formulation of country frameworks, technical assistance programmes, capacity building.

Civil society interface mechanism: Adopts the classification of NGOs into three categories of Consultative Status. Overall interface mechanism is the CONGO.

6. United Nations Human Settlements Programme (UN-Habitat)

Name of civil society unit: Partners and Youth Section.

Activities undertaken by the entity in which the unit is located: Global policy dialogue/ negotiation, normative work, policy advice at national/regional levels, field programmes, public information

Intergovernmental forums for which the unit manages civil society participation: Governing Council, World Urban Forum, Commission on Sustainable Development.

Outreach capacity at country level: No country offices. The four regional offices (Africa, Asia, Latin America and Europe) act as civil society focal points. Human Settlements Programme Officers stationed in some UNDP country offices.

Activities at country level: Policy advice, formulation of country frameworks, technical assistance programmes, humanitarian/emergency programmes, capacity building, gender and youth programmes.

Civil society interface mechanism: Has an Advisory Committee to the Executive Director with one civil society member.

7. United Nations Conference on Trade and Development (UNCTAD)

Name of civil society unit: Civil Society Outreach.

Activities undertaken by the entity in which the unit is located. Global policy dialogue, normative work, technical cooperation, capacity building.

Intergovernmental forums for which the unit manages civil society participation: UNCTAD Quadrennial Conferences, Trade and Development Board and its commissions, Expert Meetings, United Nations Conference on the Least Developed Countries.

Outreach capacity at country level: No field offices.

Activities at country level: No reply.

Civil society interface mechanism: Cooperation is with international organizations and self-organized networks. No global interface mechanism.

8. United Nations High Commissioner for Refugees (UNHCR)

Name of civil society unit: NGO Liaison Unit.

Activities undertaken by the entity in which the unit is located: Global policy dialogue/ negotiation, policy advice at national/regional levels, field programmes, public information.

Intergovernmental forums for which the unit manages civil society participation: Executive Committee and its three Standing Committees (Annual NGO Consultation prior to ExCom).

Outreach capacity at country level: 220 field offices; each has a civil society focal point.

Activities at country level: Policy advice, formulation of country frameworks, humanitarian/emergency programmes, capacity building.

Civil society interface mechanism: Formal interface conducted through annual NGO consultations and through NGO umbrella groups and their forums.

9. United Nations Environment Programme (UNEP)

Name of civil society unit: Major Groups and Stakeholder Branch.

Activities undertaken by the entity in which the unit is located: Global policy dialogue/ negotiation, normative work, policy advice at national/regional levels, public information.

Intergovernmental forums for which the unit manages civil society participation: Annual Global Civil Society Forum in conjunction with Governing Council/Global Ministerial Environment Forum, preparatory regional forums, ad hoc civil society meetings in connection with ad hoc intergovernmental meetings.

Outreach capacity at country level: Six regional offices, each with a civil society focal point, and about ten outposted offices. Thirty-two UNEP national committees, mostly in European countries.

Activities at country level: Policy advice, formulation of country frameworks, capacity building.

Civil society interface mechanism: A proposal for establishing a UNEP Major Group Facilitating Committee with one representative of each Major Group and two from each UNEP region adopted at the 9th Global Civil Society Forum in February 2008.

10. United Nations Development Programme (UNDP)

Name of civil society unit: Bureau for Resources and Strategic Partnerships.

Activities undertaken by the entity in which the unit is located: Global policy dialogue/ negotiation, normative work, policy advice at national/regional levels, field programmes.

Intergovernmental forums for which the unit manages civil society participation: None.

Outreach capacity at country level: 137 field offices. Two Regional Hubs (Pretoria and Bratislava) and one governance centre (Oslo) have CSO advisors.

Activities at country level: Policy advice, formulation of country frameworks, investment programmes, technical assistance programmes, humanitarian/emergency programmes, capacity building.

Civil society interface mechanism: Has established a CSO Advisory Committee to the Administrator with 15 members appointed in their individual capacity to advise and guide UNDP in its substantive policy areas.

11. World Food Programme (WFP)

Name of civil society unit: NGO Unit.

Activities undertaken by the entity in which the unit is located: Global policy dialogue/ negotiation, normative work, policy advice at national/regional levels, field programmes, public information.

Intergovernmental forums for which the unit manages civil society participation: Executive Board Session.

Outreach capacity at country level: 82 field offices, of which each has at least an informal civil society focal point.

Activities at country level: Policy advice, formulation of country frameworks, humanitarian/emergency programmes, capacity building.

Civil society interface mechanism: Annual consultation conducted with some 25 major NGO partners and networks.

Specialized UN Agencies

12. Food and Agriculture Organization of the United Nations (FAO)

Name of civil society unit: Resources and Strategic Partnerships Unit.

Activities undertaken by the entity in which the unit is located: Global policy dialogue/ negotiation, normative work, policy advice at national/regional levels, field programmes, public information.

Intergovernmental forums for which the unit manages civil society participation: FAO Conference and Council and standing Technical Committees and Commissions, Regional Conferences, special global forums (for example, World Summit, International Conference on Agrarian Reform and Rural Development).

Outreach capacity at country level: Five regional offices, five subregional and five liaison offices, all with an informally named civil society focal point; 78 country offices.

Activities at country level: Policy advice, formulation of country frameworks, investment programmes, technical assistance programmes, humanitarian/ emergency programmes, capacity building.

Civil society interface mechanism: Two self-organized global interface mechanisms. The International NGO/CSO Planning Committee for Food Sovereignty (IPC) emerged from the parallel forums to the World Food Summit and its +5 review. It groups some 50 constituency, regional and thematic focal points concerned with food and agriculture, with emphasis on facilitating involvement of social movements in the South (peasant farmers, fisherfolk, indigenous peoples, pastoralists, agricultural workers). The Ad Hoc Group of representatives of international non-governmental organizations (INGOs) in formal status with FAO is a forum of Rome-based representatives of these INGOs.

13. International Labour Organization (ILO)

Name of civil society unit: Bureau for External Relations and Partnerships.

Activities undertaken by the entity in which the unit is located: Global policy dialogue/ negotiation, normative work, policy advice at national/regional levels, field programmes, public information, training.

Intergovernmental forums for which the unit manages civil society participation: International Labour Conference.

Outreach capacity at country level: About 50 field offices, about half of which have officers specifically responsible for activities targeting employers' and workers' organizations.

Activities at country level: policy advice, formulation of country frameworks, technical assistance programmes, capacity building.

Civil society interface mechanism: In a special category because of its tripartite structure which fully involves workers' and employers' organizations in governance. Maintains a Special List of other categories of NGOs.

14. United Nations Industrial Development Organization (UNIDO)

Name of civil society unit: Strategic Direction, Management and Coordination, Officer of the Director-General.

Activities undertaken by the entity in which the unit is located: Global policy dialogue/ negotiation, normative work, policy advice at national/regional levels, field programmes, public information.

Intergovernmental forums for which the unit manages civil society participation: UNIDO policy-making organs which foresee civil society participation, conferences, forums and meetings.

Outreach capacity at country level: 30 field offices, none with civil society focal points.

Activities at country level: policy advice, formulation of country frameworks, investment programmes, technical assistance programmes, capacity building.

Civil society interface mechanism: No formal interface mechanism. Consultation with CSOs conducted through seminars, workshops and conferences.

15. World Health Organization (WHO)

Name of civil society unit: Civil Society Initiative.

Activities undertaken by the entity in which the unit is located: Global policy dialogue/ negotiation, normative work, policy advice at national/regional levels, field programmes, public information.

Intergovernmental forums for which the unit manages civil society participation: World Health Assembly and Executive Board.

Outreach capacity at country level: 28 field offices, none of which have civil society focal points.

Activities at country level: Policy advice, technical assistance programmes, humanitarian/emergency programmes, capacity building.

Civil society interface mechanism: No single global mechanism. Relations are maintained with various categories of NGOs: academic, scientific, professional, development, special interest (youth, women, patients, consumers, trade unions, local authorities, parliamentarians).

International Financial Institutions

16. Asian Development Bank (ADB)

Name of civil society unit: NGO Centre.

Activities undertaken by the entity in which the unit is located: Field programmes.

Intergovernmental forums for which the unit manages civil society participation: Annual meeting of Board of Governors.

Outreach capacity at country level: 24 field offices, nearly all with civil society focal points.

Activities at country level: policy advice, formulation of country frameworks, investment programmes, technical assistance programmes, humanitarian/emergency programmes, capacity building.

Civil society interface mechanism: No global advisory committee. Works through existing CSO networks like the NGO Forum on ADB. Some country-level Resident Missions hold regular meetings.

17. African Development Bank (AfDB)

Name of civil society unit: Sustainable Development and Poverty Reduction Unit.

Activities undertaken by the entity in which the unit is located: Global policy dialogue/ negotiation, normative work, policy advice at national/regional levels, field programmes.

Intergovernmental forums for which the unit manages civil society participation: Annual meeting of Board of Governors.

Outreach capacity at country level: Eight field offices, none of which have civil society focal points.

Activities at country level: Policy advice, formulation of country frameworks, investment programmes, technical assistance programmes, capacity building.

Civil society interface mechanism: AfDB–CSO Committee.

18. Inter-American Development Bank (IDB)

Name of civil society unit: Public Information and Publications Sector.

Activities undertaken by the entity in which the unit is located: Global policy dialogue/ negotiation, normative work, policy advice at national/regional levels, field programmes, public information.

Intergovernmental forums for which the unit manages civil society participation: None.

Outreach capacity at country level: 26 field offices, all with a civil society focal point.

Activities at country level: Policy advice, formulation of country frameworks, investment programmes, technical assistance programmes, humanitarian/ emergency programmes, capacity building.

Civil society interface mechanism: No global interface mechanism. Civil Society Advisory Councils exist in about half of the 26 country offices.

19. International Fund for Agricultural Development (IFAD)

Name of civil society unit: NGOs and Civil Society Partnerships Unit.

Activities undertaken by the entity in which the unit is located: global policy dialogue/ negotiation, policy advice at national/regional levels, field programmes.

Intergovernmental forums for which the unit manages civil society participation: Governing Council (and Farmers' Forum held in conjunction with it).

Outreach capacity at country level: No field offices.

Activities at country level: Policy advice, investment programmes, technical assistance programmes, capacity building.

Civil society interface mechanism: In the past an IFAD/NGO Consultation Steering Committee facilitated preparation of biennial IFAD/NGO Consultations. Now a forum of representatives of small-scale farmers, the Farmers' Forum, interacts with the Governing Council and oversees an effort to replicate such dialogue at country level.

20. International Finance Corporation (IFC)

Name of civil society unit: Corporate Relations.

Activities undertaken by the entity in which the unit is located: Global policy dialogue/ negotiation, policy advice at national/regional levels, field programmes, public information.

Intergovernmental forums for which the unit manages civil society participation: World Bank Spring and Annual Meetings, international conferences.

Outreach capacity at country level: 55 country offices and 5 regional offices, none with civil society focal points.

Activities at country level: Policy advice, investment programmes, technical assistance programmes, capacity building.

Civil society interface mechanism: No formal interface mechanism. It is felt difficult to establish one since NGOs are not representative of global civil society. Sector- or issue-specific groups are being considered.

21. International Monetary Fund (IMF)

Name of civil society unit: Policy Communication Division, External Relations Department.

Activities undertaken by the entity in which the unit is located: Global policy dialogue/ negotiation, normative work, policy advice at national/regional levels, public information.

Intergovernmental forums for which the unit manages civil society participation: IMF Annual Meetings (joint with World Bank).

Outreach capacity at country level: 88 field offices, none with civil society focal points.

Activities at country level: Policy advice, formulation of country frameworks, technical assistance programmes, capacity building, financing for balance-of-payments support.

Civil society interface mechanism: No formal interface.

22. World Bank

Name of civil society unit: Civil Society Team (global level – six staff), Civil Society Group (regional and departmental levels – 34 staff), Civil Society Country Staff (some 80 staff in 70 countries).

Activities undertaken by the entity in which the unit is located: Global policy dialogue/negotiation, normative work, policy advice at national/regional levels, field programmes, public information.

Intergovernmental forums for which the unit manages civil society participation: World Bank–IMF Annual and Spring Meetings and associated World Bank–Civil Society policy dialogue sessions, regional and sectoral forums.

Outreach capacity at country level: Approximately 100 field offices of which 70 have civil society focal points. Regional civil society teams cover the other countries.

Activities at country level: Policy advice, formulation of country frameworks, investment programmes, technical assistance programmes, humanitarian/emergency programmes, capacity building.

Civil society interface mechanism: Wide range of constituency and thematic mechanisms for consultation at all levels, using also new technologies such as video conferencing. Interface conducted with CSOs on global policy reviews (for example, indigenous peoples, environmental safeguards). World Bank–Civil Society Joint Facilitating Committee, an outgrowth of the former World Bank NGO Working Group, established to explore transparent and effective mechanisms for dialogue and engagement between civil society and the World Bank at the global level.

Other

23. Organisation for Economic Co-operation and Development (OECD)

Name of civil society unit: Public Affairs Division, Public Affairs and Communication Directorate.

Activities undertaken by the entity in which the unit is located: Global policy dialogue/ negotiation, normative work.

Intergovernmental forums for which the unit manages civil society participation: Annual civil society OECD Forum in conjunction with OECD Council meeting, sectoral forums

Outreach capacity at country level: Four OECD centres (Germany, United States, Japan, Mexico). Heads of centres act as civil society focal points.

Activities at country level: Policy advice.

Civil society outreach mechanism: Formal Business and Industry and Trade Union Advisory Committees created at the same time as the OECD. No formal mechanism for other CSOs.

24. World Trade Organization (WTO)

Name of civil society unit: External Relations Division.

Activities undertaken by the entity in which the unit is located: Global policy dialogue/ negotiation, normative work, policy advice at national/regional levels, public information.

Intergovernmental forums for which the unit manages civil society participation: WTO Ministerial Conferences, NGO briefings on meetings of major WTO bodies, public symposia.

Outreach capacity at country level: No field offices.

Activities at country level: Technical assistance programmes, capacity building.

Civil society outreach mechanism: Works with informal business and NGO advisory bodies.

Index